CRITIQUE
of
LEGAL ORDER

Law & Society Series

CRITIQUE
of
LEGAL ORDER
Crime Control in Capitalist Society

Richard Quinney

Law and Society Series

With a new introduction by Randall G. Shelden

Transaction Publishers
New Brunswick (U.S.A.) and London (U.K.)

New material this edition copyright © 2002 by Transaction Publishers, New Brunswick, New Jersey 08903. Originally published in 1974 by Little, Brown and Company.

This book is printed on acid-free paper that meets the American National Standard for Permanence of Paper for Printed Library Materials.

Library of Congress Catalog Number: 2001034716
ISBN: 0-7658-0797-1
Printed in the United States of America

Library of Congress Cataloging-in-Publication Data

Quinney, Richard.
    Critique of legal order : crime control in capitalist society / Richard Quinney ; with a new introduction by Randall G. Shelden.
        p. cm.
    Originally published: Boston : Little, Brown, c1974.
    Includes bibliographical references and index.
    ISBN 0-7658-0797-1 (pbk. : alk. paper)
    1. Criminal law—Pilosophy. 2. Sociological jurisprudence. 3. Critical legal studies. I. Title.

K5018 .Q56 2001
340' .115—dc21   2001034716
                                                          CIP

Contents

3

Preservation of Domestic Order
by the Ruling Class   51

4

Crime Control in the Capitalist State   95

Introduction To The Transaction Edition

After more than three decades, the works of Richard Quinney continue to be influential. During the past few years I have assigned graduate students in a seminar on "law and social control" to read excerpts from three of Quinney's books: *Crime and Justice in Society* (1969), *The Social Reality of Crime* (1970) and *Critique of Legal Order: Crime Control In Capitalist Society* (1974). Most of these students know little of Quinney's works, except perhaps what they have read in other books (usually undergraduate criminology or criminal justice textbooks). Without exception the students have consistently marveled at the contemporary relevance of most of what Quinney wrote so many years ago. The same can be said of several generations of criminologists, for Quinney ranks among the giants of twentieth-century criminology, as indicated by the many awards he has received (especially the prestigious Edwin Sutherland Award from the American Society of Criminology), plus the fact that he has been cited more than any other American criminologist, save for Sutherland and Donald Cressey (largely because of their classic text, *Criminology*).

What is most interesting about Quinney is the evolution of his thinking and writing over the years. In a recent interview appearing in *Contemporary Justice Review* Quinney notes that "one lifetime isn't enough for all that we need to experience.... I guess I see so many possibilities of experiencing the world, that you experience it one way and that opens up another way and then, rather than continue on that one experience, you want to see the world in another way. That's one reason why I think I've gone from one theory to another, at least in early times." This helps explain Quinney's seemingly dramatic shifts in perspectives over the course of his career, especially during the 1970s and early 1980s. His earlier writings reflected a classic "liberal" perspective, as one of the foremost representatives of the popular "labeling" approach in the late 1960s and early 1970s (as evidenced in *Crime and Justice in Society, The Problem of Crime* and especially in *The Social Reality of Crime*). *Critique of Legal Order*, however, represented a rather significant shift toward a Marxist view of crime and the legal order. This perspective was expanded upon with the publication of *Class, State and Crime* in 1977, which Quinney revised in 1980 for a second edition. But just when we were getting used to his Marxist orientation toward crime and justice, Quinney wrote something totally different in *Providence: The Reconstruction of Social and Moral Order* (1980). In this book his aim was to connect the material life (exemplified in the works of Marx) with the spiritual life; more specifically, he wrote about the possible fusion between material existence and sacred essence; about Marx's critical analysis of material existence and the prophetic theology of culture. Here Quinney's writings took him back to one of his original interests in graduate school, the sociology of religion. With his *Social Existence: Metaphysics, Marxism and the Social Sciences* (1982) it was obvious that Quinney was heading in a completely different direction, as he began to take a more existentialist and spiritual path.

Quinney wasn't entirely leaving the world of criminology, however, as he co-edited (with Hal Pepinsky) *Criminology as Peacemaking* in 1991, along with a third edition of *The Problem of Crime* in 1991 (but with a significant subtitle added: *A Peace and Social Justice Perspective*) and a third edition of his classic

Criminal Behavior Systems in 1994. Most recently he has completed a co-edited book (with Kevin Anderson), *Erich Fromm and Critical Criminology*, bringing forth a series of articles that link Fromm's work with the problem of crime and justice, including two new translations of Fromm's early articles on crime and justice, previously unpublished in English.

During the past twenty years or so Quinney has, through several different writings (including two auto-biographical books, *Journey to a Far Place* and *For the Time Being*), demonstrated his existentialist views and his Buddhist orientation toward life, along with his skills as a photographer. Today he remains an inspiration to many generations of criminologists, as is clearly demonstrated by the large attendance whenever he is on a panel at a conference (especially the American Society of Criminology).

Placing *Critique of Legal Order* in the context of Quinney's lifetime of work is not an easy task. It seems best to begin by reiterating that this book represented a significant break from Quinney's previous work. It may seem appropriate to suggest that Quinney was offering a new "paradigm" for criminology, in the sense used by Thomas Kuhn (1970). Here he clearly provided a new way of looking at the phenomenon of crime control. The emphasis of this work is on the *control* of crime, and the manner in which it is done in a *capitalist* society. He was practically alone among American criminologists in connecting the Vietnam War with what was occurring in America. In the preface Quinney writes that: "The legal system at home and the military apparatus abroad are two sides of the same phenomenon; both perpetuate American capitalism, the American Way of Life." This is a serious charge, and one that has been amply documented in the works of such well-known critics as Noam Chomsky, Howard Zinn, and Michael Parenti (to name just three) who have written about the various forms of repression abroad, supported by American tax dollars, which served "American interests"—meaning in reality, the interests of the ruling class.

Quinney's overall critique of capitalism and criminology's role in crime control is still relevant and provides some guidelines for the future. One of the leading points Quinney makes is that crime control in modern capitalist societies is not so much aimed at reducing crime and suffering as it is at preserving the established order and controlling the "dangerous classes," the "rabble" or the "surplus population" (Shelden and Brown, 2000; Shelden, 1999a, 1999b; Shelden, 2001).

It becomes obvious in the first chapter of this book that Quinney is extending his analysis of the criminal justice system, begun years earlier in *Crime and Justice in Society* with his "sociological theory of criminal law," in which he proposes, via four propositions, an "interest group" theory of law. In *Crime and Justice in Society*, he was clearly departing from conventional practice by suggesting that powerful interests shape the law, rather than the interests of all (known as the "consensus" view). This theory was expanded upon in *The Social Reality of Crime*, where he offered six propositions, among which included the proposition that criminal definitions describe behaviors that conflict with powerful interests. The theory was based on the social constructionist mode of thought, which suggests that rather than being some objective truth, reality is socially created. Thus, "crime" and the "criminal justice system," are *social products*.

In *Critique of Legal Order*, however, Quinney engages in a critique of all previous modes of criminological thought, including his own. In the first chapter he outlines and critiques three of the ways we normally think about reality: the positivist, the social constructionist and the phenomenological. He then proceeds to outline a critical mode of thinking, one which involves the "demystification, the removal of the myths — the false consciousness — created by the official reality." He completes this first chapter by outlining six propositions for a "critical philosophy of the legal order." In these propositions he clearly departs from his previous work by advancing a version of what has come to be called *instrumental Marxism*, arguing that the state serves the interest of the ruling class and that criminal law is "an instrument of the state and ruling class to maintain and perpetuate the existing social and economic order" (p. 16). In his sixth proposition he offers a form of socialism as a solution to the crime problem. It can be said that in this light the volume represents more than a mere critique of the legal order; it represents a "call to arms," so to speak, for citizens (and criminologists) to help bring about the replacement of American capitalism with a new society, based upon socialist principles. Quinney was treading on ground rarely covered then (and now) by mainstream criminology.

Critique of Legal Order was perhaps a reflection of someone who had become disenchanted with American capitalism. As a humanist, Quinney was deeply and genuinely disturbed by what he saw around him. In the preface, Quinney suggests that capitalism is in deep trouble and thus "will increasingly rely on repressive, authoritarian measures to secure its own survival" (p. vi). Writing at the time of Watergate, COINTELPRO, the Vietnam War, and other key socio-political events, it is understandable that he would predict that worse things would transpire. However, it seems obvious that Quinney, like Marx, underestimated the resiliency of capitalism and the power of the ruling class. It could even be argued that he underestimated the predictive power of his own analysis of the role of ideology and the ways in which, as Noam Chomsky has suggested, "necessary illusions" are produced, thereby "manufacturing consent" (Chomsky, 1989; Herman and Chomsky, 1988). In other words, it could be argued that Quinney did not go quite far enough in his own analysis. A more careful reading of Marxist literature reveals the importance of ideological rule ("hegemony"), that ruling classes in "democratic" societies cannot become too authoritarian.

The balance of the book consists of a critical analysis of not just the legal order per se, but of how such an order fits into society as a whole. He begins, in chapter 2, with an analysis of the relationship between "knowledge and order" and levels one of his most serious charges, calling his fellow criminologists "ancillary agents of power" who provide "the kinds of information that governing elites use to manipulate and control those who threaten the system" and who "inform the managers of social order" (p. 27).

Quinney noted that conventional knowledge tends to support the established social order. He further noted that the "official reality of the state and the interests of social scientists are the same" (p. 17). Moreover, it is the "search for order" (the so-called "Hobbesian problem of order") that has dominated intellectual thought since the seventeenth century. The solution to this "problem" came to be the establishment of a set of norms that limit legitimate action. There are, of course, serious threats to this "order." What is most interesting here is Quinney's observation that, as de Tocqueville noted long ago (and more recently Noam Chomsky) that the biggest threat to the prevailing order is *democracy*, not its traditional notions, but true democracy which would involve extending democratic principles to the economy and to everyday life (Chomsky, 1996).

For Quinney the ultimate source of social order is the "legitimacy" of the system, noted by Max Weber. Weber was famous for developing his ideal types of "authority," noting that in modern, bureaucratic societies "legitimate" authority (based on *positions* supported by *law*) is the most prevalent. This legitimacy lies not in the people, but rather in the state. Law, from this view, is one of the ultimate and most rational forms of authority. The legal system is not to be questioned because it is legitimate. Therefore it is to be obeyed. The demand for "law and order" was of paramount importance when Quinney wrote this, as it certainly is today. We constantly hear the phrase that this is a nation under the "rule of law," not the rule of men. Quinney's observation a quarter of a century ago, however, rings just as true today: while it is technically true that there is due process, that is, a system of basic rights theoretically accorded to all, such an ideal "is negated by the fact that the entire legal system is played according to rules formulated and enforced by a legal establishment that is part of the capitalist ruling class" (p. 21). In other words, we have "rights" but only within narrowly defined parameters (for a similar view see Chomsky, 1989, 1994 and Herman and Chomsky, 1988).

Quinney has consistently argued throughout his career for a need to visualize possibilities other than the taken-for-granted existing social order. That requires a *critical* perspective. This was made clear when he noted that the present legal order "is being presented to us (by the legalists in a capitalist society) as the only rational means for the achievement of social order. Other possibilities for social existence are excluded" (p. 22).

Finally, Quinney, in chapter 2, becomes a critic of established criminology. In a statement that is almost identical to a thesis offered by Chomsky in his famous essay "On the Responsibilities of Intellectuals" (1987), Quinney argues that criminologists "provide the kinds of information that governing elites use to manipulate and control those who threaten the system. As 'experts,' criminologists inform the managers of social order." Rather than being an explicit conspiracy, the relationship "is much more natural and subtle" because criminologists rarely question their own assumptions. "By pursuing a narrow scientific model, supported by an ideology of social order, the criminologist finds his interests tied to those of the state. Both parties have an interest in preserving existing arrangements" (pp. 27-28). In many of his published works and public speeches, Chomsky has criticized intellectuals for providing "scientific" rationalizations of the existing social order, with all of its injustices. Such intellectuals have been gradually socialized through established schools of higher education so that by the time they receive their degrees they have become fully indoctrinated and begin to receive handsome rewards for serving the interests of the powerful.

Quinney provides a superb example of how criminologists serve the existing order and those in power - by the mere fact that they unquestioningly rely on a state definition of "crime." The control and prediction of "crime" is the goal of the criminologist, since he or she follows the scientific tradition of positivism. Quinney quotes one of the most famous textbooks, that of Sutherland and Cressey, in which they note that "theoretical knowledge is increased most significantly in the efforts at social control" (p. 29). Indeed, Quinney states "crime control is good business for the criminologist." He notes that many criminologists have specialized in the field of corrections, since the prison provides a steady supply of data for which to test various criminological theories. Quinney notes that if we eliminated prisons we would remove "one of the crucial sites for criminological research" (p. 30). This continues to be true today as crime control has become a huge industry, which has even captured the attention of Wall Street. Indeed, several noted brokerage houses (e.g., Smith-Barney, Merril Lynch) have on several occasions issued "buy orders" to invest in various crime-control businesses, such as Corrections Corporation of America. Likewise many criminologists "follow the money" dripping from the almost unlimited coffers of the federal government (Shelden, 1999).

The remainder of Chapter 2 consists of a sampling of what Quinney calls "Scholarship in the Service of Social Control." Here he begins a lengthy analysis of various research projects funded by government agencies through universities all over the country. Especially prominent is the money coming from the (now defunct) Law Enforcement Assistance Administration (LEAA). One could easily update his list to include the most recent research projects, the bulk of which, says Quinney, are "intended to make the existing [criminal justice] system more rational or more respectable" (p. 30).

Quinney notes sarcastically that a good deal of funding goes toward the development of criminal justice programs in colleges and universities. He was one of the first criminologists to critically examine this new phenomenon. Most of these programs were, in effect, little more than "police training" programs, begun partly as a result of President Johnson's Crime Commission reports (the various "Task Forces" that appeared in the late 1960s) which strongly urged that we "professionalize" and "humanize" the police and the rest of the criminal justice system. Quinney sums up what this really meant in practice, by quoting a report by Lee Webb in an obscure publication, *The University-Military-Police Complex* (published by the North American Congress on Latin America). Webb stated that "professionalization of the police means exactly what it does in the Army: a fascination with technique and modern equipment, a de-politization of the department, and a readiness to carry out any orders from above" (p. 34). By the early 1970s LEAA was in full gear. The Department of Justice was funding a variety of research projects in an attempt, said Quinney, to secure the allegiance of scholars. As the "crime control industry" was beginning Quinney wrote prophetically that: "The study of crime, from an approved perspective, becomes a worthwhile subject for the young scientist" (p. 35).

It is appropriate to quote two other scholars who have made their mark in fields other than criminology, but whose writings nonetheless relate strongly to the field. First, Howard Zinn once criticized mainstream historians. In his book *The Politics of History* (1990), Zinn begins a chapter appropriately titled "Knowledge as a Form of Power" (which reads much like Chapter 2 of *Critique of Legal Order* and has a similar title), with comments about how the usual publications of historians have produced "the largest number of inconsequential studies in the history of civilization." Zinn further remarks that "historians occasionally emerge from library stacks to sign petitions or deliver a speech, then return to produce even more of inconsequence." He suggests that historians "read the titles of doctoral dissertations published in the past twenty years, and the pages of leading scholarly journals for the same period, alongside the lists of war dead, the figures on per capita income in Latin America, the autobiography of Malcolm X." In short, Zinn states that historians "publish while others perish" (1990: 5).

It is interesting to note that Zinn first published the above remarks in 1970, meaning he was actually writing them in the late 1960s. About the same time, another leading social critic, Noam Chomsky, wrote a piece in the *New York Review of Books* (Feb. 23, 1967), entitled "The Responsibility of Intellectuals." At the time Chomsky was best known for his work in linguistics. He crossed the line into politics with this famous article and stated that: "It is the responsibility of intellectuals to speak the truth and to expose the lies." His reasoning was simple. Intellectuals are in a unique position in that they have the time and access to a wide variety of information and freedom of expression. They do not have to rely solely on "official" publications. Chomsky further noted that, "For a privileged minority, Western democracy provides the leisure, the facilities, and the training to seek the truth lying behind the veil of distortion and misrepresentation, ideology, and class interest through which the events of current history are presented to us" (1987:60).

It should be noted that both Chomsky and Zinn remain two of the most outspoken critics of American foreign and domestic policies. In their writings and public speeches both continue to follow these responsibilities. It is clear that what they wrote four decades ago seems just as relevant today—perhaps more so. Clearly, Quinney's writings have played the same role over the years.

How does one assess the importance of *Critique of Legal Order* nearly thirty years later? In making a few general observations about some of Quinney's assertions in that book, the evidence seems quite overwhelming. Since that time numerous studies have extensively documented the following charges that he made:

(1) That there is in fact a "ruling class" and they indeed *rule* the country (Domhoff, 1998; Rothman, 1999);

(2) That members of this class play a major role in defining not only what is designated as "criminal" but also in defining the dominant crime control policies, both on the national and local level; what Quinney never explored is the impact of local or regional ruling class members on crime control policies within states and municipalities (some examples include: Chambliss and Zatz, 1993; Reiman, 1998; Greenberg and Humphries, 1993; Barnett, 1993; Humphries and Greenberg, 1993; for an example of elite influence on the "war on drugs" see Baum, 1997 and Webb, 1998); No one, except Baum and Webb, actually identified specific offenders to the extent that Quinney did. Ironically, both Baum and Webb are journalists, rather than criminologists;

(3) That the brunt of enforcement efforts is felt very disproportionately by minorities in particular and the "dangerous" classes in general, who obviously pose a threat to the established order and that this is especially evidenced by the "war on drugs" and the "war on gangs" (Klein, 1995; Shelden, Tracy and Brown, 2001; Baum, 1997 and Currie, 1995 and 1998);

(4) That the bulk of criminological research continues to follow the proverbial money trail and is concerned primarily with assisting the state in controlling conventional crime which is

committed by members of the underclass and minorities; much of this research still focuses on improving the criminal justice system, making it more "efficient" and making better use of available technology to identify "potential criminals;" if anything, this tendency is even greater than what Quinney described in his book (consider the latest advertisements for funded projects by the National Institute of Justice or Office of Juvenile Justice and Delinquency Prevention and casually review articles appearing in mainstream journals);

(5) That this research is further adding to what we have called the "crime control industry" or "criminal justice industrial complex;" it is important to note that Quinney was one of the first to point this out when he talked about "crime control bureaucracies" in *Critique of Legal Order* and then had a chapter devoted to the "criminal justice industrial complex" in *Class, State and Crime*; little did he realize how expansive this system would become within the next 25 years (more than $150 billion spent yearly on the formal criminal justice system alone; see Chambliss, 1999);

(6) That it is rare for criminologists to focus much attention to crimes committed by corporations and especially the state; a few isolated studies have documented such crimes and they are extensive, but other than Quinney, Reiman and a handful of other criminologists (notable examples include, Coleman, 1994, Friedrichs, 1996 and Simon and Hagan, 1999), there has been little consistent effort to link such crimes to the very nature of capitalism itself (some of the best work on crimes of the state is found in the works of non-criminologists, such as Chomsky and Michael Parenti);

(7) That the media contribute greatly to the standard images of crime was a major part of *The Social Reality of Crime* and Quinney continued this line of thinking in *Critique of Legal Order*; a good deal of work has been done since that time, documenting the critical role of the media (a set of giant corporations in itself) in perpetuating certain images of "crime" and "criminals" (see Surette, 1998 and Anderson, 1995), an image of street crimes, drug crimes and gang-related crime committed almost exclusively by African-Americans and Hispanics (crimes by the rich are buried in the back pages of the

Wall Street Journal, if they are reported at all); some excellent work on "moral panics" and crime have appeared in recent years (see McCorkle and Miethe, 1998; Goode and Ben-Yehuda, 1994).

These seven statements are just a few of the key portions of *Critique of Legal Order* that are still relevant today, and well supported by research. What is especially relevant here is Quinney's critique of not only crime control policies but especially the crime control bureaucracies like the Department of Justice and its various branches (e.g., the FBI). This is where Quinney broke fresh ground, for few criminologists dared to seriously question the concept of crime control in the context of state bureaucracies and the vested interest they have in perpetuating themselves and preserving the capitalist system. While most criminologists were (and still are) busy conducting "empirical studies" of the police, prosecution, the prison subculture, and treatment modalities, Quinney was the only one at that time looking at the entire structure of crime control and the overall role of the state, of which the criminal justice system is merely one part, and how the "state" supports the ruling class and the capitalist order. Quinney, along with a few other radical criminologists, has consistently tried to make connections between the very nature of capitalism (e.g., the inherent inequality, the class structure, alienation, the creation of a "surplus population") and crime.

In the final chapter of *Critique of Legal Order*, entitled "Toward a Socialist Society," Quinney offers some rather vague sketches of what is to be done and how a socialist society should look. For those who wanted (and still desire) a blueprint of the "ideal society" Quinney fell short. But a "blueprint" is not what is needed, for such a model may end up as a confining straightjacket that does not allow for alternative visions. What Quinney offers is merely a vision, with the lament that "we have much to do." His last paragraph is one of caution, as he argues that we make changes in society through constant struggle suggesting that, "Our theory and practice are formed in the struggle to make a socialist society."

One of the major weakness of Quinney's argument appears in Chapter 3 where he extends his instrumentalist perspective and tries to demonstrate that the ruling class has some sort of direct control over crime policies by noting the class backgrounds of members of various commissions (e.g., President's Commission, Riot Commission). His definition of the "ruling class" would have benefited from a closer look at the work of William Domhoff, whom he cites in this chapter. Quinney says that this class consists of those who "own the means of production" and "those who benefit in some way from the present capitalist economic system" (p. 55). To include those who benefit "in some way" lacks precision and opens the door to criticism. Subsequent pages in this chapter consist of a listing of dozens of names of those sitting on these various commissions, which many readers will doubtless find boring and repetitious.

Quinney's analysis of the "state" took the *instrumentalist* Marxist perspective. Marx once stated that, the *state* was originally a system set up to support ruling class interests and was, in effect, an inevitable outgrowth of a division of labor based upon class exploitation. In fact, the "state" was only necessary when class divisions arose. This instrumentalist perspective has received a number of important criticisms, which can be applied to *Critique of Legal Order* (Lynch and Groves, 1989: 23-24). First, there is a tendency to exaggerate the cohesiveness of the ruling class and the ability of this class to always act in a unified manner (sounding too much like a "conspiracy" theory). Second, this approach is overly deterministic, emphasizing the economic variable above all else. Third, there is an assumption that *every* law serves the interests of the ruling class only, and that the state never serves (and cannot by definition serve) the interests of ordinary people. Finally, such a simplistic view ignores the various conflicts and contradictions within the ruling class itself (Chambliss and Zatz, 1993).

Critique of Legal Order was frequently subjected to scathing criticism, much of which was overdone. To many in the mainstream of criminology, Quinney had gone "off the deep end" or was out there in "fantasy land" and his writings were too "bombastic and polemical" (Gibbons and Garabedian, 1974). It is also interesting that Quinney was not only criticized by mainstream criminology, but by many on the Left (see Platt and Takagi, 1982; see Wildeman, 1984, for an excellent response to these criticisms). As already noted, Quinney was sensitive to the criticisms, especially those concerning his instrumentalist perspective. With the publication of *Class, State and Crime*, Quinney addressed some of his critics and wrote from a more structuralist perspective. Despite these criticisms, what Quinney wrote in *Critique of Legal Order* more than a quarter century ago is still relevant today. It should be re-read by criminologists and the doors and windows he opened should be re-opened, this time with new visions, new methodologies and hopefully greater wisdom. As Quinney says in the final passage of this volume, this is indeed a "critical life." As we begin a new millennium, life remains critical indeed.

Randall G. Shelden

References

Anderson, D. C. *Crime and the Politics of Hysteria.* New York: Times Books, 1995.

Barnett, H. "The Enforcement of Anti-Monopoly Legislation." Pp. 641-648 in D. Greenberg (ed.), *Crime and Capitalism* (2nd ed.). Philadelphia: Temple University Press, 1993.

Baum, D. *Smoke and Mirrors: The War on Drugs and the Politics of Failure.* Boston: Little Brown/Back Bay Books, 1997.

Chambliss, W. J. *Power, Politics, and Crime.* Boulder, CO: Westview, 1999.

Chambliss, W. J. and M. S. Zatz (eds.) *Making Law: The State, the Law, and Structural Contradictions.* Bloomington, IN: Indiana University Press, 1993.

Chomsky, N. *The Chomsky Reader.* New York: Pantheon Books, 1987.

————————— *Necessary Illusions: Thought Control in Democratic Societies.* Boston: South End Press, 1989.

—————————. *Class Warfare.* Monroe, ME: Common Courage Press, 1994.

—————————. *Year 501: The Conquest Continues.* Boston: South End Press, 1993.

Coleman, J. W. *The Criminal Elite* (3rd ed.). New York: St. Martin's Press, 1994.

Currie, E. *Crime and Punishment in America.* New York: Metropolitan Books, 1998.

——————— *Reckoning: Drugs, the Cities, and the American Future.* New York: Hill and Wang, 1993.

Domhoff, W. *Who Rules America? Power and Politics in the Year 2000.* Mountain View, CA: Mayfield, 1998. (originally published by Prentice-Hall in 1967).

Folbre, N. and the Center for Popular Economics. *The New Field Guide to the U.S. Economy.* New York: The New Press, 1995.

Friedrichs, D.O. *Trusted Criminals: White Collar Crime in Contemporary Society.* Belmont, CA: Wadsworth, 1996.

Gibbons, D. C. and P. Garabedian. "Conservative, Liberal and Radical Criminology: Some Trends and Observations." Pp. 51-65 in C. Reasons (ed.), *The Criminologist: Crime and Criminology.* Pacific Palisades, CA: Goodyear, 1974.

Goode, E. and N. Ben-Yehuda. *Moral Panics: The Social Construction of Deviance.* Cambridge, MA: Blackwell, 1994.

Greenberg, D. and D. Humphries. "The Co-optation of Sentencing Reform." Pp. 621-640 in D. Greenberg (ed.), *Crime and Capitalism* (2nd ed.). Philadelphia: Temple University Press, 1993.

Hanh, T. N. *Peace is Every Step.* New York: Bantam Books, 1991.

Herman, E. and N. Chomsky. *Manufacturing Consent: The Political Economy of the Mass Media.* New York: Pantheon, 1988.

Humphries, D. and D. Greenberg. "The Dialectics of Crime Control." Pp. 463-508 in D. Greenberg (ed.), *Crime and Capitalism* (2nd ed.). Philadelphia: Temple University Press, 1993.

Klein, M. *The American Street Gang.* New York: Oxford University Press, 1995.

Kuhn, T. *The Structure of Scientific Revolutions* (2nd ed.). Chicago: University of Chicago Press, 1970.

McCorkle, R. and T. Miethe. "The Political and Organizational Response to Gangs: An Examination of a `Moral Panic' in Nevada." *Justice Quarterly* 15:41-64, 1998.

Messner, S. and R. Rosenbaum. *Crime and the American Dream* (2nd ed.). Belmont, CA: Wadsworth, 1997.

Miliband, R. *The State in Capitalist Society.* New York: Basic Books, 1969.

Parenti, M. *Power and the Powerless.* New York: St. Martin's Press, 1978.

——————. *Land of Idols: Political Mythology in America.* New York: St. Martin's Press, 1994.

——————. *Against Empire.* San Francisco: City Lights Press, 1995.

Platt, A. M. *The Politics of Riot Commissions, 1917-1970.* New York: Collier Books, 1971.

Platt, T. and P. Takagi. "Meeting the challenge of the 1980s." *Crime and Social Justice* (Summer, 1982).

Quinney, R. *The Social Reality of Crime.* Boston: Little, Brown. 1970.

——————— *Criminal Justice in America: A Critical Understanding.* Boston: Little, Brown, 1974.

—————— *Class, State and Crime.* (2nd ed.) New York: Longman, 1980.

—————— and J. Wildeman. *The Problem of Crime: A Peace and Social Justice Perspective* (3rd ed.). Mountain View, CA: Mayfield, 1991 (originally published by Quinney in 1970 as *The Problem of Crime*, New York: Dodd Mead).

Reiman, J. H. *The Rich Get Richer and the Poor Get Prison* (5th ed.). Chicago: Allyn and Bacon, 1998.

Rothman, R. A. *Inequality and Stratification: Race, Class and Gender* (3rd ed.). Englewood Cliffs, NJ: Prentice-Hall, 1999.

Shelden, R. G. "The Prison Industrial Complex." *The Progressive Populist* 5, 11 (Nov. 1) 1, 12-12 1999a.

—————————. "The Prison Industrial Complex and the New American Apartheid." *The Critical Criminologist* 10, 1 (Fall) 1, 7-9, 1999b.

—————————. *Controlling the Dangerous Classes: A Critical Introduction to the History of Criminal Justice.* Boston: Allyn and Bacon, 2001.

Shelden, R. G. and W. B. Brown. "The Crime Control Industry and the Management of the Surplus Population." *Critical Criminology* 9 (Autumn), 39-62, 2000.

Shelden, R.G., S. K. Tracy and W. B. Brown. *Youth Gangs in American Society* (2nd ed.). Belmont, CA: Wadsworth, 2001.

Simon, D. R. and F. E. Hagan. *White Collar Deviance.* Boston: Allyn and Bacon, 1999.

Surette, R. *Media, Crime and Criminal Justice* (2nd ed.) Belmont, CA: Wadsworth, 1998.

Webb, G. *Dark Alliance: Crack, the CIA and the Contras.* New York: Seven Stories Press, 1998.

Wildeman, J. "Richard Quinney vs. the New Orthodoxy: Some Recent Developments in Radical Criminology." Paper presented at the annual meeting of the American Society of Criminology, November, 1984.

Zinn, H. *The Politics of History* (2nd ed.). Urbana, IL: University of Illinois Press, 1990.

Preface

Once there was a way — or so it seemed — to get there from here. All we had to do was follow our procedures; all would be well. But then we began to understand. It was no longer possible to gain a better collective life under the established order or to comprehend the current reality according to conventional wisdom. Other sources became necessary.

This book is an attempt to understand some of the important events that have been going on in the United States in the last decade. I am concerned with developments in the American legal order, with occurrences that get to the deeper meaning of the American experience. To accomplish an adequate understanding I found it necessary to develop a critical form of thought. Rejecting the common assumptions of legal scholarship and criminological theory, I am suggesting a critical Marxian philosophy that allows us to demystify the existing social order. At the same time my purpose is to create a form of life that will move us out of the oppression of the capitalist age.

With a critical philosophy we begin to recognize that the legal order (that which supposedly makes for civilization) is actually a construction of the capitalist ruling class and the state that serves it. Law, contrary to the dominant ideology, promotes the survival of the capitalist system. Moreover, as capitalism is further threatened by its own contradictions, the legal order is increasingly used to maintain domestic order. The legal system at home and the military apparatus abroad are two sides of the same phenomenon; both perpetuate American capitalism, the American Way of Life. With a critical Marxian philosophy we are able to understand how the capitalist ruling class establishes its control over those it must oppress. This is a philosophy that no longer serves the existing capitalist state; instead, it promotes our liberation through socialist revolution.

As I was completing this book, Watergate was just beginning to surface. All those things that I had been writing about the American state and the ruling class were given further support. But more to the point, the kinds of things I had uncovered in the crime control measures of the last decade were now obviously correct rather than being merely the product of a writer's paranoid imagination. Yet many persons in the United States will likely feel that "the system" has been purged once the functionaries associated with Watergate have been brought "to justice." Too easily it can be assumed that a critical understanding of American legal order is only a description of an abnormal period in American history. But it is my contention that Watergate is only the surface of the deeper reality of American social and political life, that law and the state in America exist for the promotion of the capitalist system. Capitalism, in not being able to solve its own contradictions, will increasingly rely on repressive, authoritarian measures to secure its own survival. That the legal system — including the various agencies of crime control — will be an integral part of this effort is the meaning of my analysis of legal order in America. That our future for some time to come will be a dialectic between resistance and revolution, on the one hand, and counterrevolution by the state on the other, is the conclusion of a critical analysis.

Where do we go from here? Our purpose in a critical imagination is to act collectively to bring about a world liberated from the oppression of capitalism. We are engaged in socialist revolution. The thoughts and actions appropriate to an emerging socialist society can be developed only in the struggle of creating a socialist society. Given a socialist vision, the actual nature of our future, including the nature of the state, will be realized only in the course of the creation. It is in the struggle today that we realize ourselves and our future.

CRITIQUE OF LEGAL ORDER

1
A Critical Philosophy of Legal Order

We do not adequately understand our contemporary existence. Our comprehension of the present, as well as of the past, is obscured by our current consciousness — a consciousness developed within the existing order and serving only to maintain that order. If we are ever to remove the oppression of the age, we must critically understand the world about us. Only with the development of a new consciousness — a critical philosophy — can we begin to realize the world of which we are capable. My position is thus a critical one: critical not only in an assessment of our current condition, but critical in working toward a new existence — toward a negation of what *is* through thinking about and practicing what *could be*. Any possibility for a different life will come about only through new ideas formed in the course of altering the way we think and the way we live. What is required is no less than a whole new way of life. What is necessary is a new beginning — intellectually, spiritually, and politically.

Nowhere is the inadequacy of our understanding more apparent than in our thoughts and actions in relation to legal order. Our thinking about law and crime only confirms an official ideology that supports the existing social and economic order. As long as we fail to understand the nature of law in contemporary society, we will be bound by an oppressive reality. What is urgently needed is a critical philosophy of legal order.

The development of a critical philosophy of legal order should allow us to contemplate and act toward the fulfillment of a new reality. To accomplish this, it is necessary to understand where we have been in regard to our thinking about the legal order and also to understand the relation of our thoughts and actions to the official reality. In order to determine where we have been and where we are going, several modes of thought must be distinguished. Each mode embodies its own epistemology and ontology — its own way of thinking and its own assumptions about reality. Each takes a particular stance toward the philosophical issues of objectivity, reflexivity, and transcendence. Furthermore, each mode carries with it a specific relation to the dominant order. Each has its own potential for either oppressing us or liberating us. The four modes of thought are: (1) the positivistic, (2) the social constructionist, (3) the phenomenological, and (4) the critical. My objective in analyzing them is to develop a critical philosophy of legal order. The result will be a Marxian theory of crime control in capitalist society. This theory will be expanded in subsequent chapters into a critique of legal order.

THE POSITIVISTIC MODE

The positivistic mode of thought begins with the realist assumptions about existence. These assumptions are shared by anyone who has not reflected about the problems of perception and experience. At best, the positivist has only a naive acquaintance with epistemological and ontological concerns. Rather, "methodology" is the positivist's chief concern — how to develop a method to grasp or "discover" the laws of the physical world.

Positivism follows the simple epistemology that absolutely separates the knower from the known. Objectivity is assumed to be possible because order is believed to exist independent of the observer. The observer's cognitive apparatus supposedly does not affect the nature of what is known. Given enough knowledge, ac-

2

cumulated systematically, the scientist presumably could predict future events and control their occurrence. An orderly universe could be established through man's knowledge and manipulation of the external world.

The overriding emphasis of positivistic thought is on the *explanation* of events. And in following a mechanistic conception of the relation of social facts, the positivist usually couches his explanations in terms of causality. What is ignored in this approach to explanation is an *examination* (or even an awareness) of the philosophical assumptions by which the observer operates.[1] There is neither a recognition that the nature of explanation depends upon the kinds of things investigated nor that explanation requires a description of the unique context in which events occur. Likewise, the positivist refuses to recognize that to assess and make statements about human actions is to engage in a moral endeavor. Instead, the positivist regards his activity as being "value free."

The intellectual failure of positivism is that of not being reflexive. It makes little or no attempt to examine or even question the metaphysics of inquiry, to turn the activity of explanation back upon itself. The positivist refuses to be introspective. His concern is to get on with the task of explaining, without considering what he is doing. Positivistic thought is of a particular kind; it is calculative thinking as described by Heidegger: "Its peculiarity consists in the fact that whenever we plan, research, or organize, we always reckon with conditions that are given." [2] In other words, there is little time to ask the crucial philosophical questions that ultimately affect the operations of investigation. "Calculative thinking races from one prospect to the next. Calculative thinking never stops, never collects itself. Calculative thinking is not meditative thinking, not thinking which contemplates the meaning which reigns in everything that is." [3]

The political failure of positivist thought, as related to its intellectual failure, is its acceptance of the status quo. There is no questioning of the established order, just as there is no examination of

---

[1] See A. R. Louch, *Explanation and Human Action* (Berkeley: University of California Press, 1969).

[2] Martin Heidegger, *What Is a Thing?*, trans. W. B. Barton, Jr. and Vera Deutsch (Chicago: Henry Regnery Company, 1967), p. 46.

[3] *Ibid.*

scientific assumptions. The official reality is the one within which the positivist operates — and the one that he accepts and supports. The positivist takes for granted the dominant ideology that emphasizes bureaucratic rationality, modern technology, centralized authority, and scientific control.[4] Positivistic thought, in fact, naturally lends itself to the official ideology and the interests of the ruling class. Little wonder that the talents of positivistic social scientists are in such demand by those who rule. Social scientists have failed to break out of the interpretations and practices of the official reality, that reality within which they comfortably operate, never asking what could be and never seeking to transcend the established order.

Most of the research and theoretical developments in the sociology of law have been dominated by the positivistic mode of thought.[5] The legal order is taken for granted, and research is directed toward an understanding of *how* the system operates. Little attention is devoted to questions about why law exists, whether law is indeed necessary, or what a just system would look like. If the value of justice is considered at all, the concern is with the equitability of the system rather than with whether the system should exist in the first place. Suggestions may be made for changing particular laws, but the outlines of the legal system are to remain intact.[6] Inadequacies in the administration of justice may be noted, but prescriptions for change merely call for more technical and efficient procedures.

The efforts of criminologists have been devoted almost solely to the most conservative interests. Attention traditionally has been on the violator of criminal law rather than on the legal system itself.[7] Solutions to the crime problem have proposed changing the lawbreaker rather than the legal system. Only recently have some crim-

---

[4] See John H. Schaar, "Legitimacy in the Modern State," in Philip Green and Sanford Levinson (eds.), *Power and the Community: Dissenting Essays in Political Science* (New York: Vintage Books, 1970), especially pp. 303–308.

[5] For example, see the issues of the journal of the Law and Society Association, *Law and Society Review*.

[6] Norval Morris and Gordon Hawkins, *The Honest Politician's Guide to Crime Control* (Chicago: University of Chicago Press, 1970).

[7] See C. Ray Jeffery, "The Structure of American Criminological Thinking," *Journal of Criminal Law, Criminology and Police Science*, 46 (January, 1956), pp. 658–672.

inologists, realizing that law is problematic, turned their attention to a study of criminal law. But for the most part these studies have been based on the positivistic mode of thought.[8]

The conservative nature of most research and theory on law and crime is logically related to the social scientist's emphasis on social order. In the search for the natural laws of society, social scientists have favored any existing arrangements that would assure an orderly society. Anything that would threaten the existing order has been regarded as a violation of natural law, a social pathology to be eradicated, ameliorated, or punished in some way. Social scientists have formed an easy alliance with the ruling class that profits from the preservation of the status quo. Research and theory in criminology and the sociology of law have done little more than provide a rationale for the established order. A social theory that would allow for human liberation has been excluded. It now seems evident that positivistic thought cannot provide a liberating conception of human existence. Instead, we must turn to alternative modes of thought.

THE SOCIAL CONSTRUCTIONIST MODE

Social constructionist thought begins with a recognition of philosophical idealism. Social constructionists work with an ontology that questions the existence of an objective reality apart from the individual's imagination. Whether there are universal essences is indeed problematic. What can be assumed is that objects cannot exist *independently* of our minds, or at least that any such existence is important only as long as it can be perceived.

The epistemological assumption of social constructionist thought is that observations are based on our mental *constructions*, rather than on the raw apprehension of the physical world. The concern of the social constructionist is not primarily with the correspondence between "objective reality" and observation, but between observation and the utility of such observation in understanding our own subjective, multiple worlds. Therefore, the social scientist's constructs have to be founded upon the world created by social actors. As Schutz conceptualized the problem: "The constructs of the social

[8] For example, see most of the research studies collected in Richard Quinney (ed.), *Crime and Justice in Society* (Boston: Little, Brown and Company, 1969).

5

sciences are, so to speak, constructs of the second degree, that is, constructs of the constructs made by the actors on the social scene, whose behavior the social scientist has to observe and to explain in accordance with the procedural rules of his science." [9] The world that is important to the social constructionist, then, is the one created by the social actions of human beings, through interaction and intercommunication with others. This *social reality* involves the social meanings and the products of the subjective world of actors.[10] People construct activities and patterns of action as they attach meanings to their everyday life.

The social constructionist mode of thought makes a major advance over positivistic thought in respect to the crucial matter of reflexivity. The social constructionist questions the process by which he knows, instead of taking it for granted. In the course of this consideration, he reflects on his activity as observer, using to advantage the social and personal nature of his observation. That this reflexivity does not extend to a political stance, and possibly to political action, is a shortcoming inherent in the social constructionist mode.

Since social constructionist thought generally concentrates on the world of meanings created by social actors, its emphasis, especially in ethnomethodological studies, is on the construction of social order. Such concentration tends to ignore a world of events and structures that exists independent of the consciousness of social actors. This conservative side of social constructionist thought makes it inadequate for a critical perspective. As Richard Lichtman has written about this inadequacy: "It is overly subjective and voluntaristic, lacks an awareness of historical concreteness, is naive in its account of mutual typification and ultimately abandons the sense of human beings in struggle with an alien reality which they both master and to which they are subordinate. It is a view that tends to dissolve the concept of 'ideology' or 'false consciousness' and leaves

[9] Alfred Schutz, "Concept and Theory Formation in the Social Sciences," in Maurice Nathanson (ed.), *Philosophy of the Social Sciences* (New York: Random House, 1963), p. 242.

[10] See Alfred Schutz, *The Problem of Social Reality: Collected Papers I* (The Hague: Martinus Nijhoff, 1962); and Peter L. Berger and Thomas Luckmann, *The Social Construction of Reality* (Garden City, N.Y.: Doubleday, 1966).

6

us, often against the will of its advocates, without a critical posture toward the present inhuman reality." [11]

Therefore, it is often necessary to revise or reject the world as some social actors conceive it. To accept the world that social actors portray is often to accept the view of reality that the ruling class perpetuates to assure its own dominance. Social constructionist thought fails to provide a stance that would allow us to transcend the official reality and, ultimately, our current existence. Although social constructionists furnish us with the beginnings for an examination of multiple realities, they fail to provide a yardstick for judging the goodness of one reality over another. Social relativism prevails at the expense of a critical understanding of the social world.

The social constructionist perspective, however, has given new vitality to the study of crime and the law. Departing significantly from positivistic studies, social constructionists have turned attention to the problematic nature of the legal order. They view crime and other forms of stigmatized behavior first as categories created and imposed upon some persons by others.[12] Crime exists because of the social construction and the application of the label.

Similarly, criminal law is not autonomous within society, but is itself a construction, created by those in positions of power. The administration of justice is a human social activity that is constructed as various legal agents interpret behavior and impose their order on those they select for processing.[13] The social reality of crime is thus a process whereby conceptions of crime are constructed, criminal laws are established and administered, and behaviors are developed in relation to these criminal definitions.[14]

The legal order, accordingly, is a human activity. It is an order created for political purposes, to assure the hegemony of the ruling class. However, social constructionist thought stops at this point.

[11] Richard Lichtman, "Symbolic Interactionism and Social Reality: Some Marxist Queries," *Berkeley Journal of Sociology*, 15 (1970–71), pp. 75–94.

[12] Howard S. Becker, *Outsiders: Studies in the Sociology of Deviance* (New York: The Free Press, 1963).

[13] Aaron V. Cicourel, *The Social Organization of Juvenile Justice* (New York: John Wiley & Sons, 1968).

[14] Richard Quinney, *The Social Reality of Crime* (Boston: Little, Brown and Company, 1970).

To be sure, there are critical implications. There is the libertarian ideal that individuals should not be controlled by others, that people must be free to pursue their human potential. But there is, nevertheless, a failure to provide an image of what a new world should look like. Without such an image of what could be, an understanding of the current reality lacks a critical perspective. The ideal of liberation may be present, but unless that ideal is accompanied by a critique of the present and an image of an authentic existence, transcendence of the existing order is unlikely. Critical thought and action must be informed by a critical philosophy.

THE PHENOMENOLOGICAL MODE

Phenomenological thought departs markedly from positivistic and social constructionist thought in its basic intention. Whereas the other modes of thought are concerned with the explanation of social life, phenomenological thought begins by examining the process by which we understand the world. Explanation as a form of thought is itself examined. Hence, the philosophical problems of epistemology and ontology are a major concern of the phenomenologist.

Phenomenologists, though differing considerably among themselves, generally agree that our knowledge of the physical world comes from our experiences. But, they continue, when we talk about the physical world we are not limited by our experiences. That is, we are not limited by our actual experiences; we are able to talk about *possible* experiences, thus altering our perception of things in the world. As long as a physical object exists in the world, it is possible to experience it. What is important is that an object is perceivable.

The phenomenologists may proceed by "bracketing," setting aside, the question of objective reality in order to turn attention to the reality in *consciousness*. The phenomenon in question, then, is that which manifests itself immediately in consciousness. Following Kant's distinctions, the phenomenologist is primarily concerned with the *phenomenon*, or the appearance of reality in itself.[15] Yet it is

[15] See Quentin Lauer, *Phenomenology: Its Genesis and Prospect* (New York: Harper Torchbooks, 1965), pp. 1–2; and Pierre Thévenaz, *What is Phenomenology?* ed. James M. Edie (Chicago: Quadrangle Books, 1962), pp. 42–43.

8

possible to think about what is not known, the "thing-in-itself," or the *noumenon*, of which the phenomenon is the known aspect. Our knowledge of phenomena, therefore, is always subject to revision.

Consciousness itself is the source of our understanding of the world. Any knowledge of an objective thing can come about only through our consciousness of the thing. Reality is not to be found existing independently of our consciousness.[16] Any objectivity is to be achieved by means of our own subjectivity — that is, through our consciousness. Essence, or the essential, is what the human mind understands through its consciousness, in the course of its experiences in the world. We are thus capable of perceiving the essence of things.

Phenomenological thought is thought in its purest form. Following Kant's further distinction between thinking and knowing, phenomenologists are engaged in thinking beyond the limitations of knowledge. There is the urge to think and understand in contrast to the urge solely to construct verifiable knowledge.[17] Though knowledge is not denied, room is made for thinking, for thinking about the possibilities. This allows the phenomenologist to think about such otherwise unthinkable topics as the meaning of our existence.

The urge to think forces us to transcend our conventional knowledge about the world and our place in it. It allows us momentarily to remove ourselves from our concrete experiences. This is, as Heidegger has termed it, meditative thinking: "Meditative thinking demands of us not to cling one-sidedly to a single idea, nor to run down a one-track course of ideas. Meditative thinking demands of us that we engage ourselves with what at first sight does not go together at all." [18] A comportment that enables us to keep open the meaning hidden in the world, in the arrangements of modern society, is what Heidegger further describes as the "openness to the mystery." Related to this is a "releasement toward things." Through the two, in the course of meditative thinking, we seek our true

16 Kant made this clear, and on this Husserl agreed. See Lauer, *Phenomenology*, p. 21.

17 This distinction is found in Immanuel Kant, *Critique of Pure Reason*, trans. Norman Kempt Smith (New York: Macmillan, 1929).

18 Martin Heidegger, *Discourse on Thinking*, trans. John M. Anderson and E. Hans Freund (New York: Harper & Row, 1966), p. 53.

nature. And, as Heidegger writes, "They grant us the possibility of dwelling in the world in a totally different way. They promise us a new ground and foundation upon which we can stand and endure in the world of technology without being imperiled by it." [19]

The idea of some form of transcendence has been basic to most phenomenological thought. For Kant the phenomenological method was transcendental in that we attend to our experiencing of an object, rather than to the object directly. Therefore, to be transcendental is to be reflexive. Phenomenology, as Richard Zaner has recently written, "is 'transcendental' because it is *foundational,* seeking to uncover and explicatively analyze the necessary presuppositions of every actual and possible object and process of consciousness, leading ultimately to the grounds for philosophical reflection itself (reflexivity)." [20] The essence of a thing can be attained only through a transcendental philosophy — by being reflexive.

It is in the transcendental thinking of some of the phenomenologists that we find the inspiration for moving beyond the conventional wisdom of the age, including our contemporary knowledge of the legal order. Instead of reifying the social order in the manner of the positivists, or giving an account of ordered existence in the manner of the social constructionists, the phenomenologists move toward a transcendence of our experience. This is a necessary step as we begin to act in a way that will truly reveal the social world. Our primary interest is not in the development of a new social science (which would still be a reified science) but in the creation of a new existence, an existence free of all reifications.

Phenomenological thought by itself, however, is incomplete for attaining our objectives. Although it provides a drastic and necessary move beyond the other modes of thought, it lacks the critical edge that would allow us to truly transcend the present, in life as in mind. Phenomenology does make us question the assumptions by which we know and by which we live. This is its major achievement. But what is needed is a philosophy that would allow us to actively transcend the existing order, one that would allow us to be committed. We must turn to the development of a critical philosophy.

[19] *Ibid.*
[20] Richard M. Zaner, *The Way of Phenomenology: Criticism as a Philosophical Discipline* (New York: Pegasus, 1970), p. 203.

CRITICAL PHILOSOPHY

A critical philosophy is one that is *radically* critical. It is a philosophy that goes to the roots of our lives, to the foundations and the fundamentals, to the essentials of consciousness.[21] In the rooting out of presuppositions, we are able to assess every actual and possible experience. The operation is one of demystification, the removal of the myths — the false consciousness — created by the official reality. Conventional experience is revealed for what it is — a reification of an oppressive social order. The underside of official reality is thereby exposed. The liberating force of radical criticism is the movement from relevation to the development of a new consciousness and an active life in which we transcend the established existence. A critical philosophy is a form of life.

Thinking in itself is the beginning of a critical philosophy. For in the act of thought we engage in a particular kind of life, a reflective life that liberates us from preconceptions. Such theorizing, Alan Blum contends, expresses self, is a display of mind. Furthermore: "This 'calling to mind,' following an interpretation of Wittgenstein, is a way of recovering what one has all along, it is a way of seeing and as such it is inextricably tied to a way of living. More than this, it is to reconstitute or re-create out of one's life and history of a society another possibility for seeing. To theorize is to re-formulate one's self." [22] The theorist is thus showing another possibility for seeing and living. Such theorizing has the potential of allowing us to comprehend a version of a possible society. Our selves are transformed in the course of theorizing.

The concept of thought in relation to a form of life is firmly based in the classic philosophical tradition. This is the theoretical attitude that ideas are to inform actions, that life is to be enlightened by thought. A critical philosophy, as Jurgen Habermas has suggested, is one that destroys the illusion of objectivism (of a reality apart from consciousness).[23] Conceived in this way, thought itself is

21 See Zaner, *The Way of Phenomenology,* especially pp. 112–113, 117, 196, and 203.

22 Alan F. Blum, "Theorizing," in Jack D. Douglas (ed.), *Understanding Everyday Life: Toward the Reconstruction of Sociological Knowledge* (Chicago: Aldine, 1970), p. 305.

23 See Jurgen Habermas, *Knowledge and Human Interests,* trans. Jeremy J. Shapiro (Boston: Beacon Press, 1971), pp. 301–317.

necessarily critical. In demystifying our lives of all presuppostions, our attention is directed to a critique of our current existence. In a critical philosophy, truth is linked to the intention of finding the good and true life.

The chief characteristic of thinking, as Hannah Arendt notes in an essay on thinking and moral considerations, is that it interrupts all doing, all ordinary activity.[24] We are momentarily removed from our worldly associations; it is as though we entered into a different existence. Arendt adds that "thinking, the quest for meaning — rather than the scientist's thirst for knowledge for its own sake — can be felt to be 'unnatural,' as though men, when they begin to think, engage in some activity contrary to the human condition." [25] Arendt then concludes that only with thought that is aimed toward certain ideals (with the desiring of love, wisdom, beauty, and justice) are we prepared with a kind of thought that promotes a moral existence. Only when we are filled with what Socrates called *eros*, a love that desires what is not, can we find what is good.

Without critical thought we are bound to the only form of social life we know — that which currently exists. We are not then free to choose a better life; our only activity is in further support of the system in which we are enslaved. Our current cultural and social arrangements, supported as they are by a bureaucratic-technological system of production and distribution, are a threat to individual freedom — including the freedom to know that this system is oppressive and may be altered. Such a system tends to preclude the possibility of an opposition emerging within it. In aspiring to the rewards that the system holds out to us, we are unable to consider an alternative existence. Such is the message of Herbert Marcuse in his discussion of the "one-dimensional" character of our present reality.[26] Only in a negation of the present can we experience something else.

It is apparent, then, that what prevents us from seeing clearly is the ideology of the age. The modern institutional order finds its legitimation in an ideology that stresses the rationality of science

[24] Hannah Arendt, "Thinking and Moral Considerations," *Social Research,* 38 (Autumn, 1971), pp. 417–446.

[25] *Ibid.,* p. 424.

[26] Herbert Marcuse, *One-Dimensional Man* (Boston: Beacon Press 1964), p. 9.

and technology.[27] A generalized belief in the importance of controlled scientific-technical progress gives legitimacy to a particular class — the one that utilizes science and technology. The extent to which this ideology pervades the whole culture limits the possibility of emancipation, limits even the perception of the need for liberation. Moreover, the technocratic consciousness prevents a critical philosophy. Our understanding about the legal order, in particular, is limited by the ideology on which the legal order itself rests. That is, the legal order is founded on the rationality of science and technology, and the dominant mode of thought in understanding that order is based on this same ideology. Little wonder that we have been unable to break out of our conventional wisdom.

It is in a critical philosophy that we are able to break with the ideology of the age. For built into the process of critical thinking is the ability to think negatively. This dialectical form of thought allows us to question current experience.[28] By being able to entertain an alternative, we can better understand what exists. Rather than merely looking for an objective reality, we are concerned with the negation of the established order. Through this negation we are better able to understand what we experience. Possibly only by means of this dialectic can the present be comprehended. Certainly the present cannot be surpassed until the dialectic is applied to our thought.

But more than negative thinking is required in a philosophy that will move us to a radical reconstruction of our lives — indeed, to revolution itself. In order to reject something, we must have some idea of what things could be like. It is at this point that a critical philosophy must ultimately develop a Marxist perspective. In the Marxian notion of the authentic human being, we are provided with a concrete image of the possible. Current realties are judged according to how they alienate human beings. Only in the conscious grasp of the world can we change the world. The process is a collective one — consciousness and action developed in association with others. The imagery is transcendental — to attain what is natural to us by removing that which obstructs our lives. It is in the contradiction of

Marxist thought

27 Jurgen Habermas, *Toward a Rational Society: Student Protest, Science, and Politics* (Boston: Beacon Press, 1970), pp. 81–121.
28 Herbert Marcuse, *Reason and Revolution* (Boston: Beacon Press, 1960), especially pp. vii–xiv and 3–29.

13

an oppressive existence, between what exists and what is authentically human, that we understand our reality and act to bring about a liberating existence.

To think in a Marxian fashion is to be genuinely critical, to the fullest extent of our critical resources. For most of us, however, Marxian thought has been presented in two forms: either in the liberal reactionary version, as a response to the Cold War mentality of the last twenty years, or in the orthodox realpolitik version. That we accepted these versions and resorted to positivistic thought, is the stark measure of our lack of critical faculties.

In contrast, what we are experiencing today is the creation of an underground Marxism.[29] In the course of developing our critical capacities, we are rediscovering and recreating a form and body of thought that finds its grounding in Marxian analysis. Marxism is the one philosophy of our time that takes as its focus the oppression produced by a capitalist society. It is the one form of analysis that is historically specific and locates the problems of the age in the economic-class relations.[30] A Marxian critique provides, most importantly, a form of thought that allows us to transcend in thought and action that kind of existence. Contrary to both liberal and orthodox interpretations, Marxism is highly creative thought, open to the interpretations of each generation. And with the changes in capitalism itself, from industrial capitalism to advanced monopoly capitalism,

[29] See, for example, Karl E. Klare, "The Critique of Everyday Life, Marxism, and the New Left," *Berkeley Journal of Sociology*, 16 (1971–72), pp. 15–45.

[30] Horowitz writes in this regard: "There already exists, of course, a traditional *corpus* of Marxian theory which would logically form the starting point of any new analytical approach. But revision of the analytic tools and propositions of traditional Marxist theory is inevitable if the theory is to develop as an intellectual doctrine, and not degenerate into mere dogma. In principle, it may even be possible to create a theory which is 'Marxist' in the restricted sense urged here, but which has little surface relation to the traditional Marxist categories and conclusions. Nonetheless, at this historical juncture, the traditional Marxist paradigm is the only economic paradigm which is capable of analyzing capitalism as an historically specific, class-determined social formation. As such it provides an indispensable framework for understanding the development and crisis of the present social system and, as an intellectual outlook, would occupy a prime place in any scientific institution worthy of the name." David Horowitz, "Marxism and Its Place in Economic Science," *Berkeley Journal of Sociology*, 16 (1971–72), p. 57. Also see Jean-Paul Sartre, *Search for a Method*, trans. Hazel E. Barnes (New York: Alfred A. Knopf, 1963).

new and critical readings of Marx are necessary.[31] Critical thought makes possible a new understanding of Marx in each age. Which is also to say, a new understanding of Marx makes critical thought possible.

All thinking, all life, is subject to critical philosophy. A critical philosophy of legal order, in particular, allows us to understand what has been otherwise unexamined. In an understanding of the true meaning of the legal order, in a Marxian critique, we are able to transcend the present and create an alternative existence. Liberation is the ultimate objective of a critical philosophy of legal order.

DEVELOPING A CRITICAL PHILOSOPHY OF LEGAL ORDER

To summarize thus far, I have argued that current modes of thought have prevented us from understanding the legal order. The dominant modes of thought, including the positivistic, social constructionist, and much of the phenomenological, have been tied to an age that can do little more than oppress, manipulate, and control human beings as objects. The legal order has been viewed in the social sciences as a necessary force to assure order in capitalist society. Positivists have regarded law as a natural mechanism; social constructionists have regarded it relativistically, as one of man's conveniences; and even the phenomenologists, though examining underlying assumptions, have done little to provide or promote an alternative existence. We must conclude that our thoughts and our ways of thinking are wanting, are inappropriate and inadequate.

With a sense of the more authentic life that may be possible for us, I am suggesting that a critical philosophy for understanding the legal order should be based on a development of Marxist thought for our age. Marx had little to say about criminal law and crime control. Our purpose, then, will be to develop a critical-Marxian analysis of crime control in capitalist society.

Although the legal order consists of more than criminal law, criminal law is the foundation of that order. It is the coercive instrument of the state, used by the state and its ruling class to main-

[31] For example, Paul A. Baran and Paul M. Sweezy, *Monopoly Capitalism: An Essay on the American Economic and Social Order* (New York: Monthly Review Press, 1966).

15

tain the existing social and economic order. A critical theory of crime control in American society can be outlined systematically as follows:

1. American society is based on an advanced capitalist economy.
2. The state is organized to serve the interests of the dominant economic class, the capitalist ruling class.
3. Criminal law is an instrument of the state and ruling class to maintain and perpetuate the existing social and economic order.
4. Crime control in capitalist society is accomplished through a variety of institutions and agencies established and administered by a governmental elite, representing ruling class interests, for the purpose of establishing domestic order.
5. The contradictions of advanced capitalism — the disjunction between existence and essence — require that the subordinate classes remain oppressed by whatever means necessary, especially through the coercion and violence of the legal system.
6. Only with the collapse of capitalist society and the creation of a new society, based on socialist principles, will there be a solution to the crime problem.

Criminal law is used by the state and the ruling class to secure the survival of the capitalist system, and, as capitalist society is further threatened by its own contradictions, criminal law will be increasingly used in the attempt to maintain domestic order. The underclass, the class that must remain oppressed for the triumph of the dominant economic class, will continue to be the object of crime control as long as the dominant class seeks to perpetuate itself, that is, as long as capitalism exists. Only with the building of a socialist society will there be a world without the need for crime control. Never before has our understanding of legal order been so crucial. Never before has our understanding been so related to the way we must live our lives. To think critically and radically today is to be revolutionary. To do otherwise is to side with the oppression of the capitalist state. Our understanding of the legal order and our actions in relation to it must work to remove that oppression, must be a force in liberation.

2

Knowledge and Order

The intellectual sources of law and order are to be found in the minds of reasonable men. Though it is customary for the liberal intelligence to locate repression in the ideology of the masses and the programs of pragmatic politicians, the actual ideas and justifications have been developed by the liberal intelligence itself. Men of knowledge have advocated theories based on a very restricted image of human existence. The research of social scientists has only confirmed the narrowness of this vision. Little wonder that social scientists have so readily served the government. The official reality of the state and the interests of social scientists are the same.

But why, if knowledge is supposed to be liberating, have we been oppressed by it? Knowledge has failed us because it has been pursued without a critical intelligence; it has been devoid of the crucial element of thought, lacking a sense of the possible. With a new conception of knowledge — knowledge as an emerging consciousness — our efforts would be much different. Knowledge would be a searching for that which will liberate us all, rather than being merely a static judgment of our fate. It would cease to support existing authority.

But let us turn to our current state of knowledge. Conventional

17

knowledge supports the established legal order. This is evident in several areas of scholarship, particularly in the social sciences. Academic scholarship is immersed in a conventional wisdom that prevents a solution to the problems of our age. Current knowledge lacks the intellectual resources for transcending legal order. Only in a critical understanding of legal order can we begin to break out of the boundaries of existing intelligence.

THE SEARCH FOR ORDER

The search for order has been the principal concern of the social theorist. Indeed, the very emergence of the social sciences was a reaction to social and political change.[1] The early social theorists were disturbed by the many conflicts and upheavals occurring in Europe at the end of the eighteenth century and during the first half of the nineteenth. They hoped that knowledge of the natural world could be discovered and would provide a program for social stability.

The social sciences never broke from their reactionary background. To this day social scientists, in their attempt to discover the laws of social order, tend to favor existing social arrangements.[2] Whatever threatens social order is regarded as a violation of the natural laws of society. Social theorists have supported anything that would uphold order and rejected anything that would disrupt that order. Social order is regarded as the basic good. The social theorist therefore asks, "How is social order to be established and maintained?"

The problem, first formulated by Thomas Hobbes, is what social theorists today call the "Hobbesian problem of order." Hobbes assumed that man was innately violent and selfish, and that the life of man was no more than "solitary, poor, nasty, brutish, and short."

[1] See Herbert Marcuse, *Reason and Revolution* (Boston: Beacon Press, 1960), pp. 323–388; Irving M. Zeitlin, *Ideology and the Development of Sociology* (Englewood Cliffs, N.J.: Prentice-Hall, 1968); and Sheldon S. Wolin, *Politics and Vision* (Boston: Little, Brown and Company, 1960).

[2] For a more detailed discussion of the reactionary nature of the social sciences, see Richard Quinney, "From Repression to Liberation: Social Theory in Radical Age," in Robert A. Scott and Jack D. Douglas (eds.), *Theoretical Perspectives on Deviance* (New York: Basic Books, 1972), pp. 317–341.

Because of this, Hobbes reasoned, man must enter into the social contract, whereby the "war of all against all" is checked. On this point, Talcott Parsons recommended the Hobbesian problem of order to generations of sociologists. The solution to the problem of order was to be found in the "institutionalization of a set of norms defining the limits of legitimate action"; we were thereby to be assured of "the integration of stable systems of social interaction." [3]

There are, of course, threats to the maintenance of a stable social order. A basic threat to social order, as Tocqueville wrote, is democratic government.[4] In promoting individualism and equality, democracy undermines the authority of traditional rule. How to preserve authority in a democracy thus becomes the crucial problem of the modern social theorist. In *The Sociological Tradition*, Robert Nisbet provides a statement of the problem:

> But when men become separated, or feel themselves separated, from traditional institutions, there arises, along with the specter of the lost individual, the specter of lost authority. Fears and anxieties run over the intellectual landscape like masterless dogs. Inevitably in such circumstances, men's minds turn to the problem of authority. What, it is asked, shall be the source and nature of an authority sufficient to replace lost authority, to restrain the natural anarchy that even in civilized society thrusts itself now and then through the crevices of law and morality? And, paralleling this question: What shall be the means of checking the kind of power that always threatens to rise on the ruins of constituted authority? [5]

The ideological commitment of the social theorist, then, is to a stable social and political order. And the ultimate source of that stability, for the modern theorist, is the "legitimacy" of the system. According to Max Weber's ideas on legitimate authority, rulers have the right to command and be obeyed when those who are ruled regard the power of the rulers as legitimate.[6] In other words, it is

---

[3] Talcott Parsons, *The Social System* (New York: The Free Press, 1951), p. 118.

[4] Alexis de Tocqueville, *Democracy in America*, Vol. II, ed. Philip Bradley (New York: Alfred A. Knopf, 1945).

[5] Robert A. Nisbet, *The Sociological Tradition* (New York: Basic Books, 1966), p. 108.

[6] Max Weber, *The Theory of Social and Economic Organization*, trans. A. M. Henderson and Talcott Parsons (New York: The Free Press, 1947), pp. 324–386.

19

legitimate authority that gives a government by an elite the right to rule over the rest of the population. Sovereignty is in the state, not in the people. In modern terminology, "Legitimacy involves the capacity of the system to engender and maintain the belief that the existing political institutions are the most appropriate ones for the society." [7]

Legitimacy in modern society is, for the social theorist, represented by the legal system itself; law is the most rational form of authority. In this conception of legal authority, obedience is owed to the legally and rationally established impersonal order. There is little room in this image of law for questioning the rightness of the legal order; it exists, therefore it is legitimate. The legal system is not to be questioned but to be obeyed.

Law is assumed to be necessary in human society. Although this has been debated, legal scholars inevitably conclude that law is the great civilizer and source of progress.

> Leading philosophers, from Plato to Marx, may have urged that law is an evil thing of which mankind would do well to rid itself. Yet, for all the philosophic doubts, experience has shown that law is one of the great civilizing forces in human society, and that the growth of civilization has generally been linked with the gradual development of a system of legal rules, together with machinery for their regular and effective enforcement. [8]

Probably the unquestioning acceptance of the existence of law rests on the naive assumption that order can only be achieved and maintained through law. A case in point: "The idea that human society, on whatever level, could ever conceivably exist on the basis that each man should simply do whatever he thinks right in the particular circumstances is too fanciful to deserve serious consideration." [9] The fear is carried to the point that such a society would be regarded not merely as a "society without order" but as the very negation of society. The radical proposal that law be eliminated seldom receives a welcome reception.

The legal mentality is an integral part of today's demand for law

[7] Seymour Martin Lipset, *Political Man: The Social Base of Politics* (Garden City, N.Y.: Doubleday, 1960), p. 64.

[8] Dennis Lloyd, *The Idea of Law* (Harmondsworth, England: Penguin Books, 1964), p. 7.

[9] *Ibid.*, p. 24.

20

and order. Human beings, we are told, even in the best of times, must be restrained. But given what seems to be a time of chaos and disorder, even more drastic measures are justified. Liberals today are among the first to support the assumptions of law and order, although their rhetoric may be prettier than that of the right. Staughton Lynd, in an article that touches on the demand for law and order, comments exactly on this repressive legal mentality of modern liberals:

> Rather than moving with life, like a gardener or a teacher, our society rigidly confronts life like a policeman. Repression and authoritarianism are on the rise in America because at its highest levels the society believes it is better (for other people) to be dead than different. And so in every institution, at every age, in every meeting of those with more power and those with less, there is indeed a crisis of law and order. The people who talk most about it are those who have the power, hence the law and order, and feel no need for change. They — and I am talking not of George Wallace but of the Ivy League graduates in Wall Street and government — are apparently prepared to destroy the world rather than let it become something which they don't run.[10]

The liberal terminology for what passes as law and order in everyday parlance is the "rule of law." That rule has been raised to a kind of moral absolute. To obey the law becomes a good in its own right, beyond the goals that underlie each law. And though such ideas as "due process" are attractive, they become in their administration devices that further a particular authority structure. Supposedly the law protects the rights of each of us and promotes a just existence. But this ideal is negated by the fact that the entire legal system is played according to rules formulated and enforced by a legal establishment that is part of the capitalist ruling class.

ruling class

The legalists continually justify and rationalize the existence of law. We are told that the rule of law must be the core value of our society, that all other values depend on this rule. In response to the demands for change that are coming from all directions, the legal establishment is again promoting the necessity of law. The rhetorical question is asked, "Is law dead?" And Eugene Rostow, in a book

[10] Staughton Lynd, "Again — Don't Tread on Me," *Newsweek,* July 6, 1970, p. 31.

devoted to that question, sponsored by the Association of the Bar of the City of New York, writes: "Thus the concern of the Association has been not merely to justify the ways of law to the community, but to vindicate the law as a means of achieving justice — not merely to defend the law, but to help make it worthy of defense, as the supreme and all-embracing instrument of social progress, and of social peace." [11] The legal order is being presented to us (by the legalists in a capitalist society) as the only rational means for the achievement of social order. Other possibilities for social existence are excluded.

In the name of knowledge the existing order is being rationalized and supported by the social theorists and legal scholars. The role of social theory in capitalist society is to legitimize existing authority, thereby securing the dominant social and economic arrangements. Such knowledge is actually an ideology for the existing order; and those who engage in this kind of knowledge are the ideologues and servants of the ruling class.[12] Certainly the existing economic basis of society is not called into question, although there may be occasional debates within the capitalist framework. By excluding other possibilities of existence, these men of knowledge not only support capitalist society but also prevent the emergence of an alternative consciousness. A socialist alternative to the existing social and economic order is not found in the dominant theories of our time.

SOCIOLOGY OF LAW

In recent years a body of knowledge has developed regarding law as a social phenomenon, subject to sociological investigation. To the exclusion of other possibilities, the sociology of law presents a particular image of the role of law in society. That image was expressed earlier in sociological jurisprudence, a school of legal philosophy that drew its inspiration from early sociology. Its leading figure, Roscoe Pound, saw law as a specialized form of social control which brings pressure to bear upon each man "in order to constrain him to do his part in upholding civilized society and to deter him from anti-

[11] Eugene V. Rostow, "Introduction," in Eugene V. Rostow (ed.), *Is Law Dead?* (New York: Simon and Schuster, 1971), p. 15.

[12] See Ralph Miliband, *The State in Capitalist Society* (New York: Basic Books, 1969), pp. 259–261.

social conduct, that is, conduct at variance with the postulates of social order." [13]

Moreover, Pound, in formulating his theory of interests, looked upon law as reflecting the needs of the well-ordered society. In fact, the law was a form of "social engineering" in a civilized society:

> For the purpose of understanding the law of today I am content to think of law as a social institution to satisfy social wants — the claims and demands involved in the existence of civilized society — by giving effect to as much as we may with the least sacrifice, so far as such wants may be satisfied or such claims given effect by an ordering of human conduct through politically organized society. For present purposes I am content to see in legal history the record of a continually wider recognizing and satisfying of human wants or claims or desires through social control; a more embracing and more effective securing of social interests; a continually more complete and effective elimination of waste and precluding of friction in human enjoyment of the goods of existence — in short, a continually more efficacious social engineering.[14]

According to Pound's theory, law serves those interests that are for the good of the whole society. Only the right law could emerge in a civilized society.

Furthermore, a *pluralistic* model dominates this sociological conception of law. Law, supposedly, orders human relations by restraining individual actions and by settling disputes between competing groups. Again Pound:

> Looked at functionally, the law is an attempt to satisfy, to reconcile, to harmonize, to adjust these overlapping and often conflicting claims and demands, either through securing them directly and immediately, or through securing certain individual interests, or through delimitations or compromises of individual interests, so as to give effect to the greatest total of interests or to the interests that weigh most in our civilization, with the least sacrifice of the scheme of interests as a whole.[15]

[13] Roscoe Pound, *Social Control Through Law* (New Haven: Yale University Press, 1942), p. 18.
[14] Roscoe Pound, *An Introduction to Legal Philosophy* (New Haven: Yale University Press, 1922), pp. 98–99.
[15] Roscoe Pound, "A Survey of Social Interests," *Harvard Law Review,* 57 (October, 1943), p. 39.

In sociological jurisprudence, then, law is regarded as an instrument that controls diverse interests according to the requirements of social order.

The image of law as presented in sociological jurisprudence dominates the sociology of law today. Law is viewed as a form of social control that regulates and integrates the competing interests in a well-ordered pluralistic society. Through such a conception of law, not only is support given to the legal order (no matter what its content) but pluralism itself is advocated. The unity of pluralism and law is noted by Parsons when he concludes: "Finally, it may perhaps be suggested that law has a special importance in a pluralistic liberal type of society. It has its strongest place in a society where there are many different kinds of interests that must be balanced against each other and that must in some way respect each other." [16]

Sociologists of law take the existence of a pluralistic society and the necessity of law for granted. Rather than questioning these assumptions, they attempt to explain the "law in action." They fail to realize that in American society — because of gross inequality of power — only a few groups are ever able to be represented in the formulation of law. Contrary to the pluralist assumptions, law is determined by those few — representing a power elite with similar interests — who dominate the political process. Although law is supposed to protect all citizens, it starts as a tool of the dominant class and ends by maintaining the dominance of that class. Law serves the powerful over the weak; it promotes the war of the powerful against the powerless. Moreover, law is used by the state (and its elitist government) to promote and protect itself. Yet we are all bound by that law, and we are indoctrinated with the myth that it is our law. A sociology of law only confirms this myth.

In a book devoted to the problem of social change through law, Joel Grossman says: "Insofar as we are able to evaluate our own premises, the book proceeds from a view that law is a desirable

[16] Talcott Parsons, "The Law and Social Control," in William M. Evans (ed.), *Law and Sociology: Exploratory Essays* (New York: The Free Press, 1962), p. 72. A pluralist model of law is used in Edwin M. Lemert, *Social Action and Legal Change: Revolution Within the Juvenile Court* (Chicago: Aldine Publishing Company, 1970).

and necessary, if not a highly efficient means of inducing change, and that, wherever possible, its institutions and procedures are preferable to others of which we are aware." [17] Such a belief in "the adequacy of law as an instrument for bringing about necessary change" is firmly based in a conventional wisdom that regards established institutions as the most appropriate. Critical examination of the assumption of the necessity of law will produce a conception of law quite different from that found in present-day sociology of law.

It is difficult for sociologists of law to consider alternatives to legal order. An orderly existence in a developed society, they assume, is achieved only through law. They may even hold that as societies advance there is a natural development of legality. [18] Eventually, they suggest, ever wider realms of social life — churches, universities, corporations — will develop legal systems. Law, accordingly, is the realization of rationality.

Knowledge in the sociology of law is based on the assumption that legal order is the most *rational* form of human organization. The scientific study of law is bound to the belief in legal rationality, as well as to the belief that all problems of human existence can be solved by applying scientific methods. Philip Selznick writes, in an essay on the sociology of law, that "legal reasoning cannot but accept the authority of scientifically validated conclusions regarding the nature of man and his institutions. Therefore, inevitably, sociology and every other social science have a part in the legal order." [19] Hence, the sociology of law — narrowly construed as the scientific study of law — not only studies law but supports the legal order. The fate of the legal order and the fate of the scientfic study of law are tied together.

To base a legal system on the scientific ethos is the objective of the sociologist of law. With the accumulation of empirical research, and communication with legal agencies, the reasoning goes, human af-

[17] Joel B. Grossman, "Introduction," in Joel B. Grossman (ed.), *Law and Change in Modern America* (Pacific Palisades, Calif.: Goodyear Publishing Company, 1971), p. 2.
[18] See Jerome H. Skolnick, "The Sociology of Law in America: Overview and Trends," *Social Problems*, Supplement (Summer, 1965), pp. 29–32.
[19] Philip Selznick, "The Sociology of Law," in Robert K. Merton, Leonard Broom, and Leonard S. Cottrell, Jr. (eds.), *Sociology Today* (New York: Basic Books, 1959), p. 126.

fairs will become rational. An editor of the *Law and Society Review* is thus able to write:

> As more empirical studies of the legal process emerge, we may ultimately be able to construct a scientific model of law in society which can serve to refine and supplement the traditional models. We need to learn more about the manner in which law creates, supports, and regulates the various institutions of a complex society; how its actions affect its own position in society; what leads to the acceptance of its legitimacy and to the effectiveness of its sanctions; how these effects in turn relate to the influences exerted on law by public opinion, interest groups, and agencies of government; and how these influences are in turn translated into action. Such a model is certain to differ from the models implicitly held at present by legal decision makers and explicitly by men of jurisprudence. As the models of jurisprudence and social science become more consistent and find expression in the legal process we will have made an advance in the eternal battle to increase rationality in human affairs.[20]

A sociology of law as presently conceived and practiced cannot break out of the ideology of the age. It can only confirm the existing order; problems of the age are only exacerbated by the sociological-scientific study of law. Studies of law — by focusing solely on law in action — systematically ignore moral questions about the legal order. The sociology of law thereby opts for social order at the expense of informing us about the morality of that order. A sociology of law much different from what we know today is necessary if we are to be liberated from the problems of the existing society.

CRIMINOLOGY

Criminology — as the scientific study of crime — has served a single purpose: legitimation of the existing social order. The established system has been taken for granted; departures from and threats to social order have been the objects of investigation. In the name of developing knowledge about crime, most criminologists have supported current institutions at the expense of human freedoms and social revolution. Through a special form of reasoning and adherence to a particular ideology, the needs of the individual have been

[20] Richard D. Schwartz, "Introduction," *Social Problems*, Supplement (Summer, 1965), p. 3.

identified with the need to maintain and perpetuate the existing order.

Criminologists have traditionally asked the question, "What causes crime?" The answer has been sought in the study of the "criminal." That is, the sources of crime are believed to reside in the person who violates the law. This emphasis has meant that criminal law and political theory have been ignored. Rather than understanding crime as a product of the authority that defines behavior as criminal, criminologists have concentrated on the behavior of the offender. To critically understand and question the existing legal system falls outside the scientific and ideological interests of most criminologists. Their theories of crime, then, have been theories of criminal behavior. And in most instances, that criminal behavior has been, by definition, a threat to social order, something that must be controlled or eliminated in order to ensure social stability. The criminologist's efforts have been directed as much to the search for order as to an understanding of crime. Criminological theory has provided a rationale for the maintenance of social order.

The major theoretical perspective in criminology is that of the socialization of the law violator. This perspective is, of course, sociological: "The approach to crime which is distinctively sociological assumes that the criminal acquires his interest, ability, and means of self-justification in crime through his relationship to others." [21] There is little in this perspective that will allow the criminologist to examine the process by which the person becomes defined as criminal by the state. And there is no room for questioning the rightfulness of the laws that are imposed on the citizen. The value of justice traditionally falls outside the realm of criminology.

The result is that criminologists have become the ancillary agents of power. They provide the kinds of information that governing elites use to manipulate and control those who threaten the system. As "experts," criminologists inform the managers of social order.[22] This alliance between criminology and the state, however, is far

[21] Daniel Glaser, "The Sociological Approach to Crime and Correction," *Law and Contemporary Problems,* 23 (Autumn, 1958), p. 683.

[22] See Clayton A. Hartjen, "Legalism and Humanism: A Reply to the Schwendingers," *Issues in Criminology,* 7 (Winter, 1972), pp. 59–69. The problem was originally raised, with different emphasis, in Herman and Julia Schwendinger, "Defenders of Order or Guardians of Human Rights?" *Issues in Criminology,* 5 (Summer, 1970), pp. 123–157.

from being an explicit conspiracy; rather, the relationship is much more natural and subtle. Criminologists automatically serve the interests of the state by following their own unexamined assumptions about the nature of the world and the process of understanding it. By pursuing a narrow scientific model, supported by an ideology of social order, the criminologist finds his interests tied to those of the state. Both parties have an interest in preserving existing arrangements.

The criminologist has held fast to a scientific conception of his field. Indeed, it has been argued that the term "criminology" "should be used to designate a body of *scientific* knowledge about crime." [23] And in an attempt to show that this is not a restricted definition, Marvin Wolfgang adds:

> This conceptualism of criminology is neither narrow nor confining. A scientific approach to understanding the etiology of crime may include the statistical, historical, clinical, or case-study tools of analysis. Moreover, there is nothing inherently quantitative in scientific methodology, albeit the most convincing evidence, data, and presentation in general sociological replications of propositions appear to be quantitative. Probably the most fruitful source of analysis of empiric uniformity, regularity, and systems of patterned relationships can be found in the statistical studies of causation and prediction. However, interpretive analyses that may occasionally go beyond the limits of empirically correlated and organized data (but not beyond empiric reality) can be useful and enlightening. If description of the phenomena of crime is performed within a meaningful theoretical system, the methods and the goals of science are not necessarily discarded in the process but may be retained with all the vigor commonly attributed to sophisticated statistical manipulation.[24]

A difficulty for the criminologist, in his scientific pursuit of crime, is in the area of "corrections." Whether to admit those who "apply" criminology is the question. Should, for example, probation officers, social workers employed in prisons, and agency members of various kinds be regarded as criminologists, especially when they write about crime? Wolfgang maintains that none of these persons, by reason only

[23] Marvin E. Wolfgang, "Criminology and the Criminologist," *Journal of Criminal Law, Criminology and Police Science,* 54 (June, 1963), p. 155. Italics in the original.
[24] *Ibid.*

of his professional role, is a criminologist. However, "if any of these persons in pursuance of his occupational role is principally devoted to the task of *scientific* study, research, and analysis of the phenomenon of crime, criminal behavior, or treatment of the offender, his role is that of a criminologist." [25] And there is the possibility that criminology will even be strengthened by the applied interests. As Stanton Wheeler writes: "The movement toward professionalism in the practicing fields should lead to an increased number of competent and skilled practitioners and the recognition of need for more systematic research on crime and its control. Increased public attention to problems of delinquency and crime, particularly as reflected in increased budgets for prevention and research efforts, may attract a larger number of social scientists to problems of delinquency and crime." [26]

To be sure, crime control is good business for the criminologist. Crime control and scientific prediction go hand in hand. Science and politics are united: "If control and prediction in experimentation are integral goals of research and, regardless of the substantive area, if analysis proceeds by means of the scientific method, then we may include within the scope of criminology any correctional research that embraces these goals and this method." [27] Scientific criminology and the state's correctional aims are mutually supportive of one another.

We are told in criminology textbooks that not only is criminology a body of verified principles about crime but that, in addition:

> Criminology is concerned with the immediate application of knowledge to programs of crime control. This concern with practical programs is justified, in part, as experimentation which may be valuable because of its immediate results but at any rate will be valuable in the long run because of the increased knowledge which results from it. If practical programs wait until theoretical knowledge is complete, they will wait for eternity, for theoretical knowledge is increased most significantly in the efforts at social control. [28]

---

25 *Ibid.*, p. 161. Italics in the original.
26 Stanton Wheeler, "The Social Sources of Criminology," *Sociological Inquiry*, 32 (Spring, 1962), pp. 158–159.
27 Wolfgang, "Criminology and the Criminologist," p. 159.
28 Edwin H. Sutherland and Donald R. Cressey, *Criminology*, 8th edition (Philadelphia: J. B. Lippincott, 1970), p. 3.

Would a scientific criminology be possible without a state that controls citizens? At least, we are informed, theoretical knowledge is increased in the efforts of social control. A critical criminology, a radical criminology, would certainly depart significantly from the control interests of current scientific criminology.

The citizen, as long as the state defines him as criminal, is thus subject not only to the repressive measures of political authority but to the experimentations of criminologists as well. The criminologist has become more interested in developing knowledge — knowledge that will in turn be useful to the state for further repression — than he is in the human needs of the individual. In fact, prisons as they currently exist present a "unique opportunity":

> The prison system, in short, provides an opportunity for controlled sociological observation and comparative analysis which is very much needed from a practical and theoretical standpoint in criminology. It provides a unique opportunity for sociologists to test sociological theories, propositions, and insights, and to refine and develop them in the context of the correctional setting.[29]

To eliminate the prison would be to remove one of the crucial sites of criminological research.

It is in the important area of values that criminology ultimately reveals itself. The scientific model, in fact, neatly eliminates the possibility of value considerations. This means that the state is not usually criticized; it is right merely because it exists and has the authority to rule. The only time that a policy might be questioned is when "scientific evidence" appears to show that the policy is unsound, that is, either inefficient or uneconomical. A criminologist might advocate a new program within the prison if, for example, the one currently being used does not change the offender according to expectations. At any rate, few criminologists will make moral judgments about the legal system, other than talking vaguely about a more "humane" system or removing some of the minor criminal sanctions. And in these instances the recommendations are usually intended to make the existing system more rational or more respectable. Seldom is there a moral basis for criticism. The scientific-

[29] Lloyd E. Ohlin, *Sociology and the Field of Corrections* (New York: Russell Sage Foundation, 1956), p. 12.

technocratic control ethos has made the criminologist morally bankrupt.

The moral condition of criminology is evident when criminologists attempt to give some attention to ethical considerations. They take the position that ethical considerations must be based on scientific judgments. This also means that ethical judgments are unnecessary for scientific evaluation. Leslie Wilkins expresses this idea in a discussion of corporal punishment:

It may be believed that it is wrong to flog offenders, but it is difficult to make such a claim unless it is known whether or not those flogged tend afterwards to commit more or fewer offenses than those not flogged. It could be that flogging resulted in fewer offenses than those not flogged. It could be that flogging resulted in fewer reconvictions by offenders so dealt with, and yet may still be held that it would be wrong to flog. But suppose that *all* those flogged subsequently led good lives and *all* those not flogged returned to a life of crime, could flogging then be considered to be unethical? It might be so argued if other aspects of flogging could be found which were relevant to the issues, but these other facts would need similar assessment. Again, some would argue that flogging is ethical — the offender, they believe, must be given a taste of his own medicine. But if *all* those flogged lived good lives, it would be difficult to sustain the view that flogging was right. The extreme views on either side of the controversy regard the outcome of flogging as irrelevant. But can such a position be regarded as reasonable or ethical? If we have no information of the outcome, how can we make sound ethical judgments?" [30]

As Richard Korn observes regarding Wilkins's reasoning: "It is not the flogging but rather the making of such ethical judgments (pro or con) which is wrong, in the absence of evidence. It is the activity of scientifically unsupported moralizing which he opposes." [31]

This is not to imply that criminologists do not think on a large scale, or that they avoid grand schemes. Most criminologists probably have some idea of how crime should be handled authoritatively. Not to think of such a design would be a failure to carry their as-

[30] Leslie Wilkins, *Social Deviance* (Englewood Cliffs, N.J.: Prentice-Hall, 1965), p. 3.
[31] Richard Korn, "Reflections on Flogging: An Essay-Review of the Work of Leslie Wilkins and Tom Merton," *Issues in Criminology,* 6 (Summer, 1971), p. 99.

sumptions and perspectives to conclusion. The following passage describes a national, scientific approach to crime, utilizing (of course) a wide variety of "data sources."

All of these data are only likely to be collected, co-ordinated, and fully interpreted in terms of national and local crime problems, if a national research agency is created for this purpose. What appears to be needed is a federal office or bureau for criminological research, comparable in its research and dissemination activities to such diverse existing agencies as the Bureau of Labor Statistics, the Children's Bureau, the Department of Agriculture, and the Council of Economic Advisors. The optimum administrative status and place-ment of such an agency within the federal government probably is as a separate office or bureau within the Department of Justice. It would have to use the FBI criminal-record data, and ultimately other information on criminal careers from the files of judicial and correctional agencies, in addition to gathering survey information itself or contracting for such research. It should work with all agencies concerned with the policing, adjudication, correction, or prevention of crime and delinquency, yet not be dominated by any one of them. To assure this breadth of perspective it would be most desirable that such an agency operate under an advisory board representing all the major academic professional and public service groups highly concerned with the control of crime, in addition to the representatives of all concerned types of government agency on the national, state, and local level.[32]

Not only would law and order prevail, but the criminologist would be assured of steady employment. In contrast, a criminology would not be likely to exist in a truly free society.

SCHOLARSHIP IN THE SERVICE OF SOCIAL CONTROL

In spite of the intellectual arguments for social order, the myth of independent scholarship still prevails. The myth serves to justify the supposed objectivity of the intellect. Nevertheless, there is a close relation between the ideas of scholars and the interests of political authorities. And the myth is made most obvious in the actual support of scholarly research by government agencies.

[32] Daniel Glaser, "National Goals and Indicators for the Reduction of Crime and Delinquency," *Annals of the American Academy of Political and Social Science*, 371 (May, 1967), p. 126.

Social scientists, especially, have made contributions to the art of government, that is, to the perpetuation of government by the ruling elite. These explicit contributions have been made in several different ways. Social scientists have conducted research, supported by government grants, which provides information for manipulating and controlling the rest of the population. This information has come either from research sponsored for the explicit purpose of obtaining information or from studies that supposedly were independent of applied interests. In the latter case, the interests of government determine what kinds of projects are proposed by social scientists and which projects will be approved. Then there are the programs developed to train government agents (for example, policemen, parole officers, and prison guards) within the curriculum of the university. In addition, social scientists have served on numerous government commissions, providing research information and on occasion making suggestions for the benefit of the state. In all of these efforts, few social scientists have been able to separate themselves from the interests of the ruling class. There is little evidence to suggest a scholarly independence of mind. A critical philosophy has seldom guided the scholarship of social scientists.

In recent years specialized training programs in law enforcement have been instituted in American universities.[33] Over 750 colleges and universities currently offer courses or degree programs in "police science" or "criminal justice." About 65,000 students in 1970 received Department of Justice funds for their studies. At the same time, the Law Enforcement Assistance Administration (LEAA) of the Department of Justice made over 20 million dollars available to 735 colleges and universities for "law enforcement education programs." [34] The program awards ranged from $4,308 at Alabama A & M College to $24,599 at the University of Wyoming. The funds were widely distributed, including $299,699 awarded to New Haven College, $180,806 to Michigan State University, $60,304 to Southern Illinois University, $14,600 to Sacramento City College, and $600 to Point Park College.

[33] International Association of Chiefs of Police, *Directory: Law Enforcement Education 1970* (Washington, D.C.: International Association of Chiefs of Police, 1970).

[34] Law Enforcement Assistance Administration, *Grants and Contracts Fiscal Year 1970* (Washington, D.C.: Department of Justice, 1970), pp. 110–122.

These college and university programs are providing the training for personnel who will preserve domestic order. The programs are military models for the war on crime.

> These police training programs are mirror images of the Pentagon's ROTC programs. Both police and military officials believe that the sophisticated systems and weapons being introduced require manpower with more than a high school education. Supported with grants from LEAA, police departments are attempting to utilize the new military systems developed for use in Vietnam. New "command and control" systems, communications equipment, "night vision devices," and computerized intelligence systems can only be operated by skilled and trained personnel.[35]

Any hostility from students and some faculty is countered by the argument that these training programs will "professionalize" and "humanize" the police. But "professionalization of the police means exactly what it does in the Army: a fascination with technique and modern equipment, a de-politization of the department, and a readiness to carry out any orders from above." [36]

The National Institute of Law Enforcement and Criminal Justice (the research arm of LEAA) provides yearly fellowships to graduate students in the social sciences. Stipends of about $8,000 are awarded to students with a specific criminal justice focus. Some of the student awards (with the names of the students omitted) for the year 1970–71 are as follows:[37]

Economics, Virginia Polytechnic Institute
Topic: A Cost-Benefit Analysis for the Commonwealth of Virginia.

Political Science, University of Minnesota
Topic: Study of Information Transmission Between Police and Prosecutors.

Criminal Justice, State University of New York at Albany
Topic: Study of the Application of Operational Research to the Dynamics of the Criminal Justice System.

Management, Texas Technological University

[35] Lee Webb, "Training for Repression," in North American Congress on Latin America, *The University-Military-Police Complex: A Directory and Related Documents* (New York: NACLA, 1970), p. 63.
[36] *Ibid.*
[37] LEAA, *Grants and Contracts Fiscal Year 1970*, pp. 101–104.

34

Topic: Aspects of the Correctional Program of the U.S. Army Correction Facility Having Transfer Potential to Selected Civilian Institutions.

Economics, University of California at Los Angeles
Topic: Investigation of the Applicability of Planning, Programming, Budgeting Systems to Municipal Criminal Justice Systems.

Law and Social Science, Yale Law School
Topic: Use of Legal and Physical Design Criteria for Models of Criminal Rehabilitation and Administration of Justice.

Criminology, University of California at Berkeley
Topic: Exploration of the Administrative Aspects of Public Agencies Within the Criminal Justice System.

Criminology and Criminal Justice, Michigan State University
Topic: Development of Sensitivity-Training Materials for Criminal Justice Personnel.

One might well ask: By offering financial rewards for approved topics on criminal justice, is not the U.S. Department of Justice securing allegiance from developing scholars? Although the research of the graduate students may provide some useful intelligence information for the Department of Justice in controlling crime, the long term investment is in securing the minds of social scientists. The study of crime, from an approved perspective, becomes a worthwhile subject for the young scientist.

The Department of Justice (through LEAA) is not the only government agency involved in supporting law and order studies. The National Institute of Mental Health (NIMH), through its Center for Studies of Crime and Delinquency, provides substantial grants to graduate departments that design training programs in some aspect of crime and corrections. Of the fifty-one training programs being administered in 1971, which were being supported over a period of several years, a few are described as follows:[38]

T01 MH02564   7/1/61–6/30/73
Social Work — Juvenile Delinquency, Louisiana State University
This is a training program in social work to prepare students to work in the field of corrections with juvenile delinquents. Field

[38] National Institute of Mental Health, Center for Studies of Crime and Delinquency, *Active Training Grants,* mimeograph (Rockville, Md., July 1, 1971). (Names of the directors have been omitted.)

instruction is given through casework experience with delinquent and neglected adolescents and their families. Group treatment procedures are taught as are intervention-correctional procedures involving other community service agencies.

T01 MH08254   7/1/63–6/30/73
Social Work — Corrections, Ohio State University
This is a graduate Social Work training program to furnish course and field instruction in group work, psychiatric criminology and work with hostile and aggressive juveniles at various correctional institutions. Field experience includes exposure to the criminally insane, the sociopath, the sex offender and the deviate as well as inmates in correctional institutions who become mentally ill.

T01 MH10811   7/1/67–6/30/74
Research Training — Social Sciences, Department of Sociology, University of Pennsylvania
This program is designed to provide doctoral candidates in sociology with specialized training in research methods and techniques and in the substantive content of criminology. In addition to the regular requirements for a doctorate in sociology, trainees are required to take courses in the sociology of crime and delinquency, treatment of the offender and theory in criminology. Training facilities include the University's Center of Criminological Research, the Philadelphia Police Department, local courts, and county and State prisons.

T21 MH11505   7/1/68–12/31/71
Prevention and Control of Juvenile Delinquency, Law School, University of Minnesota
This is a program directed at strengthening the juvenile system through improving teamwork between police and courts, including juvenile probate personnel. Juvenile police officers, inservice training officers, juvenile probation and juvenile court judges are brought into a common training program.

T01 MH12093   7/1/69–6/30/73
Training Program in Sociology of Criminal Law, Department of Sociology, New York University
This is a training and research program for doctoral students in sociology, focusing on criminal law and social deviance. Development of a consortium of sociologists, lawyers, and judges involved in criminal law is planned, to share knowledge and experience.

T15 MH12501   7/1/70–6/30/73
Law and Social Deviance, American University, Washington College of Law

> These training seminars provide an inter-university and multi-
> disciplinary forum on law and social deviance, offering participa-
> tion to law students, psychiatric residents and graduate students
> in psychology, sociology, social work, political science and related
> disciplines. The training program will consist of two parts: the
> first semester devoted to class discussions in general topics of law
> and social deviance and the second semester requiring involve-
> ment of the students in special field projects.

T01 MH12553   9/1/70–6/30/74
Training in the Sociology of Justice, University of Washington

> This proposal establishes a training and research program for
> doctoral students in sociology, focusing on crime and delin-
> quency. Included is a strong sequence of courses in theory and
> methodology, research experience in a variety of correctional
> agencies, and establishment of a data bank to follow offenders
> through stages in a justice system. The focus of research atten-
> tion is on both deviant behavior, including juvenile, and society's
> reaction, especially on the machinery of justice.

In these programs students learn scientifically about law and
crime; they also learn that it is worthwhile to be interested in the
preservation of social order. Their future academic careers will
likely reflect their training in these programs and the ideology associated with them. Alternative perspectives to law and order are
being systematically excluded in these programs.

The mature scholar, once obtaining his academic degree, continues to benefit from the good graces of government agencies.
Which is to say, also, that it is difficult to break out of a perspective
that grants legitimacy to the existing order. Social scientists receive
funds from a number of government agencies to conduct research on
the crime problem. NIMH, for example, supported fifty-three projects
during 1971, of which a few are described below:[39]

R01 MH14806   6/66–5/74
Maturational Reform and Rural Delinquency, University of Oregon

[39] National Institute of Mental Health, Center for Studies of Crime and Delinquency, *Active Research Grants,* mimeograph (Rockville, Md., July 1, 1971).
(Names of the researchers have been omitted.)

This is a study of the extent to which stresses and pressures in adolescence contribute toward or influence social deviance. The subjects are groups of delinquent and non-delinquent rural high school males (16–21 years) who will be followed from adolescence into early adulthood. Effort will be made to analyze maturational reform (alleviation of major adolescent stress problems) by methods of repeated interviewing, with focus on the interplay of educational and occupational status, academic aspiration, community and family status. The uncertainties of military service and its impact on civilian maturation will have special attention.

R01 MH16029   5/69–4/72
Socializing Capabilities of Wives of Offenders, Department of Sociology, Rutgers State University
This is a study of the socializing capabilities of wives/girl friends of offenders. To be examined are what traits, knowledge and interpersonal skills they have in order to better guide the offender's behavior. Counseling will be given by the parole officers. Maturity level, cooperativeness, conventionality and relationships between offender and wives/girl friends will also be studied.

R01 MH17452   6/70–6/72
Interpersonal Relationships of Prisoners, Center for the Study of Crime, Delinquency & Corrections, Southern Illinois University
This is a study of the interpersonal relationships of imprisoned offenders with non-prison individuals; interpersonal dyad (wife, parent, male or female friend). Conversations are taped, letters are examined and implications will be drawn regarding confinement effects on friendship patterns and potentially on offenders. Fifty prisoners serve as paid volunteers.

R03 MH17899   7/70–10/71
Detection Analysis of Deviant Aggression, University of Denver
This investigator will examine, with a questionnaire measuring aggressive satisfaction or expected consequences, groups of white, Negro and Hispano subjects. Test items will be correlated and revised for analysis of bases of deviant aggression. The approach utilized combines techniques developed in signal detection research with social learning theory.

P01 MH18468   6/70–5/73
A Program of Research on Antisocial Behavior and Violence, Department of Psychology, Florida State University
This is a multi-dimensional research plan on personality factors involved in antisocial and aggressive behavior. Results are to be

38

applied to prediction of vocational and academic achievement and success of treatment. Studied will be background characteristics of prison inmates, the patterns of behavior and attitude change during incarceration, psycho-dynamics of aggression, and the role of anxiety and self-concept in the phenomena of violent behavior.

R01 MH18966   6/70–5/72
Behavior Modification Training for Community Agents, Oregon Research Institute

The objective of this project is to develop a program of training in behavior modification skills designed for the community mental health para-professional who deals with conduct-disorder, "pre-delinquent" children and their families. Trained will be community agents such as child welfare, juvenile court, mental health clinic and school counseling services; training to be in social learning theory, data collection, and behavior modification techniques for intervention in family and school settings.

The criminological research interests of NIMH (through its Center for Studies of Crime and Delinquency) are made quite explicit.

The activities of the Center for Studies of Crime and Delinquency include the development of greater knowledge (through basic and applied research) about deviant, maladaptive, and problem behaviors which are viewed, labeled, and handled as delinquency and crime; the development of innovative and more efficient training models and approaches for mental health and related manpower to work in both research and service activities in the fields of crime and delinquency, and social deviance; the dissemination of information and utilization of significant research findings; and consultation with and technical assistance to regional, State, and local agencies and decision-makers.[40]

In other words, the interests of the state are being served by the findings from the NIMH-funded programs. The knowledge that is developed is to be used by those in power rather than by those who are defined as deviant or criminal. Certainly there is no information

[40] "The Center for Studies of Crime and Delinquency," offset, National Institute of Mental Health (Rockville, Md., n.d.), pp. 1–2. Private foundations are similarly tied to the official conceptions of crime, deviance, and law, and they fund projects according to this conception. See Jay Schulman, Carol Brown, and Roger Kahn, "Report on the Russell Sage Foundation," *The Insurgent Sociologist,* 2 (Summer, 1972), pp. 2–34.

here that can be used to overturn authority as presently constituted. This is research for the preservation of the established order.

The National Institute of Law Enforcement and Criminal Justice for several years has been giving grants for research projects. Under the Omnibus Crime Control and Safe Streets Act of 1968, the National Institute (as the research arm of LEAA) was authorized to make grants or give contracts for "the development of new or improved approaches, techniques, systems, equipment, and devices to improve and strengthen law enforcement." Social scientists have been granted funds to implement research proposals that fall under the interests of the Department of Justice. For example, in 1970, the grants included the following:[41]

NI 70–016   4/15/70–4/14/71
Summary and Appraisal of Criminological Survey Techniques and Findings, Bureau of Social Science Research, Inc., Washington, D.C.
   The project staff will inventory and critically review applications of the sample survey method in studies of crime, delinquency, criminal justice, law enforcement and closely related areas. The objective is to take stock of the rapid accumulation of experience since 1965 in developing information in the crime field by interviews with samples of the public, to distill the knowledge that has been gained, to examine methodological problems that arise in these areas of the survey method, and to appraise the adaptability of survey methods to criminological problems with due regard both for the potential and the limitations of these techniques relative to other available sources of information.

NI 70–027   4/15/70–7/14/71
Study of Delinquency and Criminal Careers, Temple University
   This project is a longitudinal investigation of 600 families to study the manner and social processes by which their sons enter into, maintain and abandon delinquency, adult crime, and use of alcohol, soft and hard drugs, legitimate and illegitimate work careers and gang life. Dropping out of school, courtship and marital patterns and involvement in militant movements are also being examined. This analysis will permit determination of when, how and why some youths, but not others, begin and retain or abandon some forms of prescribed and proscribed behavior.

[41] LEAA, *Grants and Contracts Fiscal Year 1970,* pp. 81–98. (Names of the directors have been omitted.)

NI 70–028   4/20/70–9/20/70
Crime Control Activities and Programs in San Mateo County, San
Francisco State College

The objective of this study is to describe the ways in which the
agencies of crime control in an urban county are related to each
other as they process suspects and engage in other crime control
activities. Specifically, it will describe: (1) some of the day-to-
day operations and practices of police, prosecutors, judges, and
probation officers; (2) the views the above officials have of their
own and each other's roles in the crime control process; and (3)
the views that suspects, defendants and those who are convicted
and sentenced hold of officials at different points in the criminal
justice process. It will identify and document instances of official
as well as unofficial cooperation between criminal justice agents.

NI 70–029   5/8/70–11/8/71
The Prevention and Control of Robbery, University of California at
Davis

This project consists of a series of substudies on the robbery
problem. The substudies include a detailed study of police response to robbery, a statistical analysis of the robbery system as a
whole, a study of the geography of robbery (determining in detail the location of robberies and how location relates to possible
methods for control), a study of the offenders and robbery (including the ideas held by offenders for prevention and control), a
study of street robbery, studies of other specific kinds of robbery,
an evaluation of improved police practices and other innovations
in robbery control, a study of the role of the courts, corrections,
and other criminal justice agencies and a study of the impact of
legal decisions upon robbery.

NI 70–039   6/30/70–6/30/71
Illegal Behavior in the Student Community, Scientific Analysis Corp.,
San Francisco, California

This study will examine the social and cultural bases of youthful
drug use, with particular reference to the process by which this
form of deviant behavior is engaged in and legitimated by different types of drug users. School performance, political orientation, involvement in crime and participation in campus conflict
will be considered in terms of their relationship to the culture
of drug use. The study will also consider the techniques of ac-
quisition and control of drugs by a sample of those most heavily
involved in drug use.

NI 70–065–PG–1   6/1/70–5/30/71
An Analysis of the Police Investigation Process, California State College, Long Beach

The grantee intends to analyze the police investigation process in order to provide police administrators with information on the dimensions of their investigation programs, guidelines for development of departmental policies and procedures and criteria for determining the workloads of detectives, juvenile officers and field officers.

NI 70–077   7/1/70–6/30/71
Analysis of Defense Counsel's Effect on the Processing of Criminal Cases, Institute for Defense Analyses, Arlington, Virginia

This study is designed to examine the strategies and tactics of retained, appointed, defender and legal aid counsel as they relate to the time and manner of criminal case processing and disposition. The specific objectives of the study are: (1) to identify areas where delay in processing of cases can be attributed to the strategy and tactics of defense and how these vary with type of counsel and type of case; and (2) to develop predictive techniques and cost/benefit measures that are applicable not only to the role of defense counsel but as useful inputs to a study of the total system of criminal justice. To the extent date requirements and availability permit, several urban jurisdictions would be studied on a comparative basis in order that more generally applicable results and recommendations can be developed.

The above research can best be regarded as "counterinsurgency research": "Nowhere is research and development for the police more important than in counterinsurgency research. And here the cooperation of the colleges and universities is critical to the success of the Justice Department's plans. More crucial than hardware is the information, intelligence, and knowledge that social science can bring to the Justice Department and the police departments. College faculty and graduate students have been aggressively courted. The Justice Department hopes to have available the same counterinsurgency capability the Army has in its think-tanks and university affiliations." [42]

This is social science research that serves the state. Scholars have

---

[42] Lee Webb, "Back Home: The Campus Beat," in National Action/Research on the Military-Industrial Complex, *Police on the Homefront* (Philadelphia: American Friends Service Committee, 1971), p. 17.

taken as their own the perspective and interests of the ruling class. The official reality is the one that social scientists have accepted. No longer can research on law and crime be regarded as independent scholarship.

SOCIAL SCIENCE AND THE VIOLENCE COMMISSION

Social scientists have been especially active in recent years in lending their support to government commissions. It was with considerable enthusiasm that a staff of nearly one hundred social scientists contributed to the reports of the National Commission on the Causes and Prevention of Violence, the commission formed in 1968 and chaired by Milton Eisenhower. They wrote task force papers, acted as advisers and consultants, and engaged in research. The two directors of research for the Commission, both sociologists, have written of their involvement:

> That scholarly research is predominant in the work here presented is evident in the product. But we should like to emphasize that the roles which we occupied were not limited to scholarly inquiry. The Directors of Research were afforded an opportunity to participate in all Commission meetings. We engaged in discussions at the highest levels of decision-making, and had great freedom in the selection of scholars, in the control of research budgets, and in the direction and design of research. If this was not unique, it is at least an uncommon degree of prominence accorded research by a National Commission.[43]

In spite of the considerable amount of research on violence, and the diversity of findings, the staff members found themselves associated with a final Commission report (*To Establish Justice, To Insure Domestic Tranquility*) that proclaimed a single conception of violence. That particular conception or reality is summarized in a Commission report: "Violence is the breakdown of social order. Social order is maintained, and violence is prevented, by the effective functioning of society's primary legal, political and social insti-

[43] James F. Short, Jr. and Marvin E. Wolfgang, "Preface," *To Establish Justice, To Insure Domestic Tranquility,* The Final Report of the National Commission on the Causes and Prevention of Violence (New York: Bantam Books, 1970), pp. 252–255. This Preface appears in each of the staff research reports.

43

tutions, including, among others, the agencies of law enforcement."[44] (To this the social scientist might only add that continued research by scholars will be useful for policy-making.) This particular reality of violence is very close to the conception shared by most social scientists today.

Were the social scientists involved in the Violence Commission co-opted? One Commission staff member, an author of one of the reports, indeed suggests that the whole staff was co-opted in that their efforts were associated with a final report which they did not write.[45] Social scientists thus granted legitimacy to the Commission reports and to the Commission's particular conception of violence. However, though the Violence Commission predetermined the orientation to the study of violence, it is likely that few of the social scientists on the staff would have sought a different perspective on violence. In this regard, social scientists were not co-opted; they shared the same perspective as the Commission in general. Commenting on the efforts of social scientists on previous commissions, particularly the riot commissions, Anthony Platt observes:

> While it is true that riot commissions often misuse and exploit social scientists, it should be recognized that social scientists have often been willing, even enthusiastic, "victims" of this kind of relationship. The image of social scientists as value-free technical experts ready for hire is one which social scientists have themselves helped to build. Academics are not forced to work for government commissions; they are free to negotiate the terms of their work; they can resign if they feel that their intellectual freedom is restricted; they can publicly criticize a commission for dishonest or inadequate research; and they can write dissents and minority reports. Unfortunately, too many social scientists sacrifice their intellectual obligations for prestige and narrow self-interest. Moreover, there are a large number of academics who are not only willing to do "agency-determined" research but who also share the "agency's" perspective on the problem to be studied.[46]

[44] *Law and Order Reconsidered,* A Staff Report of the National Commission on the Causes and Prevention of Violence, Prepared by James S. Campbell, Joseph R. Sahid, and David P. Stang (New York: Bantam Books, 1970), p. xxvii.

[45] Jerome H. Skolnick, "Violence Commission Violence," *Transaction,* 7 (October, 1970), pp. 32–38.

[46] Anthony M. Platt, *The Politics of Riot Commissions 1917–1970: A Collec-*

44

In accepting and sharing the Commission's conception of violence, few social scientists were able to entertain an alternative conception. But there is a distinct alternative reality. It can be summarized in this way: Violence is a definition of human conduct that is subject to considerable manipulation. Conceptions of violence have been a monopoly of those who have the power to enforce their realities on others. Violence is the product of strong social institutions; it can be prevented only by eliminating these institutions. The government itself commits violence against the people. And further research is not necessary for policy-making. This alternative reality of violence is, unfortunately, far removed from the ideology of the social sciences. Only a critical social theory will allow us to move beyond the assumptions and realities of the Violence Commission.[47]

It was in the preparation of a three-volume staff report that social scientists expressed their position to the Violence Commission. In the course of presenting much of their research in *Crimes of Violence,* the staff members offered the conventional sociological wisdom regarding discontent and violence. The sources of our discontent, the reports noted, are the traditional ones: poverty, relative deprivation, lack of economic opportunity, and a failure to have a "stake" in the established order. Why raise the problem to a moral level, a level that requires a questioning of the very existence of institutions, when solutions can be found in a simple reformation of the same old institutions? The social science staff on the Violence Commission could only offer changes within the context of the existing capitalist society. Their perspective for action and research on crimes of violence, or any other type of crime, was made plain:

> The perspective advocated here accepts the present system as the framework within which changes should be made. It does not call for total change; it does not denounce major institutions in their entirety. It argues rather, that there are significant defects in the operating social institutions; that these defects place a disproportionate burden on the backs of certain segments of society, especially the poor and the black; that the provisions for the incorpora-

tion of Official Reports and Critical Essays (New York: Collier Books, 1971), p. 29.

[47] See Richard Quinney, "National Commission on the Causes and Prevention of Violence: Reports" (A Review Symposium), *American Sociological Review,* 36 (August, 1971), pp. 724–727.

tion of young people into adult society are generally inadequate; and that, in sum, these basic inequities and burdens must be redressed substantially and promptly, lest they continue to generate increasing disrespect for our society, its institutions, and its laws. Such changes are not likely to occur overnight, but immediate movement in their direction can and must be initiated.[48]

Rather than move beyond the existing reality, most social scientists suggest ways of preventing and controlling threats to the established order.

Combined with this perspective, of course, is the sociologist's call for law and order.

> Law and order we must have. We must also have social justice, fair play, and genuinely equal opportunity; society must assume the responsibility for those who have found themselves at the bottom of the socio-economic ladder. We must engender a sense of social responsibility which will make it possible for each of us to coexist in decency and security, with some degree of confidence in the good opinion and mutual concern of others. To each of us there must be made more available a greater sense of stake in the society, in its institutions, and in its norms. In that stake we will find the key to law and order.[49]

Whether public policy will be affected by the Violence Commission, through the efforts of social scientists, is not the issue. The reports of the Violence Commissions, and other commissions as well, already fit into the established pattern of policy and reform. The reports prepared by social scientists are themselves an integral part of today's problems. The liberal, reformist response to contemporary experiences is bankrupt. Following obsolete theories of government, law, and social order, we are unable to act in a way that would begin to solve our problems. The only reaction of those who govern and those who advise is one of manipulation, control, and repression. Only if we start anew, with a radical image of our reality, can a new world be created.

[48] *Crimes of Violence*, vol. 12, A Staff Report Submitted to the National Commission on the Causes and Prevention of Violence, Donald J. Mulvihill and Melvin M. Tumin, Co-Directors (Washington, D.C.: U.S. Government Printing Office, 1969), p. 727.
[49] *Ibid.*, p. 520.

BEHAVIOR MANIPULATION AND CONTROL

It is finally in the control and manipulation of human behavior that knowledge serves the established order. At the expense of human freedoms and an alternative existence, social order scholars foster ideas that attempt to justify and secure a stable society. Law is accepted as a necessary means of social control, and devices are suggested to assure conformity to the established legal system. A controlled social environment and a manipulated human being are the objects of such knowledge.

As conceived by social scientists, society is a self-contained "social system" that includes the necessary elements for its own survival. The "system" and its interrelated elements have been described in a discussion of crime and violence:

- *Goals* and *functions* that specify the system's objectives or purposes.
- *Achievement strategies* that spell out the methods by which the objectives are to be attained and state the assumptions made in selecting these methods.
- *Position networks* that indicate the division of labor among individuals who belong to the system, the channels of communication and authority, the pattern of access to information and other resources, and the like.
- *Roles* that detail the behavioral requirements of the members assigned to any given position, including duties and responsibilities as well as rights and privileges.
- *Sanctions* that encourage the members' conformity to their role requirements by the appropriate allocation of rewards and penalties.[50]

In other words, the system contains its own elements for the control and manipulation of human behavior. Ultimately there are sanctions that "encourage the members' conformity to their role requirements." The "requirements," of course, even in such abstract form, are based on the needs of those in positions of power. The "systems" approach is necessarily a ruling class conception of social

[50] Clarence C. Schrag, "Critical Analysis of Sociological Theories," in *Crimes of Violence*, vol. 13, A Staff Report Submitted to the National Commission on the Causes and Prevention of Violence (Washington, D.C.: U.S. Government Printing Office, 1969), p. 1274.

order, which requires sanctions in order to keep the underclass in its position. Law enforcement, punishment, "corrections," and environmental control are therefore taken for granted by the social order theorist. A conception of social order, or the social system, presupposes the control and manipulation of human beings.

When social scientists enter into the realm of social policy, their recommendations are based on their notions of social order, including the manipulation and control of those who threaten the social system. The recommendations of social scientists, especially criminologists, therefore involve various forms of imprisonment, rehabilitation in an institution, and methods of reintegrating the offender into the dominant society.[51] More specifically, scientific experiments are conducted on the deterrent effects of incarceration; correctional programs are designed to modify the offender's attitudes and behavior; predictive instruments for probation and parole supervision are constructed; and community-based release centers are devised for the "reintegration of the offender into the community."

In addition to these solutions to the crime problem, offered by social scientists, there are the more immediate measures for controlling crime by increasing the difficulty and risk of committing crime. Included here are the recommendations for improving the techniques of detection and arrest, such as the use of new equipment and better methods of surveillance. Technological innovations are to be developed and applied in the war on crime. The recommendations of social scientists are not only consistent with those offered by law enforcement officials, but serve equally well the law and order interests of the dominant society.

Similarly, the proposals for the future control of crime follow the assumptions of social order theory. A possible future is being created for us by the development of a "behavior control technology." This future is inevitable, we are told: "There is probably little point today, if there ever was one, in debating whether or not behavior control technology is feasible or desirable. No such choice is any longer possible. This technology, at this point in history, is scientifically inevitable, socially necessary, and psychologically prepared for. What remains is to determine the characteristics of this technology,

[51] See, for example, the recommendations in *Crimes of Violence,* vol. 12, pp. 753–787.

the rules of implementing control, and the purposes which it should serve." [52]

We are then informed about the wide range of control techniques that are being developed: therapy conditioning, electronic surveillance, control of emotions through drugs, electrical and chemical stimulating devices, brain surgery. These techniques are recommended as part of the legal system and its controls. They are more subtle and insidious than the old-fashioned methods of imprisonment and rehabilitation.

> Some aspects of behavior control technology are sufficiently established to be usefully incorporated by existing criminal justice and correction systems. Psychotherapy, mood-changing drugs, and some conditioning methods are suitable alternative or adjunctive rehabilitation procedures for a variety of offenses. They are appropriate alternative penalties for offenses where imprisonment is not necessary for the protection of society, so that probationary, voluntary correctives are in order. Precedents exist in the mandatory counseling or treatment required by some domestic and juvenile courts and the "safety classes" required of some traffic offenders. For offenses requiring mandatory restraints, these methods are useful adjuncts which may reduce length of incarceration and/or recidivism.[53]

A number of social scientists, with the support of the federal government, are now involved in developing "coercive behavior modification techniques" for the control and manipulation of those who threaten the existing social order. The techniques that these scientists are developing for the treatment and handling of offenders range from operant and classical conditioning to aversion suppression and electronic monitoring. Moreover, as Ralph Schwitzgebel, one of the leading researchers and advocates of these forms of social engineering, observes (in a monograph sponsored by NIMH): "Regardless of orientation, the basic underlying theory usually involves carefully specified changes in the environment of the person whose behavior is to be changed." [54] Scientific behavior modification, there-

[52] Perry London, "Behavior Control," in *Crimes of Violence*, vol. 13, p. 1360.
[53] *Ibid.*, p. 1374.
[54] Ralph K. Schwitzgebel, *Development and Legal Regulation of Coercive Behavior Modification Techniques with Offenders*, National Institute of Mental Health Monograph (Washington, D.C.: U.S. Government Printing Office, 1971), p. 5.

fore, is systematic and total, not limited to the "nontransferable" techniques of individual therapist or change agent.

So it is that scientific knowledge is being applied to the legal order. A science separated from morality can provide the way to a stable social order. "A science of behavior must be developed on the model of an input-output system, with adaptation to the environment as a key component." [55] The behaviorist, through "environmental design," will control the information and experiences for the rest of us. "A successful crime control model must deal with behavior before the crime occurs, must deal directly with criminal behavior, and must deal with environmental design, rather than the individual offender." [56] Of course, such planning "must be scientific, not humanistic."

Finally, a new school of "environmental criminology" is being proposed:

> A new school of *environmental criminology* must emerge, based on scientific procedures, behaviorism, and environmentalism. The basic principles of the classical school — i.e., prevention of crime before it occurs and certainty of consequences for behavior — would be retained, but the emphasis would shift from punishment to reinforcement and from the individual offender to the environment. The major form of control would be reinforcement of lawful behavior and the removal of reinforcement for illegal behavior. The focus would be the environment in which crimes are committed, not the individual offender.[57]

From rehabilitation to environmental design the objectives are the same: the control and manipulation of human beings, accomplished by those who rule and those who benefit from this rule.

These are oppressive ideas. A critical analysis of current knowledge is exposing the meaning and consequences of these ideas. An alternative to existing knowledge about the legal order is becoming evident. A radical critique of legal order provides the grounds for a new form of human existence. We cannot continue to be oppressed by current knowledge, knowledge that only serves the existing capitalist order. We must be released for the creation of a more authentic existence.

[55] C. Ray Jeffery, *Crime Prevention Through Environmental Design* (Beverly Hills: Sage Publications, 1971), p. 276.
[56] *Ibid.*, p. 278.
[57] *Ibid.*, p. 270.

3
Preservation of Domestic Order by the Ruling Class

How is crime in America to be understood critically? Current interpretations of crime are bound by official reality. Our theories fail to go beyond the dominant ideology of the age. A radical theory of crime would, in contrast, expose the underside of the prevailing reality. It would go to the roots of law and crime in the United States. We would see clearly the meaning of all efforts that relate to the creation and control of crime. A critical theory will expose the official reality and allow us to move beyond our current existence.

THE CLASS STRUCTURE OF CAPITALIST SOCIETY

According to liberal intelligence, the state exists to maintain order and stability in civil society. Law is regarded as a body of rules established through consensus by those who are governed, or rather by the "representatives" of the governed. Such a notion of the state and its law presents a false conception of reality, but one that benefits those who rule.

51

An alternative position gets to the deeper meaning of the existence of the state and the legal order. Contrary to the dominant view, the state is created by the class that has the power to enforce its will on the rest of society. The state is thus a political organization created out of force and coercion. The state is established by those who desire to protect their material basis and who have the power (because of material means) to maintain the state. The law in capitalist society gives political recognition to powerful private interests.

Moreover, the legal system is an apparatus created to secure the interests of the dominant class. Contrary to conventional belief, law is a tool of the ruling class. The legal system provides the mechanism for the forceful and violent control of the rest of the population. In the course of battle, the agents of the law (police, prosecutors, judges, and so on) serve as the military force for the protection of domestic order. Legal order benefits the ruling class in the course of dominating the classes that are ruled. And it may be added that the legal system prevents the dominated classes from becoming powerful. The rates of crime in any state are an indication of the extent to which the ruling class, through its machinery of criminal law, must coerce the rest of the population, thereby preventing any threats to its ability to rule and possess. The assumption that criminal law serves as a coercive means in establishing domestic order for the ruling class is basic to a radical critique of crime.

The idea that American society can best be understood in terms of its class structure violates another piece of liberal wisdom. The fact that 1 percent of the population owns 40 percent of the nation's wealth still comes as a surprise to many citizens — an indication that the liberal perspective dominates. Yet the evidence now overwhelmingly supports the radical critique of American society.[1] The liberal assumption of a pluralistic American economy — with corporations as just one kind of interest group among many others — is negated by the fact that the major portion of the wealth and nearly all the power in American society are concentrated in the hands of a few large corporations. Furthermore, those who benefit

[1] See Richard C. Edwards, Michael Reich, and Thomas E. Weisskopf, *The Capitalist System: A Radical Analysis of American Society* (Englewood Cliffs, N.J.: Prentice-Hall, 1972); Tom Christoffel, David Finkelhor, and Dan Gilbarg (eds.), *Up Against the American Myth* (New York: Holt, Rinehart and Winston, 1970).

from this economy make up a small, cohesive group of persons related to one another in their power, wealth, and corporate connections. In addition, the pluralistic conception ignores all the manifestations of the alliance between business and government. On the evidence of radical scholarship, government and business are inseparable.

A critique of the American political economy begins with the assumption that life in the United States is determined by the capitalist mode of production. And here as in any capitalist society, a class division exists between those who rule and those who are ruled. As Ralph Miliband writes, in reference to the class structure of capitalist societies:

> The economic and political life of capitalist societies is *primarily* determined by the relationship, born of the capitalist mode of production, between these two classes — the class which on the one hand owns and controls, and the working class on the other. Here are still the social forces whose confrontation most powerfully shapes the social climate and the political system of advanced capitalism. In fact, the political process in these societies is mainly *about* the confrontation of these forces, and is intended to sanction the terms of the relationship between them.[2]

Although there are other classes, such as professionals, small businessmen, office workers, and cultural workmen — some of these either within or cutting across the two major classes — it is the division between the ruling class and the subordinate class that establishes the nature of political, economic, and social life in capitalist society.

The ruling class is "that class which owns and controls the means of production and which is able, by virtue of the economic power thus conferred upon it, to use the state as its instrument for the domination of society."[3] The existence of this class in America, rooted mainly in the corporations and financial institutions of monopoly capitalism, is well documented.[4] This is the class that makes

[2] Ralph Miliband, *The State in Capitalist Society* (New York: Basic Books, 1969), p. 16.

[3] *Ibid.*, p. 23.

[4] G. William Domhoff, *Who Rules America?* (Englewood Cliffs, N.J.: Prentice-Hall, 1967); Gabriel Kolko, *Wealth and Power in America* (New York: Frederick A. Praeger, 1962).

53

the decisions affecting the lives of those who are subordinate to it.

It is according to the interests of the ruling class that American society is governed. Though pluralists may suggest that there are diverse and conflicting interests among groups in the upper class, what they ignore is that members of the ruling class work within a common general framework in the formulation of public policy. Superficially, groups within the ruling class may differ on some issues, but in general they have common interests and can exclude members of the other classes from the political process entirely.

> If powerful economic groups are geographically diffuse and often in competition for particular favors from the state, superficially appearing as interest groups rather than as a unified class, what is critical is not who wins or loses but what kind of socioeconomic framework they *all* wish to compete within, and the relationship between themselves and the rest of the society in a manner that defines their vital function as a class. It is this class that controls the major policy options and the manner in which the state applies its power. That they disagree on the options is less consequential than that they circumscribe the political universe.[5]

In contrast to pluralist theory, radical theory notes that basic interests, in spite of concrete differences, place the elite in a distinct ruling class.

In a radical critique of American society we are able, in addition, to get at the objective interests that are external to the consciousness of individuals. We are able, furthermore, to suggest normative evaluations of these interests. Pluralists, on the other hand, are bound by the subjective interests of individuals.[6] The critical perspective allows us to understand the actual and potential interests of classes, of the ruling class as well as of those who are ruled. What this means for a critique of legal order is that we can break with the official, dominant ideology which proclaims the diversity of interests among numerous competing groups. We are able to determine the interests of those who make and use law for their own advantage.

The primary interest of the ruling class is to preserve the existing

[5] Gabriel Kolko, *The Roots of American Foreign Policy* (Boston: Beacon Press, 1969), pp. 6–7.

[6] Isaac D. Balbus, "The Concept of Interest in Pluralist and Marxian Analysis," *Politics and Society,* 1 (February, 1971), pp. 151–177.

order and, in so doing, to protect its existential and material base. This is accomplished ultimately by means of the legal system. Any threats to the established order can be dealt with by invoking the final weapon of the ruling class, its legal system. Threats to American economic security abroad are dealt with militarily; our armed forces are ready to attack any foe that attempts (as in a revolution) to upset the foreign markets of American capitalism.[7] American imperialism fosters and perpetuates the colonial status of foreign countries, securing American hegemony throughout as much of the world as possible. This has been the history of American foreign relations, dominated by the corporate interests of the ruling class.[8]

Similarly, the criminal law is used at home to maintain domestic order. Ruling class interests are secured by preventing any challenge to the moral and economic structure. In other words, the military abroad and law enforcement at home are two sides of the same phenomenon: the preservation of the interests of the ruling class. The weapons of control are in the hands of that class, and its response to any challenge is force and destruction. The weapons of crime control, as well as the idea and practice of law itself, are dominated by the ruling class. A stable capitalist order is in its interest.

From this critical perspective, then, crime is worthy of the greatest consideration. To understand crime radically is to understand the makings and workings of the American empire.

LAW AS AN ARM OF THE RULING CLASS

What, then, is the nature of this ruling class as reflected in criminal matters? It is composed of (1) members of the upper economic class (those who own or control the means of production) and (2) those who benefit in some way from the present capitalist economic system. It is engaged in legal concerns for the purpose of preserving the capitalist order, including the welfare state associated with that order. Even when laws regulating morality are made and enforced,

[7] David Horowitz, *Empire and Revolution: A Radical Interpretation of Contemporary History* (New York: Random House, 1969).

[8] William Appleman Williams, *The Roots of Modern American Empire* (New York: Random House, 1969).

55

the intention is to preserve the moral and ideological basis of capitalism.

There is conclusive evidence on the role of the ruling class (tied to corporate wealth) in the shaping of American foreign policy. It is another question, however, whether this class also controls domestic policies. In an essay on this subject, William Domhoff demonstrates that in four areas of social legislation — protective labor legislation, the regulation of business, social security, and the recognition of labor unions — the power elite has been instrumental in determining domestic policy.[9] He discusses the institutions through which the power elite shapes social legislation and shows that the various policy research associations and institutes are directed and financed by members of the upper class. He presents evidence to show how important these organizations are in providing the context and ideas for shaping the various pieces of social legislation. By determining such legislation, the power elite is able to preserve existing economic arrangements, allowing the upper class to retain control of the important economic and political decisions in the United States.

Does a similar situation exist for policies regarding crime control in the United States? Already there is indication of a ruling class interest in crime control. In a study of "the crime fighters," voluntary members of the Citizen Action Program of the National Council on Crime and Delinquency (NCCD), John Wildeman found that the members do comprise an influential group representing dominant economic interests.[10] The Citizen Action Program, composed of 690 members in the Councils of 21 states, was established by the NCCD (a private organization) in 1955 with the aid of a grant from the Ford Foundation. On the basis of his research on these members, Wildeman found that they are influential people located in the dominant economic class. They are in the elite sectors of the corporate capitalist economy (owners, managers, and directors), and of the legal and educational institutions as well. He writes:

[9] G. William Domhoff, *The Higher Circles: The Governing Class in America* (New York: Random House, 1970), Chap. 6.

[10] John Wildeman, *The Crime Fighters: A Study of the Ideologies and Reactions to Criminally Defined Behavior on the Part of the Members of an Interest Group Operative in the Official Definition and Management of Deviance,* Unpublished Ph.D. dissertation, New York University, 1971.

56

Without exception these data lend justification to the assumption that the Crime Fighters are indeed influentials drawn from an elite segment of American society. The majority enjoy an income that is without question considerably higher than the national average; seventy-seven percent are in the middle to upper half of the 16 to 75 thousand dollar a year bracket, with ten percent above the 75 thousand dollar range. The overall educational level of the group is also far above the national average. Fifty-five percent have graduate study experience, and almost half of the members have graduate degrees. On this point it is also enlightening to examine the lower end of this distribution: only thirteen percent failed to complete college, and of these only sixteen persons reached no higher than high school or less.

With regard to occupational level, the evidence is again strongly indicative of a group of influential people. Not only are the Crime Fighters located in the critical areas of the occupational structure of industrial, capitalist society, but furthermore they are situated at the top of the hierarchies in these critical areas. The critical areas are industry, trade, and finance on the one hand and education and the professions on the other; almost one-half of all the Council members, (44 percent) are in the former areas and over a third are in the latter areas, (37 percent). Taken together, then, these two areas account for eighty-one percent of all the Crime Fighters. This accounts for and justifies their own perceptions of their levels of influence in law and policy formation.

We have seen that not only are they located in the critical segments of our occupational structure, but also that they are at the top of the hierarchies in those areas. A phenomenal ninety-five percent are in the top three ranks. For example, those in industry are administrators and managers of productive property — if not also owners. Those in finance and trade also are in the power positions of the American economic structure, directors, managers, and presidents of insurance companies and banks. As such, their decisions affect the lives of countless numbers of people. Those in education are in top administrative positions in our educational system, particularly higher education, and are consequently key policy-makers. They are part of that segment of the educational structure in our country that sets directions for educational policy. Those in the professions are from the elite strata of their professions. It is useful to note here that most of the eighty-six professionals are either lawyers in large law firms or are judges. In fact, one-fifth of all the Crime Fighters (a full 20 percent) are directly connected with the criminal justice system in their roles as lawyers, judges, or correctional or law enforcement administrators.

The assumption that the Crime Fighters are influentials is certainly reasonable in light of the data in these tables: they are members of a powerful minority in our society, one capable of exerting a considerable influence over public policy. Their interests certainly are the predominant interests that are being incorporated both into criminal law and public policy in the administration of criminal justice. These are, in short, important people. They are people located in the segments of society that have the resources necessary to protect their interests, (values, ideologies, material goods, etc.).[11]

The goal of these elite citizen groups is to shape criminal policy. In creating the Citizens Action Program, NCCD initiated a nationwide program involving influential citizens, or "laymen," in the fight against crime and delinquency. The official objective in launching the program, noted in the application to the Ford Foundation, was ". . . through State Committees, to rally and unify the efforts of responsible citizens who are aware that something must be done about the nation's burgeoning rate of crime." [12] Through these select citizen groups, policy suggestions are made in respect to criminal law, law enforcement, and crime prevention. The goal of the program is to influence state legislation and other policy-making bodies according to the interests of the dominant economic class.

To understand criminal policy, then, we must know something about those who make that policy. Rather than assuming that criminal policies are formulated by neutral persons representing the public good, let us begin by examining the backgrounds, activities, and interests of the policy-makers. In his study of the makers of American foreign policy, Gabriel Kolko has observed:

> To understand policy one must know the policy-makers — the men of power — and define their ideological view and their backgrounds. This means we must better perceive the nature of bureaucracy and state institutions in modern America, and determine whether such organizations carry with them distinctive economic and ideological attributes likely to emerge in the specific policies.

[11] *Ibid.*, pp. 76–78.
[12] Quoted in Alex Elson, *Citizen Action Program: An Evaluation*, NCCD, August, 1964.

It is, of course, the dominant fashion in the study of bureaucracy to ascribe to the structure of decision-making bureaucracy a neutral, independent rationale, and to drain away the class nature of formal institutions — indeed, to deny that men of power are something more than disinterested, perhaps misguided, public servants. The fact, of course, is that men of power do come from specific class and business backgrounds and ultimately have a very tangible material interest in the larger contours of policy. And although some are indeed seemingly perfect models of the neutral and disinterested public servant, both, in practice, implement the same policies.[13]

Furthermore, the American policy-making apparatus — the bureaucratic structure of government itself — has been created by and operates for large business.[14] Little wonder, then, that the governmental bureaucracy continues to serve the large corporate and financial interests in the United States; the policy-making structure is especially equipped to meet the needs of organized economic interests. Thus we find that the makers of criminal policy are members of or representatives of big business and finance, including the legal establishment which is tied to corporate and financial wealth. The personnel of these realms move readily and easily from one elite sector to another. In such tangible fashion, government and business come together, uniting into a single form of domination.

What, then, is the economic and political nature of criminal policy-making in America? My argument is that the ruling class formulates criminal policy for the preservation of domestic order, an order that assures the social and economic hegemony of the capitalist system. Therefore, let us look more closely at the class composition of those groups responsible for the formulation and enactment of criminal policies. We will examine in detail the composition of specially appointed commissions, legislative bodies, crime control bureaucracies, and advisory groups — especially the President's Crime Commission, the Violence Commission, the Riot Commission, the Senate Subcommittee on Criminal Laws and Procedures, the Law Enforcement Assistance Administration, and the Committee for Economic Development. All of these organizations operate to preserve domestic order for the ruling class.

13 Kolko, *The Roots of American Foreign Policy*, p. xii.
14 Gabriel Kolko, *The Triumph of Conservatism: A Reinterpretation of American History, 1900–1916* (New York: The Free Press, 1963).

CLASS BASIS OF THE PRESIDENT'S CRIME COMMISSION

During the early 1960s the nation's problems began to be focused simply and conveniently on that domestic enemy, *crime*. In a presidential message to the 89th Congress, in 1965, Lyndon Johnson launched the "war on crime." Turning the public's attention from a war that was going badly abroad, Johnson declared that "we must arrest and reverse the trend toward lawlessness." [15] Suggesting that "crime has become a malignant enemy in America's midst," the President charted a course of action based on legal control and law enforcement: "This active combat against crime calls for a fair and efficient system of law enforcement to deal with those who break the law. It means giving new priority to the methods and institutions of law enforcement." The problem was conceived to be a *national* one, with crime prevention and crime fighting to be intensified at all levels of government. The federal effort, Johnson continued, would consist of: "(1) increased federal law enforcement efforts, (2) assistance to local enforcement efforts, and (3) a comprehensive, penetrating analysis of the origins and nature of crime in modern America."

Eventually a national crime control bill, the Omnibus Crime Control and Safe Streets Act, was enacted, and an organization was established to promote its aims. Yet, the effort had to be made specific and given legitimacy by a presidential commission: "As a first step," Johnson advised Congress, "I am establishing the President's Commission on Law Enforcement and Administration of Justice. The Commission will be composed of men and women of distinction who share my belief that we need to know far more about the prevention and control of crime." The composition of that Commission suggested to the public a cross-section of the population. True to liberal etiquette, varying factions were to be represented. And true to the liberal myth, the whole population would seem to be represented by these distinguished and dedicated "public servants."

What becomes clear in an analysis of the President's Crime Commission is that its members consisted of a select group of persons

[15] "Crime, Its Prevalence, and Measures of Prevention," Message from the President of the United States, House of Representatives, 89th Congress, March 8, 1965, Document No. 103.

who represented the dominant class interests. Such a Crime Commission could do nothing more than accept the official definition of the crime problem, a definition that construed crime to be a threat to the existing system, a phenomenon that must be controlled in order to assure domestic order. To conceive of the problem in other terms would have violated the class interest of the Commission members. Yet we all were expected to believe that the public interest was being served by this Commission. The "public interest" was actually the interest of the dominant economic class.

The President's Crime Commission provided the official rationale and recommendations for a war on crime that continues to affect the nature of American criminal justice to this day. An understanding of crime control as a preservation of domestic order begins in an investigation of the composition of this Commission. What we learn is that the members of this national commission were dependent upon and involved in particular ways with the United States as it is presently constituted: The Commission consisted of members who had impressive records of employment or activity in domestic government positions, were involved in foreign policy matters, had prestigious and influential affiliations, and were closely tied to business and corporate interests. A brief sketch of the career of each member indicates the character of the President's Crime Commission.[16]

Nicholas DeB. Katzenbach, Chairman of the Commission, U.S. Attorney General.
Under Secretary of State; Rhodes Scholar, 1947–49; Attorney, Department of the Air Force, 1950–52; Professor of Law, Yale Law School, 1952–56; Professor of International Law, University of Chicago, 1956–61; Assistant Attorney General Office of Legal Counsel, 1961; Deputy Attorney General 1962–65; Attorney General of the United States, 1965–66.

Genevieve Blatt, Secretary of Internal Affairs, State of Pennsylvania.
Attorney; Member, State Board of Pardons, State of Pennsylvania, 1955–67; Vice Chairman, Interstate Oil Compact Commission.

[16] Biographical sketches as listed in the President's Commission on Law Enforcement and Administration of Justice, *The Challenge of Crime in a Free Society* (Washington, D.C.: U.S. Government Printing Office, 1967), Appendix A., with some additions (see footnote 17).

Charles D. Breitel, Justice of the Court of Appeals of the State of New York.

Deputy Assistant District Attorney, New York County, staff of Thomas E. Dewey, special rackets investigations, 1935–37; Assistant District Attorney, New York County, 1938–41, Chief of Indictment Bureau, 1941; Counsel of Governor, State of New York, 1943–50; Justice, Supreme Court of New York, 1950–52; Associate Justice, Appellate Division (First Department), Supreme Court of New York, 1952–66; Advisory Committee, Model Penal Code, American Law Institute; Chairman, Special Committee on the Administration of Criminal Justice, Association of the Bar of the City of New York; Council, American Law Institute.

Kingman Brewster, Jr., President, Yale University.

Assistant Professor of Law, Harvard Law School, 1950–53; Professor of Law, Harvard Law School, 1953–60; Provost, Yale University, 1960–63; author, "Anti-Trust and American Business Abroad" (1959); "Law of International Transactions and Relations" (with M. Katz, 1960); Member, Council of Foreign Affairs.

Garrett H. Byrne, District Attorney, Suffolk County, Mass.

Member, Massachusetts House of Representatives, 1924–28; President, National District Attorneys Association, 1963–64; President, Massachusetts District Attorney Association, 1963–64; President, National District Attorneys Foundation.

Thomas J. Cahill, Chief of Police, San Francisco.

Entered San Francisco Police Department as patrolman, 1942; Big Brother of the Year Award, 1964; Liberty Bell Award, San Francisco Bar Association, 1965; Vice President, International Association of Chiefs of Police, 1963– ; Chairman, Advisory Committee to the Governor on the Law Enforcement Section of the Disaster Office of the State of California; Chairman, Advisory Committee to the School of Criminology, City College, San Francisco; Member, National Advisory Committee, National Center on Police-Community Relations, Michigan State University.

Otis Chandler, Publisher, Los Angeles Times.

Senior Vice President, the Times-Mirror Co.; Member, Board of Directors, Associated Press, Western Airlines, Union Bank, Pan American World Airlines, Unionamerica.

Leon Jaworski, Attorney, senior partner, Fulbright, Crooker, Freeman, Bates & Jaworski, Houston.

U.S. Army, Colonel, Chief, War Crimes Trial Section, European Theater, Legion of Merit, 1942–46; President, Houston Bar Association, 1949; President, Texas Civil Judicial Council, 1951–52; President, American College of Trial Lawyers, 1961–62; President, Texas Bar Association, 1962–63; Special Assistant U.S. Attorney General, 1962–65; Special Counsel, Attorney General of Texas, 1963–65; Executive Committee, Southwestern Legal Foundation; Trustee, Houston Legal Foundation; Fellow, American Bar Foundation; U.S. Member, Permanent (International) Court of Arbitration; Member, National Science Commission; Chairman, Governor's Committee on Public School Education, State of Texas; Board of Directors, Bank of Southwest, Gulf Publishing Company, Benjamin Franklin Savings Association.

Thomas C. Lynch, Attorney General, State of California.
Assistant U.S. Attorney, 1933–42; Chief Assistant U.S. Attorney, 1943–51; District Attorney, San Francisco, Calif., 1951–64; Fellow, American College of Trial Lawyers; Advisory Committee on Prearraignment Code, American Law Institute.

Ross L. Malone, Attorney, partner, Awod & Malone, Roswell, New Mexico.
Deputy Attorney General of the United States, 1952–53; President, American Bar Association, 1958–59; President, American Bar Foundation; Trustee, Southwestern Legal Foundation; Council, American Law Institute; Board of Regents, American College of Trial Lawyers; Board of Trustees, Southern Methodist University; Vice President, General Counsel, General Motors Corporation, 1967–.

James Benton Parsons, Judge, U.S. District Court, Northern District of Illinois.
Teacher, Lincoln University of Missouri, 1934–40, city schools of Greensboro, N.C., 1940–42, John Marshall Law School, 1949–52; Assistant Corporation Counsel, city of Chicago, 1949–51; Assistant U.S. Attorney, 1951–60; Judge, Superior Court of Cook County, Ill., 1960–61; Member, Committee on Administration of Probation System, Judicial Council of the United States; Chicago Commission on Police-Community Relations; Illinois Academy of Criminology.

Lewis Franklin Powell, Jr., Attorney, partner, Hunton, Williams, Gay, Powell & Gibson, Richmond, Virginia.
Member, Virginia State Board of Education, 1961–; President, American Bar Association, 1964–65; Trustee, Washington and Lee University and Hollins College; Board of Regents, American College of Trial Lawyers; Vice President, American Bar Foun-

dation; Trustee and General Counsel, Colonial Williamsburg, Inc., Director, Ethyl Corporation, Philip-Morris, Inc., Chesapeake & Potomac Telephone Company.

William Pierce Rogers, Attorney, partner, Royall, Koegel, Rogers & Wells (New York and Washington).
Assistant U.S. Attorney, New York County, 1938–42; 1946–47; Chief Counsel, U.S. Senate War Investigating Committee, 1948; Chief Counsel, Senate Investigations Subcommittee of Executive Expenditures Committee, 1948–50; Deputy Attorney General, 1953–57, Attorney General of the United States, 1957–61; Member, U.S. Delegation, 20th General Assembly, United Nations, 1965; U.S. Representative, United Nations Ad Hoc Committee on Southwest Africa, 1967; Member, President's Commission on Crime in the District of Columbia, 1965–67; Fellow, American Bar Foundation; Director, Washington Post Company, Newsweek, 20th Century Fox Film Corporation.

Robert Gerald Storey, Attorney, partner, Storey, Armstrong & Steger, Dallas, Texas.
Order of Coif; Assistant Attorney General, State of Texas, 1921–23; Executive Trial Counsel for the United States, trial of major Axis war criminals, Nuremberg; Legion of Honor (France), 1945–46; Dean, Southern Methodist University Law School, 1947–59; President, Texas Bar Association, 1948–49; President, American Bar Association, 1952–53; Member, Hoover Commission, 1953–55; President Inter-American Bar Association, 1954–56; American Bar Association Gold Medal, 1956; Vice Chairman, U.S. Civil Rights Commission, 1957–63; President Southwestern Legal Foundation; Director, Royalty Corporation, Lakewood Bank & Trust Company, United Fidelity Life Insurance Company.

Julia Davis Stuart, President, League of Women Voters of the United States.
Governor's Tax Advisory Council, State of Washington, 1958; Chairman, Citizens Sub-committee on School Finance, State of Washington Legislature, 1960; National Municipal League Distinguished Citizen Award, 1964; Member, National Citizens Commission on International Cooperation, 1965; Board of Directors, UNA–USA, 1967–.

Robert F. Wagner, Mayor, New York City.
New York State Assembly, 1938–41; New York City Tax Commission, 1946; Commissioner of Housing and Buildings, New

York City, 1947; New York City Planning Commission, 1948; President, Borough of Manhattan, N.Y., 1949–53; Mayor, New York City, 1954–66; Partner, Law firm of Wagner, Quillnan and Tennant, 1966–.

Herbert Wechsler, Harlan Fisk Stone Professor of Constitutional Law, Columbia Law School.

Assistant Attorney General, State of New York, 1938–40; Special Assistant U.S. Attorney General, 1940–44; Assistant Attorney General of the United States, 1944–46; Member, U.S. Supreme Court Advisory Committee on Rules of Criminal Procedure, 1941–45; Oliver Wendell Holmes Lecturer, Harvard Law School, 1958–59; Director, American Law Institute; Reporter, Model Penal Code, American Law Institute; Member, New York State Temporary Commission on Revision of the Penal Law and Criminal Code; Member, Executive Committee, Association of the Bar, City of New York; author "Criminal Law and Its Administration" (with J. Michael, 1940); "The Federal Courts and the Federal System" (with Hart, Jr., 1953); "Principles, Politics and Fundamental Law" (1961).

Whitney Moore Young, Jr., Executive Director, National Urban League.

Dean, Atlanta University School of Social Work, 1954–60; Member, President's Committee on Youth Employment, 1962; Member, President's Committee on Equal Opportunity in the Armed Forces, 1963; Member, President's Commission on Technology, Automation, and Economic Progress, 1965–66; Member, Special Presidential Task Force on Metropolitan and Urban Problems, 1965–66; Member, Advisory Committee on Housing and Urban Development, Department of Housing and Urban Development; President, National Conference on Social Welfare; Member, Advisory Board, A. Philip Randolph Institute; Member, National Board, Citizens Crusade Against Poverty; Trustee, Eleanor Roosevelt Memorial Foundation; author, "To Be Equal" (1964).

Luther W. Youngdahl, Senior Judge, U.S. District Court, District of Columbia.

Municipal Court, Minneapolis, Minn., 1930–36; Judge, District Court, Hennepin County, Minn., 1936–42; Associate Justice, Supreme Court of Minnesota, 1942–46; Governor of Minnesota, 1947–51; Judge, U.S. District Court, District of Columbia, 1951–66.

Any diversity in the Commission is found only in the standard external characteristics. The Commission had blacks as well as whites, women as well as men, a civil rights worker as well as businessmen. But the similarity of the members and their common frame of reference are the striking characteristics. Of the nineteen members, fifteen were lawyers; and one of the non-lawyers was in the legal establishment as the Chief of Police of San Francisco. Even the non-lawyers had personal careers that were clearly within the legal framework. Moreover, most of the lawyers on the Commission had been or presently were members of large corporate law firms. In other words, the existing legal framework set the tone. A law and order mentality assured a Commission report that would propose solutions which would secure the dominant order. The perspective of the oppressed — those who are defined as criminal, to state this another way — was not to be found in a Commission established to understand the problem of crime. The Commission would accomplish a single task: to enforce the dominant ideology and secure the dominant class interests.

The commissioners, almost by fact of their selection, had served their nation well.[17] They had pursued careers that included appointments and elective offices in the domestic government. Eighteen of the commissioners had held at least one government position, but usually a series of them, prior to appointment to the President's Crime Commission. Over half (53 percent) of the commissioners had held foreign policy positions or positions that related to foreign affairs. Regarding their involvement in the business and corporate world, nearly two-thirds (63 percent) had business and corporate connections, as directors of corporations or members of corporations, including corporate law firms. Furthermore, nearly half of the commissioners combined their involvement in the various realms. Ten (53 percent) commissioners had careers that consisted of positions in both domestic and foreign policy-making. The preservation of world order and domestic order are necessary for maintaining the national corporate economy. Revolution, or disruption of any kind, is a threat to corporate capitalism, whether at home or abroad.

Appointment to the Commission represented to the members a consistent step in their careers. Here was an opportunity to provide

[17] Biographical sources used here included: *Who's Who in America, Current Biography, Who's Who of American Women, Congressional Directory,* and *Who's Who in the West.*

Career positions of the nineteen members of the President's Crime Commission	Number	Percentage
Domestic government positions	18	95
Foreign policy positions	10	53
Business and corporate connections	12	63
Domestic government positions *and* Foreign policy positions	10	53
Domestic government positions *and* Business and corporate connections	11	58
Domestic government positions *and* Foreign policy positions *and* Business and corporate positions	9	47

a national statement about crime and American society, under conditions corresponding to those that had promoted their earlier careers and current class interests. Furthermore, several of the commissioners rose to considerable prominence after their work on the Commission. Not that the Commission fostered promotion, but subsequent careers confirmed the conventional wisdom that characterized the Crime Commission.

For example, to mention only a few names, William P. Rogers, already a prominent "public citizen" at the time of his appointment to the Commission (being U.S. Attorney General in the Eisenhower administration), became Secretary of State in the Nixon administration. In being responsible for the direction and coordination of "government overseas activities" — the war in Vietnam, that is — Rogers continued to preserve order according to the interests of the dominant economic class in America. Nicholas Katzenbach, as U.S. Attorney General, had played a major role in the Kennedy administration. In addition to Justice Department duties, Katzenbach had served in the foreign-trade program, had drafted the new wiretapping legislation, and had drawn up the brief supporting Kennedy's decision to blockade Cuba in 1962. Later he was to become Under Secretary of State in the Johnson administration. Leaving government for the time being, he became a vice-president and general counsel of the IBM Corporation. And Lewis Powell, corporate firm lawyer and past president of the American Bar Association, director of numerous corporations, and author of a booklet on the communist threat, was appointed by Nixon in 1972 to the U.S. Supreme Court. Powell — Nixon's "strict constructionist" appointee to the Supreme Court — had earlier as a member of the President's Crime Commission led a dissenting group (including Jaworski, Malone, and Storey, with Byrne, Cahill and Lynch concurring) declaring that recent Supreme Court decisions limiting police powers had tilted the balance of justice too far in favor of defendants.

To say the least, the President's Crime Commission was a reflection of the nature of power and the force of the legal ideology in the United States. The Commission's reaffirmation of economic power and of the dominant ideology was its objective and accomplishment. The Commission members betrayed no class interests in their service to the nation. The crime problem continued to be in the hands of the ruling class.

THE RIOT COMMISSION AND THE VIOLENCE COMMISSION

Criminal law is not the only tool used by the ruling class to preserve domestic order. Any kind of perceived attack on domestic stability that may threaten the existing distribution of economic power in the country is subject to manipulation by the ruling class. Thus it is that the concepts of "riot" and "violence" are used in the attempt to maintain the status quo. Two national commissions were soon to follow the President's Commission on Law Enforcement and Administration of Justice. These two commissioners, the National Advisory Commission on Civil Disorders (the Kerner Commission, or the Riot Commission) and the National Commission on the Causes and Prevention of Violence (the Eisenhower Commission, or the Violence Commission) differed very little from the Crime Commission in general objective and the nature of the final recommendations. The 1960s furnished the ruling class with the challenge and opportunity to preserve domestic order. Its response was to invoke the authority of national commissions.

The Riot Commission of 1967 was specially created in response to the "racial violence" that had occurred in the ghettos of several large cities in the summers of 1966 and 1967. In its final report, the Riot Commission summarized its position:

> The summer of 1967 brought racial disorder again to American cities, deepening the bitter residue of fear and threatening the future of all Americans.
>
> We are charged by the President with the responsibility to examine this condition and to speak the truth as we see it. Two fundamental questions confront us:
>
> How can we as a people end the resort to violence while we build a better society?
>
> How can the nation realize the promise of a single society — one nation indivisible — which yet remains unfulfilled?
>
> Violence surely cannot build that society. Disruption and disorder will nourish not justice but repression. Those few who would destroy civil order and the rule of law strike at the freedom of every citizen. They must know that the community cannot and will not tolerate coercion and mob action.[18]

Hence, two premises guided the work of the Riot Commission: (1) "that this nation cannot abide violence and disorder if it is to ensure the safety of its people and their progress in a free society," and (2) "that this nation will deserve neither safety nor progress unless it can demonstrate the wisdom and the will to undertake decisive action against the root causes of racial disorder." [19] The final recommendations suggested action that would only confirm the national corporate economy and its own sources of violence, instead of drastically altering the existing system. Again, the surface was touched, while the core of the American political economy remained safe from examination and change.

Following close behind the Riot Commission was the appointment of the Violence Commission. The Commission was formed in June of 1968 by executive order of Lyndon Johnson, after the assassinations of Martin Luther King and Robert Kennedy. From the final report of the Commission, submitted in December of 1969, the message is clear: not only assassination but all "violent" phenomena (excepting, of course, the violent acts of the state) are considered dangerous to the established order. Violence, that very elusive

[18] *Report of the National Advisory Commission on Civil Disorders* (New York: Bantam Books, 1968), p. 31.

[19] *Ibid.*, p. 34.

category subject to gross manipulation by those in power, is to be controlled or eliminated. The emphasis is on those who commit this "violence," rather than on the nature of the existing order that underlies the American crisis. The final report observed:

> Violence in the United States has risen to alarmingly high levels. Whether one considers assassination, group violence, or individual acts of violence, the decade of the 1960s was considerably more violent than the several decades preceding it and ranks among the most violent in our history. The United States is the clear leader among modern, stable democratic nations in its rates of homicide, assault, rape, and robbery, and it is at least among the highest in incidence of group violence and assassination.
>
> This high level of violence is dangerous to our society. It is disfiguring our society — making fortresses of portions of our cities and dividing our people into armed camps. It is jeopardizing some of our most precious institutions, among them our schools and universities — poisoning the spirit of trust and cooperation that is essential to their proper functioning. It is corroding the central political processes of our democratic society — substituting force and fear for argument and accommodation.[20]

Violence may be dangerous to domestic order, but the recommendations of the Violence Commission did nothing to suggest an alteration in the existing social, political, and economic order. The existing order was to prevail.

We are still supposed to believe that the truth is told to us by these commissions. Johnson in his charge to the Riot Commission implied the impartiality and objectivity of the Commission when he said, "Let your search be free . . . As best as you can find the truth and express it in your report" — adding, "This matter is far, far too important for politics."[21] Indeed there was no search for the real truth by these two commissions. The only truth was the truth of a particular class, the ruling class, that sought to protect the existing American order. Our willingness to accept a ruling class conception of truth results from a failure to critically examine the nature of

[20] National Commission on the Causes and Prevention of Violence, *To Establish Justice, To Insure Domestic Tranquility* (New York: Bantam Books, 1970), p. xxv.
[21] *Report of the National Advisory Commission on Civil Disorders*, p. xvi.

70

national institutions, including the specially appointed commissions that serve these institutions.

There were eleven members appointed to the Riot Commission and thirteen appointed to the Violence Commission. The members were as follows, listing their positions at the time of their appointment and the characteristic aspects of their careers.[22]

National Advisory Commission on Civil Disorders

Otto Kerner, Chairman — Governor of Illinois. U.S. District Attorney, Northern District of Illinois; County Judge, Cook County.

John V. Lindsay, Vice Chairman — Mayor of New York City. Attorney, New York City; Executive Assistant to the U.S. Attorney General; U.S. House of Representatives; Member, Council on Foreign Relations.

I. W. Abel — President, United Steel Workers of America (AFL–CIO). Staff of United Steel Workers; Director, District 27 of United Steel Workers; Secretary-Treasurer, United Steel Workers.

Edward W. Brooke — U.S. Senator from Massachusetts; Attorney, Boston; Chairman of Finance Commission, Boston; Attorney General of Massachusetts.

James C. Coleman — U.S. Representative from California; Attorney, Los Angeles; Member of the Los Angeles City Council; House Judiciary Committee.

Fred R. Harris — U.S. Senator from Oklahoma; Oklahoma State Senate; "Outstanding Young Man" Award, Oklahoma and U.S. Junior Chamber of Commerce.

Herbert Jenkins — Chief of Police, Atlanta. Atlanta Police Department; President, International Association of Chiefs of Police; Member, Attorney General's Advisory Panel on Grants.

William M. McCulloch — U.S. Representative from Ohio; Ohio House of Representatives; Speaker and Republican Leader, Ohio House of Representatives; Recipient, Congressional Distinguished Service Award.

Katherine Graham Peden — Commissioner of Commerce, State of Kentucky; Owner-President, Radio Station WNVL, Nicholasville; President, National Federation of Business and Professional

[22] Information primarily from *Ibid.*, pp. 542–545 and *To Establish Justice, To Insure Domestic Tranquility*, pp. xvii–xviii.

Women; Member, National Advisory Council of the Small Business Administration; Board of Directors, American Industrial Development Council.

Charles B. Thornton — Chairman of the Board and Chief Executive Officer, Litton Industries, Inc.; Director of Planning, Ford Motor Company; Vice President, Hughes Aircraft Company; Vice President, Hughes Tool Company; Director, United California Bank, Times-Mirror Company, Union Oil Company, Lehman Corporation, General Mills, Inc.; Member, The Business Council; Member, Defense Industry Advisory Council to the Department of Defense.

Roy Wilkins — Executive Director, National Association for the Advancement of Colored People; Managing Editor, Kansas City Call; Secretary and Administer, NAACP.

National Commission on the Causes and Prevention of Violence

Milton S. Eisenhower — Chairman, President Emeritus of Johns Hopkins University; President, Pennsylvania State University and Kansas State University; Special Ambassador and Presidential Representative for Latin American Affairs; Board of Visitors, U.S. Naval Academy; Public Governor for New York Stock Exchange; Director, Baltimore & Ohio Railroad, C & O Railroad, ISI Growth and Income Funds, FAS International, Inc., Commercial Credit Company, Chesapeake and Potomac Telephone Company.

A. Leon Higginbotham — Vice Chairman, U.S. District Court Judge, Eastern District of Pennsylvania; Commissioner, Federal Trade Commission; Member, Commission on Reform of U.S. Criminal Law.

Hale Boggs — Majority Whip, House of Representatives; Member, Presidential Commission to Investigate the Assassination of President Kennedy.

Terence Cardinal Cooke — Archbishop of New York; Military Vicar to the Armed Forces of the United States; Member, Presidential Task Force on International Development.

Philip A. Hart — U.S. Senator from Michigan; Judiciary and Commerce Committees; Chairman, Judiciary Anti-Trust and Monopoly Sub-committee; Chairman, Commerce Sub-committee on Energy, Natural Resources and Environment; Member, Democratic Policy Committee.

Eric Hoffer — Longshoreman; Author; Philosopher; Author of *The True Believer* and *The Ordeal of Change*.

Roman Lee Hruska — U.S. Senator from Nebraska; Member, Senate Judiciary Committee; U.S. Representative from Nebraska; Board of Regents, University of Omaha.

Patricia Roberts Harris — Attorney at Law; Dean and Professor, School of Law, Howard University; U.S. Ambassador to Luxembourg.

Leon Jaworski — Attorney at Law; Special Assistant U.S. Attorney General; Special Assistant Attorney General of Texas; Member, President's Commission on Law Enforcement and Administration of Justice [see above]; Board of Directors, Bank of Southwest, Gulf Publishing Company.

Albert E. Jenner, Jr. — Attorney at Law; Special Assistant Attorney General of Illinois; Senior Counsel, Warren Commission; President, National Conference Commission on Uniform State Laws; Fellow, American College of Trial Lawyers.

William McCulloch — U.S. Representative from Ohio; Also a member of the National Commission on Civil Disorders [see above].

Ernest William McFarland — Justice, Arizona Supreme Court; Governor of Arizona; U.S. Senator from Arizona and Senate Majority Leader.

W. Walter Messinger — Staff Psychiatrist, Menninger Foundation; Member, National Advisory Health Council; Senior Psychiatric Consultant, Peace Corps; Consultant, Federal Bureau of Prisons.

The twenty-four members of the Riot Commission and the Violence Commission sketched above represent, to say the least, the established elements of political and economic life in the United States. Few of them would question the basic assumptions by which the United States is organized and operates. The established institutions are to remain intact, with perhaps some reforms within these institutions. And those who are the subjects of the commissions, those who riot and commit violence, find no voice in these commissions. Here is another victory for the corporate economy and the capitalist state.

Crime-related commissions have always protected the existing order. Indeed, this appears to be their primary objective. In a study of the eighty-six riot commissions that were appointed between 1917 and 1970, including the Kerner Riot Commission, Anthony Platt found that commissions fail to conform to the pluralist imagery of American politics.[23] Certainly the commissions have failed to be representative of the population, and even of the established groups in the country. For example, industry and business have provided three times as many commissioners as organized labor, and lawyers have far outnumbered representatives from other professional groups. The basic contradictions between pluralist rhetoric and the actual composition of riot commissions are summarized by Platt:

> (1) Commissions appear to be composed of and balanced by elite representatives from all established interest groups. *In fact,* representatives of politics, industry, and law predominate the composition of commissions. (2) Commissions appear to be composed of persons who unequivocally represent established interest groups. *In fact,* their representativeness is often disputed by their alleged constituencies. (3) Commissions appear to operate on the basis of an adversary system of conflict resolution. *In fact,* commissioners generally work harmoniously and cooperatively as a result of their similar class backgrounds, interchangeability of interests, and mutual ideology.[24]

What the riot commissions do represent, then, are those established groups that are likely to share a common frame of reference regarding the existing order. Only members who will agree on the basic assumptions of the existing American order are appointed to these commissions.

> This means in practice that government officials will select the members of riot commissions from established political organizations, established religions, and established economic groups. Republicans and Democrats will be favored over members of the Nation of Islam, agnostics, and atheists; representatives of big business and organized labor will be favored over small businessmen, non-unionized workers, and consumers. In this sense, riot commissions are inherently conservative, protective of existing institutions and not disposed to propose radical changes which will diminish the power of established groups. We can not find, therefore, nor expect to find official riot commissions which are critical of

[23] Anthony Platt, "The Politics of Riot Commissions, 1917–70: An Overview," in Anthony M. Platt (ed.), *The Politics of Riot Commissions* (New York: Macmillan, 1971), pp. 3–43.
[24] *Ibid.*, p. 19.

the two-party political system, of organized religion, or of corporate capitalism.[25]

We cannot count on commissions to solve the fundamental problems of modern life in the United States. Commissions can do little more than affirm the conditions that underlie our problems. To do otherwise, to carry out a radical analysis of our problems and to propose solutions that would make a difference in American life, would be to upset the established order, the national corporate economy. Since commissions are composed of men of power, such changes will not be suggested within that context. Commissions provide the ruling class with one more means of protecting the existing order, which means securing domestic order — keeping the people of the underclass in their place, as colonials.

THE OMNIBUS CRIME BILL

The American corporate ruling class triumphed at the end of the 1960s. It was able, in part through the commissions, to affirm a conceptual and actual criminal reality that assured its own existence. The ruling class pulled off another of its schemes: it survived by preserving the existing order. Domestic order was finally enforced through the ultimate weapon, the law of the state. Several pieces of legislation were enacted, following the Commission's reports, which stepped up the war on crime and domestic revolt. Rioters and potential rioters were placed under surveillance. Activists were tried for crossing state lines to organize. Defendants were denied basic civil rights. And most dramatically, the Omnibus Crime Control and Safe Streets Act was passed and instituted, profoundly determining criminal justice to this day.

The Omnibus Crime Control bill was the legislators' attempt to control any behavior that would threaten the existing order. The bill that the legislators passed was ultimately shaped by the Senate Subcommittee on Criminal Laws and Procedures. It was through this committee that the ruling class was able to have its interests represented and incorporated into legislation. The Subcommittee on Criminal Laws and Procedures (as part of the larger Senate Committee on the Judiciary) was made up of representatives of the

25 *Ibid.*, p. 20.

ruling class. It was composed of eight established senators, with John McClellan (a long-time crimebuster in the Senate) as chairman. Their biographical sketches are as follows, as listed by the senators in the *Congressional Directory:*[26]

John L. McClellan, Chairman; Democrat, of Camden, Ark.; born at Sheridan, Grant County, Ark., February 25, 1896; first lieutenant of ASSC during the First World War; lawyer; prosecuting attorney of the seventh judicial district of Arkansas, 1926–30; member of 74th and 75th Congresses from the Sixth Congressional District of Arkansas; elected United States Senator November 3, 1942, for the term beginning January 3, 1943; reelected in 1948, 1954, 1960, and 1966 for the term ending January 3, 1973.

James Oliver Eastland, Democrat, of Doddsville, Miss.; born in Doddsville, Miss., November 28, 1904; Methodist; attended the University of Mississippi, Vanderbilt University, and the University of Alabama; moved to Forest, Miss., in 1905 and was reared in Scott County, Miss.; studied law, was admitted to the bar in 1927, and commenced practice in Forest, Miss.; also engaged in farming; member of the State house of representatives from Scott County, Miss., 1928–32; appointed to the United States Senate to fill the vacancy caused by the death of Hon. Pat Harrison, and served from June 30, 1941, to September 28, 1941, when a duly elected successor qualified, elected to the United States Senate on November 3, 1942, for the term beginning January 3, 1943; unopposed for the term beginning January 3, 1949; reelected for term beginning January 1955; reelected for term beginning January 3, 1961; reelected for term beginning January 10, 1967.

Sam J. Ervin, Jr., Democrat, born at Morganton, N.C., September 27, 1896; graduated from University of North Carolina with A.B. degree, 1917, and Harvard Law School with LL.B. degree, 1922; granted these honorary degrees: LL.D., University of North Carolina, 1951, LL.D., Western Carolina College, 1955, and D.P.A., Suffolk University, 1957; served in France with First Division in First World War; twice wounded in battle, twice cited for gallantry in action, and awarded French Fourragere, Purple Heart with Oak Leaf Cluster, Silver Star, and Distinguished Service Cross; subsequently served in National Guard; admitted to North Carolina Bar, 1919; practiced law at Morganton from 1922

[26] *Congressional Directory,* 90th Congress (Washington, D.C.: U.S. Government Printing Office, 1967), pp. 10, 74, 79, 88, 95, 126, 146, 157.

until present except during service on the bench; representative from Burke County in North Carolina Legislature, 1923, 1925, 1931; member North Carolina State Democratic Executive Committee, 1930–37; judge, Burke County Criminal Court, 1935–37; judge, North Carolina Superior Court, 1937–43; member North Carolina State Board of Law Examiners, 1944–46; representative from the Tenth North Carolina District in the 79th Congress, 1946–47; chairman, North Carolina Commission for the Improvement of the Administration of Justice, 1947–49; associate justice, North Carolina Supreme Court, February 3, 1948, until June 11, 1954, when he qualified as a U.S. Senator from North Carolina under appointment of Governor William B. Umstead as a successor to the late Clyde R. Hoey; returned to the U.S. Senate by the people of North Carolina at the elections of 1954, 1956, and 1962 for additional terms ending on January 2, 1969; delegate to Democratic National Conventions, 1956, 1960, 1964; trustee, University of North Carolina (1932–35, 1945–46) and Davidson College (1948–58); chosen Morganton's Man of the Year, 1954; Grand Orator, the Grand Lodge of Masons of North Carolina, 1963; director, First National Bank of Morganton; member, American Bar Association, American Judicature Society, North Carolina Bar Association, North Carolina State Bar, Farm Bureau, Grange, Morganton Chamber of Commerce, etc.; awarded the Cross of Military Service by the United Daughters of the Confederacy, the Good Citizenship Medal by the Sons of the American Revolution, the Distinguished Citizenship Certificate by the North Carolina Citizens Association, the Patriotic Service Medal by the American Coalition of Patriotic Societies, the Religious Liberty Citation by Americans United for Separation of Church and State, and the George Washington Award by the American Good Government Society [abbreviated].

Philip A. Hart, Democrat, of Mackinac Island, Mich.; born December 10, 1912, at Bryn Mawr, Pa.; Georgetown University, A.B. cum laude, 1934; University of Michigan Law School, J.D., 1937; U.S. Army, 1941–46, with Fourth Infantry Division, wounded in D-Day assault on Utah Beach, Normandy; Michigan Corporation and Securities Commissioner, 1949–50; director, OPS, 1951; U.S. Attorney for Eastern Michigan, 1952; legal adviser to Governor Williams, 1953–54; elected Lieutenant Governor, 1954, reelected 1956; trustee and past president of Michigan Bar Foundation; elected to the U.S. Senate November 4, 1958; reelected November 3, 1964.

Roman Lee Hruska, Republican, of Omaha, Nebr.; born in David City, Nebr., August 16, 1904; son of Joseph C. and Caroline L. Hruska; attended the public schools; University of Omaha; University of Chicago Law School, 1927 and 1928; Creighton University College of Law, Omaha, LL.B. 1929; Creighton University LL.D. (hon.); Doane College (Nebr.) LL.D. (hon.); Coe College (Iowa) Doctor of Humanities (hon.); general practice of law in Omaha; member Nebraska State and American Bar Associations, Kiwanis, Shrine, Unitarian Church; University of Omaha Board of Regents 1950–57; national vice president and general counsel Western Bohemian Fraternal Association (Cedar Rapids, Iowa); past president Nebraska Fraternal Congress; 1944–52 Board of County Commissioners, Douglas County, Nebr., served as chairman 1945–52; member Advisory Committee to Nebraska Board of Control, 1947–52; president, Nebraska Association of County Officials 1950–51; vice president, National Association of County Officials, 1951 and 1952; elected to the 83d Congress November 4, 1952; elected to the United States Senate November 2, 1954, to complete unexpired term; reelected November 4, 1958 and November 3, 1964.

Edward Moore Kennedy, Democrat, of Boston, Mass.; born in Brookline, Mass., February 22, 1932, son of Joseph P. and Rose Kennedy; Milton Academy, 1950; Harvard College, A.B., 1954; International Law School, The Hague, Holland, 1958; University of Virginia Law School, LL.B., 1959; enlisted in the U.S. Army as a private and served in France and Germany from June 1951 to March 1953; President of the Joseph P. Kennedy, Jr. Foundation; trustee of: Children's Hospital Medical Center, Boston; Lahey Clinic, Boston; Museum of Science, Boston; Boston University, John F. Kennedy Library; on Board of Visitors of Fletcher School of Law & Diplomacy, Tufts University; advisory board of Emmanuel College; corporation member Northeastern University; assistant district attorney of Suffolk County; elected to the U.S. Senate November 6, 1962, to fill unexpired term of his brother, John F. Kennedy; reelected November 3, 1964.

Hugh Scott, Republican, of Philadelphia, Pa.; lawyer, Philadelphia; elected 77th Congress, reelected seven additional terms; member, House minority policy committee; member, Board of Visitors, Naval Academy, 1948; chairman, Board of Visitors, U.S. Merchant Marine Academy, 1959; Board of Visitors, Coast Guard Academy, 1963; author, "Scott on Bailments" (1931), "How to Go Into Politics" (1949), "The Golden Age of Chinese Art" (1967), and numerous articles in national magazines; national chairman, Republican Party, 1948–49; Eisenhower personal staff, 1952; chairman, Eisenhower Headquarters Committee, 1952; general counsel, Republican National Committee, 1955–60; vice chairman, Senatorial Campaign Committee, 1964–; member of Republican Coordinating Committee; active duty, United States Naval Reserve, in World War II as a lieutenant; last rank, captain; active service with North Atlantic Patrol, Occupation of Iceland and Pacific area, including Occupation of Japan; duty aboard carrier *Valley Forge* in Korean War, August and September 1950; A.B., Randolph-Macon College, 1919; LL.B., University of Virginia, 1922; LL.D., University of Pennsylvania; LL.D., Randolph-Macon; L.H.D., La Salle College; LL.D., Dickinson College, LL.D., Temple University; D. Pub. Adm., Suffolk University; LL.D., Ursinus College; LL.D. Washington and Jefferson; LL.D., Lebanon Valley College; Litt. D., Philadelphia College of Osteopathy; LL.D., Philadelphia Textile Institute; Sc.D., Delaware Valley College; LL.D., Lincoln University; LL.D., Westminster College; LL.D., Waynesburg College; LL.D. Franklin and Marshall College; D.C.L., Susquehanna University; also attended University of Pennsylvania; member of American Legion; VFW; AMVETS; Sons of the Revolution; Society of the Cincinnati; P.O.S. of A.; Capitol Press Club, Pa.; Friendly Sons of St. Patrick; Oriental Ceramic Society (U.K.); Asia House; Advisory Committee on Oriental Art, Philadelphia Museum of Art; Board of Regents, Smithsonian Institution; Alpha Chi Rho (national president 1942–46); Phi Beta Kappa, Tau Kappa Alpha and Phi Alpha Delta fraternities; Philadelphia Cricket Club; Germantown Lions Club; honorary alumnus, Philadelphia Textile Institute; Episcopalian; elected United States Senator November 1958; reelected November 3, 1964.

Strom Thurmond, Republican, of Aiken, S.C.; attorney and farmer; born December 5, 1902, in Edgefield, S.C., son of John William and Eleanor Gertrude (Strom) Thurmond; 1923 graduate of Clemson College; studied law at night and admitted to South Carolina Bar 1930, and admitted to practice in all Federal Courts, including the U.S. Supreme Court; LL.D. degrees, Bob Jones U. (1948), Presbyterian Coll. (1960), Clemson Coll. (1961); D. Mil. Sc. degree, The Citadel (1961); Doctor of Humanities, Trinity College (1965); served as teacher and athletic coach, county superintendent of education, city attorney and county attorney, State Senator, circuit judge, Governor of South Carolina 1947–51, serving as chairman of Southern Governors' Conference; practiced law in Aiken, S.C., 1951–55; volunteered for service in World War II the day war was declared against Germany, served with Headquarters First Army 1942–46, European and Pacific Theaters, participated in Normandy invasion with 82d Airborne Division; awarded 5 battle stars and 17 decorations, medals and awards, including the Legion of Merit, Bronze Star Medal with "V", Army Commendation Ribbon, Purple Heart, Presidential Distinguished Unit Citation, 3d Army Certificate of Achievement, OCAMG Certificate of Achievement, Department of Army Certificate of Appreciation, Belgian Order of the Crown, and French Croix de Guerre; major general, U.S. Army Reserve, past national president Reserve Officers Association and Military Government Association; Baptist; American Bar Association, and numerous defense, veterans, civic, fraternal, and farm organizations; Thurmond Hall (1939) at Winthrop Coll., streets in several S.C. cities, and new Edgefield County consolidated high school (1961) named in his honor; delegate to six Democratic National Conventions (chairman of South Carolina delegation and national committeeman 1948); States' Rights Democratic candidate for President of United States 1948, carrying 4 states and receiving 39 electoral votes; elected to the United States Senate November 2, 1954, as a write-in candidate, for the term ending January 3, 1961; resigned as United States Senator April 4, 1956, to place the office in a primary, pursuant to a promise made to the people during the 1954 campaign; renominated and reelected to the Senate without opposition in 1956, resuming duties on November 7, 1956; renominated and reelected in 1960; September 16, 1964, switched from Democratic to Republican Party; renominated and reelected 1966 for term ending January 3, 1973.

The hearings for the crime bill were held by this subcommittee beginning on March 7, 1967. Chairman McClellan opened the hearings by stating that "It is quite probable that these hearings and the bills we will be considering will mark the turning point in the struggle against lawlessness in this nation." The survival of the state and the current economic order ("society") were at stake:

In view of the gravity of the crime problem in this country, of which I think we are all becoming cognizant, we will have to give serious and constant study to the difficulties that confront us in trying to find ways, methods, and the means legislatively speaking to bring about a reduction in crime or at least arrest the rate of increase in order to bring the amount of crime in this country down to tolerable proportions, to where society can be reasonably safe.[27]

He then added that it was the burden of Congress to find a solution, to protect the existing order:

This committee has a tremendous task. It is a great burden, I think, upon the Congress of the United States to diligently search for legislative remedies, and that burden, that challenge, is also to the administrative branch of the Government, and in my judgment, to the judicial as well, because there must be a change. The rate of increase in crime cannot continue if our society is to remain safe and secure and our people protected against the ravages of crime.[28]

The Omnibus Crime bill that came out of this committee was an outright device to control the underclass. The Senate Subcommittee on Criminal Laws and Procedures (and the larger Judiciary Committee) operated, and continues to operate, as a legislative arm of the capitalist ruling class. The legislation of crime control is an integral part of the survival of the national economy. And as the final vote on the crime bill indicated, the ruling class interest of the subcommittee was confirmed by the rest of Congress. Indeed, most legislators were on the side of the ruling class. When the roll for the final vote was called in the Senate, on May 23, 1967, the bill was overwhelmingly approved. With its various repressive provisions and dangerous precedents, it was passed by a margin of seventy-one to four. The bill was similarly passed in the House by a vote of three hundred and sixty-eight to seventeen.

After the Senate vote, Senate leader Mansfield rose to say: "Mr. President, with a loud and clear voice the Senate has said, 'Let us reverse the growing crime rate, let us give our law-enforcement officers the help and assistance they need.' The cry of 'crime in the streets' is not, by any means, a false alarm; it exists and it is about time the Congress faced the issue squarely. With the passage of this

[27] "Controlling Crime Through More Effective Law Enforcement," *Hearings* Before the Subcommittee on Criminal Law and Procedures of the Committee on the Judiciary, United States Senate, 90th Congress (Washington, D.C.: U.S. Government Printing Office, 1967), p. 1.
[28] *Ibid.*

measure, the Senate has responded. I think this entire body may be proud of such an immense achievement." [29] Congress had once again assisted the ruling class in preserving the existing order.

SHAPING DOMESTIC POLICY: THE CED

The ruling class is able to shape social policy to its own ends by participating in a variety of advisory organizations involved in the government policy-making process. These groups are composed, almost by definition, of the owners and managers of the large corporations. They engage in the formulation of policy positions, advising government officials both formally and informally, in reports and through personal contact. Often the proposals are submitted as "reforms," to make the capitalist system more efficient and better able to adapt to other changes in the system.

One of the most prominent and powerful of these organizations is the Committee for Economic Development (CED). It is in many ways the counterpart on domestic policy of the Council on Foreign Relations (CFR). As such, it is the link between corporations and the federal government. In his examination of CED, Domhoff makes the following observations about the organization:

> Organized in the early 1940's to prepare for postwar reconversion to a civilian economy, the leaders in its formation were financier Jesse Jones, then Secretary of Commerce, and millionaires Paul Hoffman and William Benton. These three men brought together corporation executives and bankers with outstanding economists for weekend study sessions which were intensified versions of the CFR study groups. Out of these sessions came the guidelines for American economic policy in the postwar era, including some of the provisions of the Employment Act of 1946, the stabilized budget concept, long-range fiscal and monetary policy, and certain aspects of the Marshall Plan.[30]

The relationship of CED to the ruling class really does not need to be established, as Domhoff further notes, since membership is limited to big businessmen, educators who consult to corporations, and a few university presidents. And like the members of CFR, the mem-

[29] Quoted in Richard Harris, *The Fear of Crime* (New York: Frederick A. Praeger, 1969), pp. 98–99.
[30] Domhoff, *The Higher Circles*, pp. 123–124.

bers of CED readily move between corporate power, government affiliation, and domestic and foreign policy.

> Among its original and most active members have been Ralph Flanders, the Vermont toolmaker and Boston banker; Thomas B. McCabe, head of Scott Paper Company; Clarence Francis of General Foods; Marion B. Folsom of Eastman Kodak; William L. Clayton of Clayton, Anderson; William L. Batt of SKF Industries; Charles E. Wilson of General Electric; Eric A. Johnston of the Brown-Johnston Company; Chester C. Davis of the Federal Reserve Bank of St. Louis; and S. Bayard Colgate of Colgate-Palmolive-Peet. As with the CFR, many CED members become officials of the federal government: thirty-eight of the trustees during the first fifteen years of CED held elective or appointive positions. Flanders and Benton became senators, McCabe became head of the Federal Reserve Bank under President Truman, and Folsom, Clayton, William C. Foster, and Wayne C. Taylor held important posts in major departments. As of the early 1960's, forty-eight of 190 CED trustees were at the same time members of CFR.[31]

And as CED itself observes, its objective (as "nonpartisan and nonpolitical") is "to promote stable economic growth with rising living standards and increasing opportunities for all and to strengthen the concepts and institutions essential to progress in a free society."[32] In other words, the Committee for Economic Development is engaged in promoting the capitalist social and economic order.

Therefore, in its own response to domestic disorder, CED has recently prepared and released a policy report on "Reducing Crime and Assuring Justice."[33] The report panel was headed by Wayne E. Thompson, Senior Vice-President of Dayton Hudson Corporation. The chairmen of the research and policy committee of CED consisted of Emilio G. Collado (Executive Vice-President of Standard Oil Company), Philip M. Klutznick (Chairman of Urban Investment and Development Co.), Howard C. Petersen (Chairman of the Fidelity Bank), John A. Perkins (Vice-President of the University of California, Berkeley), John L. Burns (President of John L. Burns

[31] *Ibid.*, p. 124.

[32] *CED Publications 1972* (New York: Committee for Economic Development, 1972), Preface.

[33] Committee for Economic Development, *Reducing Crime and Assuring Justice* (New York: Committee for Economic Development, 1972).

and Co.), and William M. Roth (Director of Pacific National Life Assurance Co.).

At the beginning of its report, CED makes clear the nature of its interest in crime: the American capitalist economy and the crime problem are closely related.

> Crime running rampant is certainly not the mark of a healthy society. Large-scale criminal activity, whether organized or spontaneous, undermines an economy based upon opportunity and enterprise, while it fosters a sense of injustice among the poor and the minorities. No citizen can justify indifference, least of all members of the business community with their special concern for public safety. Complacency will prove suicidal.[34]

And the solution that CED proposes is a businesslike one: modernize and rationalize the criminal justice system.

> The Committee believes that the ineffectiveness of the present structure is rooted in the organizational and administrative chaos that characterizes the nation's uncoordinated system of criminal justice, and in the management weaknesses prevailing in agencies at all levels. The Committee therefore proposes a complete administrative overhaul of the criminal justice system and a redistribution of responsibilities, functions, and financial support among the various levels of government. Local governments would be relieved of all obligations other than maintenance of urban police forces, and each state would draw together all criminal justice activities under a strong, centralized Department of Justice. The federal role would be concentrated in a new, independent Federal Authority To Ensure Justice, which would coordinate the fight against crime on the national level and would provide strong financial incentives for the reorganization of state and local systems.[35]

There is no attempt here, of course, to change the capitalist system itself; the solution to the crime problem is to be found in a more effective administration.

The "administrative overhaul of the criminal justice system" that CED recommends is no less than the nationalization of crime control. The proposed "Federal Authority To Ensure Justice" could

[34] *Ibid.*, p. 9.
[35] *Ibid.*, pp. 7–8.

bypass or supersede existing agencies (local, state, and federal), including the Department of Justice, the FBI, and LEAA, agencies which are "inefficient"; it could become a new centralized national body "endowed with a sweeping range of statutory powers." This authority could be given powers to:

- set and enforce the standards — substantive, administrative, and organizational — governing large federal grants-in-aid in support of all criminal justice functions;
- establish, organize, and direct administrative mechanisms to develop strategic plans and policies, evaluate performance of ongoing programs, and provide advisory and liaison services to state and local units;
- formulate new legislative proposals, whenever necessary, and review pending legislation at the request of Congressional committees;
- advance and finance education programs on a broad front — including aids to academic institutions with appropriate programs in criminal justice and, if necessary, foundation of a federal staff college for the advancement of criminal justice — to assure suitable training for all law enforcement officers with discretionary functions, as a requirement for holding such positions;
- commission or manage research into every aspect of this field deemed worthy of serious investigation;
- make an annual Report to the President and Congress — comparable to that of the Council of Economic Adviser — describing the national condition with regard to crime and justice and outlining policy directions; and
- assure the collection and analysis of dependable, comprehensive, detailed data covering every aspect of criminal justice — either under its own or other suitable auspices.[36]

As the Committee for Economic Development admits, "The national government has no constitutional responsibility or direct authority for general law enforcement." But, it continues, "when customary patterns of federalism break down in the face of critical and widespread problems, the people of this country have on many occasions turned to the national government." [37] Since this breakdown "is now evident," CED suggests, this is the time for the federal

[36] *Ibid.*, pp. 70–71.
[37] *Ibid.*, p. 67.

85

government to fight crime on a national level, with the appropriate kind of centralized organization.

This, then, could be the final solution to instability in the capitalist system, to any threats made against the existing order. By nationalizing crime control, corporate capitalism could determine domestic policy in the same way that it determines foreign policy. The law enforcement interests of local power elites, and any public interest, could be nullified by placing crime control decisions directly in the hands of the corporate ruling class. The appeal made by CED is deceptively attractive: "An orderly and just society is not an easy goal, nor is it impossible of attainment. It is a goal that must be achieved, and soon, to restore the faith of Americans in their most basic institutions. Means suited to these ends are at hand; adoption depends only upon better public understanding, and upon determined support from the great majority of citizens and opinion leaders." [38] But in the end, the proposal for this type of crime control is a proposal for greater control by the corporate ruling class over the preservation of the capitalist system. This may well be the ultimate direction of crime control in capitalist society.

CRIME CONTROL BUREAUCRACIES

It is in the state bureaucracy that the interests of the ruling class are finally applied and enforced. Those who manage these bureaucracies in capitalist societies are, technically and ideologically, the servants of the ruling class.[39] Far from being politically neutral, these managers (or technocrats) constitute a considerable force in preserving the capitalist order. The role of bureaucrats is, indeed, to conduct the interests of the state. Whether or not they intentionally promote the interests of the ruling class is less important than the fact that, by the very nature of their work, they are allies of the existing social and economic elite. Moreover, as Miliband observes, the education and social class of these bureaucrats make them "part of a specific milieu whose ideas, prejudices and outlook they are most likely to share, and which is bound to influence, in fact to define, their view of the 'national interest.' " [40]

38 *Ibid.*, p. 17.
39 Miliband, *The State in Capitalist Society*, pp. 115–129.
40 *Ibid.*, p. 123.

86

To understand the role of these bureaucracies that manage the control of crime in America, we need to know about the top-level technocrats who make them work. The national crime control bureaucracies have their own managers who carry out the capitalist interests embodied in the crime control programs. We can sketch a few of the crime control bureaucracies and the "domestic order managers" who occupy key roles in these agencies.

The number of crime control bureaucracies has increased greatly in recent years. With the attempt by the ruling class to combat the crisis in the capitalist system, new agencies of control have been established. A few of these, along with the old standbys (the Department of Justice and the FBI), can be listed and characterized as follows:[41]

Department of Justice — Leading institution of the national criminal justice system; forty thousand employees, twenty-five hundred of whom are attorneys; located in Washington and ninety-three regional U.S. Attorney's offices; includes the Bureau of Prisons, Bureau of Narcotics and Dangerous Drugs, Immigration and Naturalization Service, LEAA and the FBI.

Federal Bureau of Investigation (FBI) — National police and investigative force of nine thousand special agents, ten thousand clerical personnel; located in Washington and fifty-nine regional offices and five hundred local "resident offices;" specializes in domestic intelligence-gathering and internal security protection. Each agent carries an average case load of thirty and controls a network of from five to seven informers. The Bureau is rigid, efficient, uncreative, better at catching bank robbers than bank bombers.

Law Enforcement Assistance Administration (LEAA) — Some of the biggest but subtlest steps toward 1984 have been taken through the Law Enforcement Assistance Administration (LEAA) — a Justice Department Agency which obtained its original legislative mandate in the 1968 Safe Streets Act, a law passed hastily in the wake of wide-spread unrest triggered by the assassination of Martin Luther King. Under Mitchell and Kleindienst, LEAA has become the fastest growing agency of government, its budget increasing twenty-five fold from $63 million in fiscal year 1969 to the latest authorization of $1.75 *billion* for fiscal year 1973. The

[41] As described in Jeff Gerth, "The Americanization of 1984," *SunDance*, 1 (April–May, 1972), pp. 59 and 66.

majority of LEAA's money goes to the purchase of weapons and electronic hardware for police departments around the country.

Internal Securities Division (ISD) — Justice Department agency bolstered considerably in November 1970 by a doubling of its legal staff to seventy-five; specializes in prosecution and investigation of white radicals (Third World radicals are handled by Civil Rights Division); is the resting place for the military intelligence dossiers supposedly destroyed by the Pentagon (according to the *Washington Post*).

Interdivisional Intelligence Unit (IDIU) — Data bank of political dossiers under supervision of ISD; relatively inactive since its inception in 1967 but reactivated by Mitchell; contains fifteen thousand name files and fifteen thousand incident files relating to political dissent; information compiled mostly from FBI but also from Secret Service and the military.

Subversive Activities Control Board (SACB) — Quasi-judicial agency created by the Subversive Activities Control Act of 1950; makes public designation of "Communist-front" or "Communist-infiltrated" groups based on information supplied by the Attorney General; reactivated in 1971 by Nixon with a broadened definition of "subversive"-type organizations.

Central Intelligence Agency (CIA) — Operates through the Domestic Operations Division, increasingly bypassing the FBI in Domestic "counter-espionage;" operates most "openly" in keeping track of Third World groups and radical groups with international links (e.g. Venceremos Brigade); also penetrates and uses key institutions as conduits, observation posts and recruitment centers (such as foundations and universities); exact scope of domestic operation undeterminable. Regulates international hard drug traffic.

What kind of men (for this is a male's occupation) operate these crime control bureaucracies? What are their interests and what interests do they serve? From a review of the backgrounds and current activities of a few of the most prominent domestic order managers, we learn that they are without exception devoted to preserving the capitalist system. Their interests and the interests of those they serve are basically the same. The single purpose is to control behavior and activity that will threaten the existing order. Hence, those who create crime control agencies and those who manage them are united in a common cause. The crime control bureaucracies and the men within them conform to a pattern: *law and order* in the name of preserving domestic order. Only in an analytical sense can the men be separated from interests and the bureaucracies they serve.

A detailed analysis of the domestic order managers is yet to be done; it is sufficient here to describe briefly some of the most prominent of these men in the first years of the 1970s:[42]

John Mitchell, ex-Attorney General.
Former Wall Street bond lawyer having connections with many political figures in state and local governments; helped develop Wisconsin's borrowing system in Fifties, installing Jerris Leonard as head (then appointed him in 1970 to head LEAA); while on Wall Street, specialized in financial manipulation. His law firm, Caldwell, Trimble and Mitchell, merged with Nixon's in 1967. Nixon's campaign manager in 1968; close political confidant of President, intimate of CIA chief Richard Helms; reads President's daily CIA briefing — a "super secret" compendium of world events of the previous twenty-four hours — only four copies of which circulate. Members of National Security Council, Forty Committee (secret NSC group, chaired by Kissinger, which screens "covert action" proposals such as last year's prisoner raid inside North Vietnam), Urban Affairs Council. Has an authoritarian, take-charge manner, runs a tight ship, is strong advocate of expanded "national security" wiretap authority; resigned from Nixon's 1972 reelection campaign after the Watergate crimes.

Richard Kleindienst, Attorney General.
Phoenix, Arizona, attorney from 1956 to 1969, represented various contracting, mining, oil, and ranching interests; was active in state Republican Party; ran for governor in 1964 but was defeated. Was very active in Goldwater's Presidential campaign as Director of Field Operations and worked closely with Denison Kitchell, former John Birch Society member, in guiding Goldwater's primary strategy. Was dubbed one of Goldwater's "bully boys" for his aggressive pigeonholing of delegates. Did field work, under Mitchell's guidance, for Nixon's 1968 campaign. Controlled day-to-day activities in Justice Department under Mitchell as Deputy Attorney General; was responsible for Supreme Court and other federal appointments; in February recommended by Mitchell for

[42] *Ibid.*, p. 66. The description of L. Patrick Gray is from *Current Biography*, 33 (September, 1972), pp. 23–25.

89

Attorney General position. Is aggressive, ambitious, tough. In fall of 1969 with anti-war demonstrations looming, urged mass arrests, and when a lawyer asked, "What about the Constitution?" snapped, "We'll worry about the Constitution later."

William Rehnquist, Supreme Court Justice.

Phoenix, Arizona, attorney from 1956 to 1969; first law firm association was with Denison Kitchell; partner in Powers and Rehnquist from 1960 to 1968, representing innocuous land development and ranching interests in bankruptcy and fraud cases. Was active, under Kleindienst's direction, in Goldwater campaign and in Arizona Republican politics; is close friend of Goldwater. Is active in harassment of radical minorities and in anti-labor activity; is associated with extreme right-wing causes in Phoenix. Was appointed Assistant Attorney General on strength of Kleindienst's recommendation in 1969, responsible for Justice Department policy in field of electronic surveillance; also formulated legal justification ("protective reaction") for Cambodian invasion in 1970; played key role in government's Mayday strategy. Was appointed and confirmed to Supreme Court in December 1971. Is ambitious, upwardly mobile, outwardly shy; married (wife is former CIA employee).

Jerris Leonard, Administor of LEAA.

Since 1971, the man heading LEAA has been Jerris Leonard, a close friend of Mitchell's for the past fifteen years. Leonard was formerly the chief of the Justice Department's civil rights division, where he was responsible for the decision not to press charges against the National Guard in the Kent State killings, or against the Chicago police in the Fred Hampton case. Earlier, in the fall of 1969, over half of the lawyers in Leonard's civil rights division publicly protested his blocking of a Mississippi school desegregation case.

John Edgar Hoover, Former Director, FBI (deceased).

Head of the FBI since 1924, worked initially in Justice Department as special assistant to Attorney General Palmer and played a large role in the Palmer Raids of 1920; given command of General Investigative Division (GID) in 1919 and compiled radical dossiers — within three months had a "complete history of over sixty thousand radically-inclined individuals." Has denied and ignored the existence of organized crime during his entire tenure, while maintaining a xenophobic proclivity for hunting "reds." Close friend of Roy Cohn and Sen. Joe McCarthy, intimate of wealthy oil barons, financiers and numerous individuals with close connections to organized crime.

L. Patrick Gray, III, Acting Director, FBI.

Upon the death in May 1972 of the Federal Bureau of Investigation's primordial director, septuagenarian J. Edgar Hoover, President Nixon hand-picked his old friend and loyal troubleshooter L. Patrick Gray to be acting director of the Justice Department's fact-finding law enforcement agency. Gray, a retired Pentagon Navy official who practises law when not in the President's service, first served Nixon in the latter's initial, unsuccessful bid for the Presidency, in 1960. When Nixon finally entered the White House, in 1969, Gray joined his administration as executive assistant to the Secretary of Health, Education and Welfare. Later he served as head of the Civil Division of the Department of Justice, and while in that position he accepted the additional burden of enforcing the administration's freeze on wages and prices. At the time of his present appointment his nomination for the post of Deputy Attorney General was pending. The fervor of Gray's patriotism is second to no man's, including J. Edgar Hoover's. Gray had earlier succeeded William Ruckelshaus as assistant Attorney General in charge of the Justice Department's Civil Division. Gray developed the strategy, later constitutionally questioned, of mass arrests of antiwar demonstrators in Washington.

Robert Mardian, Assistant Attorney General.

Former Pasadena, California attorney from 1951 to 1968, representing various contracting and investment interests, among others; vice-president, general counsel, and large stockholder of Mutual Savings and Loan Association, 1962 through 1968. (Brother Sam was mayor of Phoenix from 1960 to 1963.) Directed western region of Goldwater campaign in 1964 because of his "business and personal connections in most areas of the region." Was appointed general counsel for H.E.W. by Nixon in 1969, developed Administration's "desegregation" policies. Was appointed head of ISD in November 1970; responsible for flood of investigative grand juries, expanded intelligence and surveillance, and prosecution of Pentagon Papers and Anderson Papers leaks. Plays golf with Mitchell, rides to work each morning with his neighbor and close friend Richard Kleindienst. Is very aggressive, tough-minded, competitive.

In addition to these leading figures in the nation's crime control bureaucracies, there are such persons as Guy L. Goodwin (head of the elite Special Litigation Section of the Justice Department's Internal Security Division), Associate Deputy Attorney General Donald Santarelli (later to be appointed Administrator of LEAA), and LEAA Associate Administrators Richard W. Velde and Clarence M. Coster. With all of these men, there is the fact of close ties in the past and a common outlook regarding the problem of securing the domestic order. There is no need for an outright law and order conspiracy when the crime control managers share such a basic mental framework.

The closed and total nature of the national crime control bureaucracy becomes evident in any investigation of these agencies and their leaders. Whenever there is a change in bureaucratic positions, usually involving merely a reshuffling of personalities or a set of promotions, a sense of the common framework and relationships becomes obvious. For example, when Jerris Leonard was sworn in as the new Administrator of LEAA the old hands — from the Presidency, to the Supreme Court, to the Department of Justice, to other control agencies — were involved. The Attorney General, then John Mitchell, delivered the remarks:

> I welcome all of you here today for this noteworthy occasion. The ceremony at the White House when Jerry Leonard was sworn in at noon by Justice Blackmun, in the presence of the President, was very delightful. It was a great thing for law enforcement.
>
> I can highly commend Jerris Leonard to all of you. I have known Jerry for many years and have worked with him very closely. He has a great deal of experience in legislative and administrative matters, and, of course, he was head of the Civil Rights Division of the Justice Department for more than two years. I think his qualifications for the position he now holds are unique and outstanding. There are very few jobs in government he could not handle with great distinction. He certainly has my full confidence, and he also has the confidence of the President of the United States.
>
> His task and your task, as part of the LEAA program, will have a greater impact on our society than perhaps any other segment of government. I am sure most of you realize that the criminal justice system in this country — particularly at the state and local level — is archaic and relates more to the 18th and 19th centuries than to

the present century. It is only through improvement of the entire system that we are going to be able to reduce crime. It is a monumental job because of the absence of resources in most areas.

I believe that all of you, under Jerris Leonard's leadership, along with Clarence Coster and Richard Velde, will make a mark and will contribute to society the true potential of what LEAA can do. We in the Justice Department — from my office on down — as well as the President in the White House will be behind you one hundred percent in all your efforts.[43]

The question is whether the crime control bureaucracy will continue to increase in size and in scope. The current personalities, those who manage the control agencies, are performing their duty of assisting the ruling class in preserving domestic order. The capitalist system is being maintained, in time of crisis, by the crime control bureaucracy. And I would argue that as long as the capitalist system is threatened this bureaucracy will exist and perform the function of maintaining order. Since the capitalist system will increasingly be plagued by its own contradictions, the crime control bureaucracy will become even stronger and more pervasive. Legal repression is a basic part of capitalism. It may be the final solution to the preservation of the capitalist order. That is, until we can change to a different kind of society.

THE REVOLUTIONARY CONSEQUENCES
OF THE CAPITALIST CRISIS

Criminal law continues to secure the colonial status of the oppressed in the corporate economy of the United States. The events of the last few years relating to crime can be understood only in the light of the crisis of the American system, including the events of "disruption" and those of repression. Moreover, the oppression and repression within the United States cannot be separated from its imperialism abroad. The crisis of the American empire is complete. The war waged against the people of Indochina is part of the same war waged against the oppressed at home. The ruling class, through its control of the state, must resort to a worldwide counterrevolution. A counter-insurgency program is carried out — through the CIA

---

[43] Quoted in *LEAA Newsletter*, 1 (June, 1971), p. 2.

abroad and the FBI and local police forces at home. A military war has been fought in Asia, while a war on crime with its own weaponry is being fought within the United States. All of this to avoid changing the national corporate economy, indeed to protect it and to promote its continuation.

Crime and the criminal law can only be understood within the context of this crisis.

By posing on the national level the central issues of the international conflict, by linking the international struggle for self-determination with the internal quest for social equality and social control, the crisis of democracy increasingly presents itself as the revolutionary crisis of the epoch. The movement for the sovereignty of the people within the imperial nation coincides with the struggle for self-determination in the international sphere. Just as domestically the demand for democratic power is a demand to overthrow the corporate ruling class and to make the productive apparatus responsive to social needs, so internationally the precondition of democratic sovereignty and inter-state coexistence is the dissolution of the government of the international corporations and financial institutions which have expropriated the sovereignty of nations in order to appropriate the wealth of the world.[44]

The consequences of such an understanding are revolutionary.

[44] Horowitz, *Empire and Revolution*, pp. 257–258.

4
Crime Control in the Capitalist State

The awareness that the legal system does not serve society as a whole, but serves the interests of the ruling class, is the beginning of a critical understanding of law in capitalist society. The ruling class through its use of the legal system is able to preserve a domestic order that allows the dominant economic interests to be maintained and promoted. This class, however, is not in direct control of the legal system, but must operate through the mechanisms of the state. Thus it is to the state that we must turn for further understanding of the nature and operation of the legal order. For the role of the state in capitalist society is to defend the interests of the ruling class, and crime control becomes a major device in that defense.

THE CAPITALIST STATE

Criminologists and legal scholars generally neglect the state as a focus of inquiry. Failing to distinguish between civil society and the political organization of that society, they ignore the major fact that civil society is secured politically by the state and that a dominant economic class is able by means of the state to advance its own interests. Or, when the state *is* admitted into a criminological or legal analysis, it is usually conceived of as an impartial agency devoted to balancing and reconciling the diverse interests of competing groups. This view not only obscures the underlying reality of advanced capitalist society but is basically wrong in reference to the legal order. In a critical analysis of the legal order we realize that the capitalist state is a coercive instrument serving the dominant economic class.

Several observations must be made in a critical analysis of crime control in the capitalist state. First, we must inquire into the nature of the state, that is, into the complexity of that which we call the state. Second, we must determine how the dominant economic class relates to the state, that is, how that class becomes a ruling class and how the state governs in relation to it. Third, we must observe the development of the state in reference to capitalist economy.

"The state," as Miliband notes, is not a thing that exists as such. "What 'the state' stands for is a number of particular institutions which, together, constitute its reality, and which interact as parts of what may be called the state system." [1] Miliband goes on to observe that the state, or state system, is made up of various elements: (1) the government, (2) the administration, (3) the military and the police, (4) the judiciary, and (5) the units of sub-central government.[2] The government of the time, with its duly empowered agents, is invested with state power and speaks in the name of the state. The administration of the state is composed of a large variety of bureaucratic bodies and departments concerned with the management of the economic, cultural, and other activities in which the state is involved. The directly coercive forces of the state, at home and abroad, are the police and the military. They form that branch of the state which is concerned with the "management of violence." The judiciary is an integral part of the state, supposedly independent of the government, which affects the exercise of state power. Finally, the various units of sub-central government constitute the extension of the central government. They are the administrative devices for

[1] Ralph Miliband, *The State in Capitalist Society* (New York: Basic Books, 1969), p. 49.
[2] *Ibid.*, pp. 49–55.

96

centralized power, although some units may exercise power on their own over the lives of the populations they govern.

It is in these institutions that state power lies, and it is in these institutions that power is wielded by the persons who occupy the leading positions. Most important, these are the people who constitute the *state elite*, as distinct from those who wield power outside of state institutions.[3] Some holders of state power, members of the state elite, may also be the agents of private economic power. But when members of private economic power are not members of the state elite, how are they able to rule the state? Somehow the interests of the dominant economic class must be translated into the governing process in order for that class to be a true ruling class.

Miliband has observed the essential relation between the dominant economic class and the process of governing.

> What the evidence conclusively suggests is that in terms of social origin, education and class situation, the men who have manned *all* command positions in the state system have largely, and in many cases overwhelmingly, been drawn from the world of business and property, or from the professional middle classes. Here as in every other field, men and women born into the subordinate classes, which form of course the vast majority of the population, have fared very poorly — and not only, it must be stressed, in those parts of the state system, such as administration, the military and the judiciary, which depend on appointment, but also in those parts of it which are exposed or which appear to be exposed to the vagaries of universal suffrage and the fortunes of competitive politics. In an epoch when so much is made of democracy, equality, social mobility, classlessness and the rest, it has remained a basic fact of life in advanced capitalist countries that the vast majority of men and women in these countries has been governed, represented, administered, judged, and commanded in war by people drawn from other, economically and socially superior and relatively distant classes.[4]

The dominant economic class is thus the ruling class in capitalist societies.

Viewed historically, the capitalist state is the natural product of a society divided by economic classes. Only with the emergence of a

[3] *Ibid.*, p. 54.
[4] *Ibid.*, pp. 66–67.

division of labor based on the exploitation of one class by another, and with the breakup of communal society, was there a need for the state. The new ruling class created the state as a means for coercing the rest of the population into economic and political submission. That the state was termed "democratic" does not alter its actual purpose.

The state, as Engels observed in his study of its origins, has not existed in all societies. There have been societies with no notion of state power. Only with a particular kind of economic development, with economic divisions, did the state become necessary. The new stage of development, Engels observes, called for the creation of the state:

> Only one thing was wanting: an institution which not only secured the newly acquired riches of individuals against the communistic traditions of the gentile order, which not only sanctified the private property formerly so little valued, and declared this sanctification to be the highest purpose of all human society; but an institution which set the seal of general social recognition on each new method of acquiring property and thus amassing wealth at continually increasing speed; an institution which perpetuated, not only this growing cleavage of society into classes, but also the right of the posessing class to exploit the non-possessing, and the rule of the former over the latter.
> And this institution came. The *state* was invented.[5]

And the state, rather than appearing as a third party in the conflict between classes, arose to protect and promote the interests of the dominant class, the class that owns and controls the means of production. The state continues as a device for holding down the exploited class, the class that labors, for the benefit of the ruling class. Modern civilization, as epitomized by capitalist societies, is thus founded on the exploitation of one class by another, and the state secures this arrangement.

Law has become the ultimate means by which the state secures the interests of the ruling class. Laws institutionalize and legitimate the existing property relations. A legal system, a public force, is established: "This public force exists in every state; it consists not

[5] Frederick Engels, *The Origin of the Family, Private Property, and the State* (New York: International Publishers, 1942), p. 97.

merely of armed men, but also of material appendages, prisons and coercive institutions of all kinds, of which gentile society knew nothing. It may be very insignificant, practically negligible, in societies with still undeveloped class antagonisms and living in remote areas, as at times and in places in the United States of America. But it becomes stronger in proportion as the class antagonisms within the state become sharper and as adjoining states grow larger and more populous." [6]

It is through the legal system, then, that the state explicitly and forcefully protects the interests of the capitalist ruling class. Crime control becomes the coercive means of checking threats to the existing economic arrangements. The state defines its welfare according to the general well-being of the capitalist economy.

LEGISLATION OF CRIME CONTROL

Crime control in capitalist society is accomplished by a variety of methods, strategies, and institutions. The government, especially through its legislative bodies, establishes official policies of crime control. Supposedly representing the people, Congress enacts legislation that controls the population according to the interests of the ruling class. The administrative branch of the state, usually in conjunction with the government, establishes and enforces crime control policies. Specific agencies of law enforcement, such as the Federal Bureau of Investigation and the recent Law Enforcement Assistance Administration, have great latitude in determining the nature of crime control efforts. Local police departments enforce national policies of law enforcement, while at the same time creating their own systems of crime control. And on the national level, operating as an administrative unit of the government of the time, there is the Department of Justice. In the name of justice, the state is able through its Department of Justice to officially repress the "dangerous" and "subversive" elements of the population, that is, those who would threaten the state and its supporting economic structure.

All of these state institutions attempt to rationalize the legal system by employing the advanced methods of science and technology. And whenever any changes are to be attempted toward the end of

[6] *Ibid.*, p. 156.

reducing the incidence of crime, rehabilitation of the individual or reform within the institutions is suggested rather than a revolution in the institutions themselves. To drastically alter the society and the crime control institutions would be to alter beyond recognition the existing economic system.

The congressmen who draft and enact crime control policies are of a single mind regarding the need for crime control in the preservation of the capitalist system. Contrary to liberal political theory, political leaders are in agreement on the truly fundamental issues. The governments of capitalist countries, Miliband argues,

> . . . have mostly been composed of men who beyond all their political, social, religious, cultural and other differences and diversities, have at least had in common a basic and usually explicit belief in the validity and virtues of the capitalist system, though this was not what they would necessarily call it; and those among them who have not been particularly concerned with that system, or even aware that they were helping to run a specific economic system, much in the way that they were not aware of the air they breathed, have at least shared with their more ideologically-aware colleagues or competitors a quite basic and unswerving hostility to any socialist alternative to that system.[7]

The commitment to capitalism, therefore, determines the government's policies and, moreover, provides the rationale for social legislation, including crime control legislation. Though legislators may differ on some specific issues, they are in basic agreement on the control, through law, of behavior and activities that threaten the capitalist system — euphemistically referred to as "the American way of life."

In recent years the government has been particularly active in the areas of crime control. This activity reflects in large part the reaction of the government to a crisis in the capitalist system. The solution has been simplistic, but nevertheless consequential: to protect the existing order by controlling crime. Congress has enacted a series of crime bills. The concern of Congress over the challenges to the existing order, a concern reflected in the crime legislation, is documented in the opening statement of the 1968 crime bill:

[7] Miliband, *The State in Capitalist Society*, p. 70.

Congress finds that the high incidence of crime in the United States threatens the peace, security and general welfare of the Nation and its citizens. To prevent crime and to insure the greater safety of the people, law enforcement efforts must be better coordinated, intensified, and made more effective at all levels of government.

Congress finds further that crime is essentially a local problem that must be dealt with by State and local governments if it is to be controlled effectively.

It is therefore the declared policy of the Congress to assist State and local governments in strengthening and improving law enforcement at every level by national assistance. It is the purpose of this title to (1) encourage States and units of general local government to prepare and adopt comprehensive plans based upon their evaluation of State and local problems of law enforcement; (2) authorize grants to States and units of local government in order to improve and strengthen law enforcement; and (3) encourage research and development directed toward the improvement of law enforcement and the development of new methods for the prevention and reduction of crime and the detection and apprehension of criminals.[8]

Not only was the war on crime intensified by this legislation, but the federal government stimulated local governments to engage in the battle. With the creation of the Law Enforcement Assistance Administration, requiring large amounts of financing and guidance, local governments were enlisted in the crusade to make capitalism survive.

The government's reaction to the crisis of the 1960s — to the riots, assassinations, and "crime in the streets" — was to define the problem as one of insufficient laws and inadequate law enforcement. Rather than acknowledging that the crisis was a result of the contradiction in the capitalist system itself, which would have been against the interests of the government, the government enacted further repressive legislation. President Johnson sounded the call in a message to Congress in 1967, warning the legislators that "crime — and the fear of crime — has become a public malady," and reminded them of their "duty to seek its cure." [9] Johnson's legislative proposals

[8] "Omnibus Crime Control and Safe Streets Act," Public Law 90–351, *United States Statutes at Large*, 1968, vol. 82 (Washington, D.C.: U.S. Government Printing Office, 1969), pp. 197–198.

[9] See Richard Harris, *The Fear of Crime* (New York: Frederick A. Praeger, 1969).

gave Congress the opportunity to further define the crime problem. Hearings were held by the Senate Subcommittee on Criminal Laws and Procedures and by the House Judiciary Committee. The hearings provided the framework for defining the crime problem in modern terms, and for urging stricter law enforcement, denial of basic rights for defendants, and the use of modern technology in the war on crime.

The result of these efforts was the enactment of the Omnibus Crime Control and Safe Streets Act of 1968. The new crime legislation initially assisted state and local governments in trying more effectively to assure domestic order by increasing the effectiveness of law enforcement and criminal administration. By the time the bill was passed, several amendments were added which deliberately attempted to overturn previous Supreme Court decisions that supposedly "coddled criminals" and "handcuffed the police." For example, one amendment provided that all voluntary confessions and eyewitness identifications — regardless of whether a defendant had been informed of his rights to counsel — could be admitted in federal trials. In another provision, state and local law enforcement agencies were given broad license to tap telephones and engage in other forms of eavesdropping, even without a court order. Another provision required that any persons convicted of "inciting a riot or civil disorder," "organizing, promoting, encouraging, or participating in a riot or civil disorder," or "aiding and abetting any person in committing" such offenses be disqualified from employment by the federal government for five years. The legislation was a clear attempt to control by means of the criminal law any behavior that would threaten the established order.

The government has continued its course of enacting crime control legislation. The Congress and the Presidency have worked together to construct a comprehensive program of crime control.[10] Several congressional committees — including four Senate committees, five House committees, and two appropriations committees — are actively involved in formulating crime control policies. Coming from these efforts is a crime bill for the District of Columbia, drug control legislation, an organized crime bill, and a series of proposals for

[10] See Herbert L. Packer, "Nixon's Crime Program and What It Means," *The New York Review of Books*, 15 (October 22, 1970), pp. 26–37.

future legislation. There is no sign that the administration and the Congress will cease in their crime control interests and activities.

In July of 1970, Nixon signed into law the District of Columbia crime bill. Crime in the District of Columbia had become a symbolic issue for Nixon and the Congress, deserving an exemplary crime control program. Among the features of the bill, in addition to new laws of regulation, are the following repressive measures:

- Authorization for "no-knock" searches, under which a policeman with a warrant could force his way into a building without announcing his presence or identifying himself if there was reason to believe evidence inside would otherwise be destroyed.
- Preventive, or pretrial, detention, under which a defendant could be jailed without bail for up to 60 days if a hearing established that he might commit further crimes if he were released.
- Establishment of a mandatory five-year sentence upon a second conviction for a crime of violence in which the defendant was carrying a gun.
- Authorization for wiretaps by the police with court approval, but restricting their use when the communication involved was between physician and patient; attorney and client; clergyman and parishioner; or husband and wife.[11]

The bill not only regulates crime in the District of Columbia, but serves, as Attorney General Mitchell suggested, as a model for all states of the nation.

The government's crime control program was further advanced in October of 1970 with the signing of the Organized Crime Control Act. Although the act is labeled as an "organized crime" bill, its provisions apply to a wide range of offenses.[12] Fundamental procedural policies are instituted, covering such matters as grand jury powers, illegally obtained evidence, long-term sentencing, self-incrimination, and due process of law. In the bill, grand juries are empowered to issue reports on noncriminal misconduct by an appointed public

[11] *The New York Times,* July 24, 1970, p. 1. See District of Columbia Committee, "Anti-Crime Proposals," *Hearings* Before the Select Committee on Crime, U.S. House of Representatives, 91st Congress (Washington, D.C.: U.S. Government Printing Office, 1970).

[12] "Organized Crime Control," *Hearings* Before the Subcommittee on Criminal Laws and Procedures of the Committee on the Judiciary, United States Senate, 91st Congress (Washington, D.C.: U.S. Government Printing Office, 1970).

official, with little safeguard for protecting the accused against such reports. Federal judges are authorized to impose an additional sentence of up to twenty-five years on a class of so-called "dangerous special offenders." The additional sentence can be imposed upon a convicted person on the basis of a hearing before a judge rather than on the basis of a jury trial. The bill also revises the laws dealing with the immunity of a witness from prosecution, and other procedural safeguards, in an attempt to overcome some of the law enforcement problems of gathering evidence. In other words, another crime bill has been enacted which further extends the power of the government over the lives of citizens, overturning even the constitutional protections. The war on crime must finally suspend even the liberal guarantees of civil liberties.

Soon to follow the organized crime bill was the Comprehensive Drug Abuse Prevention and Control Act. Like the organized crime bill, the new law covered a range of activities only superficially related to drug control, and it suspended certain constitutional rights. Provisions were made to force witnesses to testify in virtually any federal case; new provisions were made for the admission of wiretapping evidence; grand jury powers were extended; search and seizure activities, without warrants, were expanded; and special offenders could be given extended sentences by judges. Drug control, like the control of other criminal activities, had become an excuse for Congress and the Presidency to control anything that seemed to threaten the existing order.

The government continues to expand its crime control program. At the beginning of the 1970s the Senate could praise itself on the passage of a good share of legislation for the program. Of twenty proposed anti-crime measures, thirteen had already been passed by the Senate by January of 1970. Senator Mansfield could state: "Only five areas remain for action and all of these will be considered in the Senate this session. Thus, in the field of proposals for additional laws in the battle against crime, the Senate has completed the lion's share of its work and tidying up of relatively minor proposals remains." [13] Mansfield then indicated the course for the future: "After the passage of these bills, we may then direct ourselves to

[13] *Congressional Record*, Vol. 16, Part 2, 91st Congress, January 28, 1970 (Washington, D.C.: U.S. Government Printing Office, 1970), p. 1690.

104

the more difficult tasks of identifying and addressing ourselves to the task of eradicating the causes of criminal behavior." [14] Even if the Senate were to turn its attention to the "causes of criminal behavior," it is unlikely that there would be a critical examination of the system that makes crime possible. There would be no critique of the capitalist system.

A new reality of crime is being constructed. This reality is an obvious attempt to perpetuate the existing social and economic order, in further oppression of those who suffer from a class-dominated society. The government, after all, is in the business of maintaining the capitalist system, a system which in its advanced stage requires a close relationship between the economic and political order.

CRIME CONTROL BUREAUCRACY: LEAA

The state creates a complex of bureaucratic agencies in the course of establishing control over the population. These agencies not only carry out the objectives of state authority but serve to solidify and protect the economic interests that underpin the state. An adequate picture of the state control of crime must therefore take into account the role of these bureaucratic agencies. The administrative, coercive, and judicial agencies of the state, and the people who function within them, reinforce the state's political and economic objectives. Indeed, "The state bureaucracy, in all its parts, is not an impersonal, un-ideological, a-political element in society, above the conflicts in which classes, interests and groups engage. By virtue of its ideological dispositions, reinforced by its own interests, that bureaucracy, on the contrary, is a crucially important and committed element in the maintenance and defence of the structure of power and privilege inherent in advanced capitalism." [15]

This applies most dramatically to the state bureaucracies that deal in crime control. The purpose of these agencies, and of the agents who constitute them, is the strengthening of the prevailing economic and political order. Agencies that deal in coercion for state ends — that is, the agencies involved in crime control — epit-

[14] *Ibid.*
[15] Miliband, *The State in Capitalist Society*, pp. 128–129.

omize the bureaucracy devoted to serving the state and its material basis. The role of the police in capitalist society has always been to preserve the existing order. In fact, the rise of local police departments in the nineteenth century was a response to attacks that were being made on the existing order.[16] And as capitalism moved into its advanced form in the twentieth century, law enforcement bureaucracies on various governmental levels grew in importance.

The coercive bureaucratic development reached its modern form in the mid-1960s. By that time crime, as a threat to the existing regime, had come to a point where modern, scientific schemes had to be developed to counteract it. Since crime could not be reduced without drastically altering the capitalist system, the only alternative open to the state was the modernization of law enforcement. Thus in the middle 1960s the federal government responded, in its "war on crime," by creating a law enforcement apparatus unparalleled in the history of any nation. The architecture for crime control in advanced capitalist society was constructed. In the end, this will likely prove to be not only repression made official and bureaucratic but also the basic contradiction of which a capitalist society is capable. A country that claims to promote freedom, equality, and social justice cannot finally survive when it also promotes the negation of these ideals. And certainly the natural desire for a humane existence, founded on a classless community, can never be achieved in capitalist society. The recent attempts at crime control are only one more indication of the inevitable end of capitalism. In the meantime, however, we will experience unprecedented repression — in the name of crime control by the state.

It was in 1965 that the federal government began to increase its role in crime control. Although the initial attempt was rather low-keyed in comparison with what was soon to follow, the government made a commitment to a new form of crime control. It had previously shied away from interfering in local police activities, but the time was now ripe for a program that would give national direction to law enforcement. At President Johnson's urging, in a special message to Congress on February 6, 1967, greater federal efforts and

[16] Allan Silver, "The Demand for Order in Civil Society: A Review of Some Themes in the History of Urban Crime, Police, and Riot," in David J. Bordua (ed.), *The Police: Six Sociological Essays* (New York: John Wiley & Sons, 1967), pp. 1–24.

expenditures for law enforcement were suggested in order "to strengthen the system and to encourage the kind of innovations needed to respond to the problems of crime in America." [17] Congress had already created the Office of Law Enforcement Assistance, within the Department of Justice. The agency, operating from 1965 to 1968, supported nearly 400 projects aimed at "helping local governments improve their overall criminal justice systems." These projects included "training, research and demonstration efforts to prevent and control crime; to improve law enforcement, corrections, courts and other criminal justice agencies; and to assist these agencies in recruiting and upgrading personnel." [18]

But this was only the beginning. In 1968 Congress passed the Omnibus Crime Control and Safe Streets Act, which contained a major provision (Title I) for the creation of the Law Enforcement Assistance Administration (LEAA). As an agency within the Department of Justice, to replace and supersede the Office of Law Enforcement Assistance, LEAA signaled a broader and more pervasive plan of federal involvement in law enforcement and crime control. Support for the enlarged program came from all quarters, since domestic security was the name of the game. The liberal contingent, led by Attorney General Ramsey Clark, gave its wholehearted support. Attorney General Clark, in fact, as a major force behind the enactment of the new crime bill, told a Senate committee that the program "is the one appropriate way the federal government can make a major difference. It is based on the demonstrated need for more resources, better applied, to improve the state of criminal justice in America." [19] So-called "soft-on-crime" liberals were as heavily involved in the new crime control legislation as "law-and-order" conservatives. When it comes to protecting the existing order, political differences become insignificant, the common interest being the survival of the capitalist system.

LEAA has grown steadily since its creation in 1968. During its first years of operation, LEAA received an annual congressional

[17] See Joseph C. Goulden, "Tooling Up for Repression: The Cops Hit the Jackpot," *The Nation*, 211 (November 23, 1970), pp. 520–533.
[18] Law Enforcement Assistance Administration, *Grants and Contracts Awarded Under the Law Enforcement Assistance Act of 1965*, Fiscal 1966–1968 (Washington, D.C.: U.S. Government Printing Office, 1968), p. 1.
[19] Quoted in Goulden, "Tooling Up for Repression," p. 520.

appropriation of $63 million. The budget increased sharply to $268 million in 1970 and was further increased to $529 million in 1971. The Senate authorized $1.15 billion for 1972 and $1.75 billion for 1973. In his annual report, the Administrator of LEAA, after citing the generous appropriations, advised the President and the Congress on the mission and impact of his agency:

> The mission of LEAA is to reduce crime and delinquency by channeling Federal financial aid to state and local governments, to conduct research in methods of improving law enforcement and criminal justice, to fund efforts to upgrade the educational level of law enforcement personnel, to develop applications of statistical research and applied systems analysis in law enforcement, and to develop broad policy guidelines for both the short and long-range improvement of the nation's Criminal Justice System as a whole.[20]

The major portion of LEAA's budget goes to states and localities for the fight against crime. Officially, the objective is stated in the following terms:

> State and local governments receive the bulk of LEAA aid. To be effective, law enforcement planning and action programs must be broad and comprehensive. Congress recognized the most meaningful primary unit to accomplish improvements is the state. Within this framework, the state and its cities can increase cooperation; there can be greater coordination among police, courts, and corrections. The bulk of the LEAA budget therefore goes in block grants to the 50 states, which in turn re-allocate most of those funds to their city and county governments.[21]

Nevertheless, though the states are the units for receiving block grants, "the goal of the LEAA program is across-the-board improvement of the Nation's criminal justice system." Thus, we are told, "For the first time in our history, all levels of government and all parts of the criminal justice system are working together in a coordinated, nationwide approach to the urgent problems of crime and criminal justice." [22]

[20] *LEAA*, 3rd Annual Report of the Law Enforcement Assistance Administration, Fiscal Year 1971 (Washington, D.C.: U.S. Government Printing Office, 1972), p. ii.
[21] Law Enforcement Assistance Administration, *A Program for a Safer, More Just America* (Washington, D.C.: U.S. Government Printing Office, 1970), p. 3.
[22] Law Enforcement Assistance Administration, *Safe Streets: The LEAA*

In order to carry out its program "more effectively and efficiently," LEAA has gone through several bureaucratic reorganizations. The function of the agency's headquarters in Washington now "is largely to develop and implement policy guidelines, to channel Federal funds to the states, to undertake research, to provide special assistance to states in such areas as applied systems analysis, and to provide technical assistance." [23] In other words, LEAA is attempting to maximize the possibility of building a comprehensive national crime control program under the guise of decentralization. However, each state, in order to receive the grants and technical assistance of LEAA, has had to set up a comprehensive law enforcement agency. Moreover, to be eligible for federal funds, each state agency must annually draw up a law enforcement plan, which must in turn be approved by LEAA, a plan for "comprehensive state-wide law enforcement improvements in police, courts, and corrections."

In addition to encouraging, or forcing, state governments to develop law enforcement plans, LEAA awards federal funds to state and local governments for the development of programs to improve and strengthen law enforcement, gives funds for the training of law enforcement agents, and supports research and the development of methods for improvement of law enforcement and reduction of crime. (These programs are administered in the three operating divisions of LEAA: the Office of Criminal Justice Administration, the National Institute of Law Enforcement and Criminal Justice, and the Office of Operations Support.) What all this means is the creation of a nationally sponsored program of crime control. In the name of "criminal justice," the national government is providing a comprehensive, coordinated system of repression.

To mention just one consequence, local police are being armed with sophisticated "crime prevention" techniques and equipment. As one critical investigator writes: "The purpose is to curb robberies, burglaries and violent street crimes. The result, however, enables police to keep citizens — the innocent and the guilty alike — under electronic and photographic surveillance while they are shopping, walking public streets, driving automobiles, and visiting both private

---

Program at Work (Washington, D.C.: U.S. Government Printing Office, 1971), p. i.

[23] *LEAA*, 3rd Annual Report of the Law Enforcement Assistance Administration, p. iii. Also see the *LEAA Newsletter*, 1 (July), pp. 1–6.

and public buildings." [24] Furthermore, massive computerized "intelligence systems" are being developed to predict disorder and to contain information on "dangerous" persons. Great amounts of money are being given for the development of techniques for the control of the populaton, for the prevention of disorder, for the preservation of domestic order.

In the course of this development, a huge bureaucracy devoted to crime control is being created not only in Washington but within each of the states. In addition, there are the ten regional offices of LEAA, each with its own director, deputy director, administrative services, technical assistance staff, and operations division. A considerable portion of the federal support of LEAA must go to the routine operation of these state and regional agencies. It gives some encouragement to those who fear governmental repression that much of the funds and energies of LEAA are being used for the sheer operation of these bureaucracies. The potential impact of LEAA is necessarily limited by the weight of the bureaucracy.[25]

But the aims of LEAA are specific and of long-term consequence. In his testimony before the Legal and Monetary Affairs Subcommittee of Congress, the Administrator of LEAA, Jerris Leonard, made clear the government's objectives in the war on crime:

> For the future, reducing crime nationally will not be an easy job. It will not be cheap, in either labor or money. But it can be done, and the present LEAA program must be the major vehicle for doing it.
>
> For those without blinders, unmistakable signs of progress already are evident. Many more will become apparent if we can have unmatched dedication by local, state, and federal officials; responsible assistance from the public; and continued support from the Congress, whose Judiciary Committees gave LEAA a remarkably sound bill of health following extended hearings last year.
>
> In many ways, American citizens are safer now than they were three years ago. A year from now, they will be safer than they are today. The decade of the 1960s ended as the most lawless in our history. The decade of the 1970s can end with crime long since under control, if we are not diverted from our task by phantoms.[26]

[24] Goulden, "Tooling Up for Repression," p. 520.
[25] See "Crime Program Held Inefficient," *The New York Times,* April 11, 1972, p. 14.
[26] Quoted in the *LEAA Newsletter,* 2 (November, 1971), p. 8.

LEGAL REPRESSION BY THE JUSTICE DEPARTMENT

The modern phase of the legal order in the United States is characterized by greater centralization of crime control and a much more organized and effective form of legal repression. Whereas crime control was formerly in the hands of local police, crime control in the 1960s and 1970s became a primary concern of the federal government. Although funds for crime control are allocated to states and local governments, the overall system is designed and dictated by the federal government. The control of crime has become of such importance in the maintenance of domestic order that the nation-state has had to manage the problem. The government — headed by the President, the Attorney General, the Law Enforcement Assistance Administration, and the Federal Bureau of Investigation — now controls crime, recognizing that what is at stake is the survival of the existing order.

The government today is concentrating its crime control efforts in the United States Department of Justice. Contrary to the popular image, the Justice Department is not a bureaucratic agency separate from the current government, serving the interests of the public. The Justice Department, instead, is an agency of the government currently in power, serving the interests of that government. And with the principal forces of crime control now centered in the Justice Department, the possibility of controlling the population is greatly increased. Not only is the Justice Department engaged in law enforcement for the government, but it is establishing the policies for crime control as well. Legal repression has reached its modern form, operating on a national level, and at the same time making local crime control more repressive. The situation can be described in the following way:

> The serious problem which America will be facing in the decade of the seventies is the transition from repression emanating almost exclusively from lower echelon levels, officially condemned from above, to a more subtle, but probably more effective form of official, legal repression aimed against those engaged in radical challenges to the system. At such times the upper echelons set the tone and rallying cry and spearhead the drive by using the courts against prominent radicals, while the reins on the police are loosened to make lower level repression more effective, less fraught with risks for the

111

police, and more respectable. In such an atmosphere, the usual lower echelon repression is not supplanted; it is supplemented and nourished.[27]

In a critical understanding of crime control today, we have to recognize that legal oppression is but a part of the problem. It is all too easy to comment on the repression that is occurring everywhere around us. But to assume that the problems of the modern state would be solved with the control of repression, with the protection of civil liberties, is to ignore the larger context within which repression is made possible. The larger issue is that of oppression, oppression that results from the capitalist system itself. Repression cannot be eliminated, or even safeguarded against, as long as that oppression remains. The only way to understand legal repression is as a consequence of the oppressive social-economic system itself. Legal repression takes place as an official act when the other social control mechanisms of the modern capitalist system are no longer effective. The problem, then, is the elimination of the oppressive system, a system that makes repression possible.

It is in the Department of Justice's Federal Bureau of Investigation that the national government of the time has traditionally centered its crime control activities. Since its creation by a secret executive order during the administration of Theodore Roosevelt, the FBI has developed into a national police and investigative force that consists of nine thousand special agents, a clerical staff of ten thousand, fifty-nine regional offices, and hundreds of local "resident offices." [28] But more important than these figures is the fact that the FBI is involved in more than simply investigating federal law violations; it specializes in domestic intelligence-gathering and internal security protection. Its history is one of controlling "domestic subversion," from the investigation of spy activities in wartime America, to the pursuit of communists, to the repression of radical political action in recent years. Under its long-time director, J. Edgar Hoover, the FBI has developed into a self-perpetuating bureaucracy that, though it is the subject of occasional criticism, operates beyond

[27] Harvey A. Silverglate, "The 1970s: A Decade of Repression?" in Bruce Wasserstein and Mark J. Green (eds.), *With Justice For Some* (Boston: Beacon Press, 1970), p. 359.

[28] For some of the history of the FBI, see Fred J. Cook, *The FBI Nobody Knows* (New York: Macmillan, 1964).

public control for the sole benefit of itself and the government.[29] The speculation that the FBI will change with the recent death of Hoover ignores the nature of the FBI's bureaucracy and the service the agency performs for the state in maintaining domestic security.

The FBI has been able to extend its surveillance activities over the years through legislative enactment overturning previous Supreme Court decisions. Since the mid-1960s the FBI has freely engaged in electronic eavesdropping, court-ordered and otherwise.[30] Each year the telephones of tens of thousands of citizens are wire-tapped, at a cost of about $5 million for these operations alone. On the basis of "national security," the FBI legally and illegally justifies this operation. Defending the government's inherent right to wiretap dissident domestic groups, then Deputy Attorney General Richard Kleindienst maintained that no distinction can be made between Americans and foreigners when the aim is to destroy the government: "It would be silly to say that an American citizen, because he is an American, could subvert the government by actions of violence or revolution and be immune from, first, identification, and second, prosecution." [31]

It came as a shock to many Americans in the early 1970s that the government was actually spying on them. In the course of a Senate investigation, led by the Subcommittee on Constitutional Rights (chaired by Sam J. Ervin, Jr.), it was disclosed that several government agencies, the FBI included, were heavily involved in obtaining intelligence information on hundreds of thousands of law-abiding yet suspect American citizens. With the justification that domestic security is in jeopardy, the government is building a "national data bank," euphemistically called a "criminal justice information center," for instantly retrievable intelligence information on "persons of interest." The government's purpose is to avert internal subversion, threats to the domestic order. Upon discovering the existence and extensiveness of such surveillance, *The New York Times* reported the following to its readers:

[29] Hank Messick, *John Edgar Hoover* (New York: David McKay Company, 1972).

[30] Tom Wicker, "A Gross Invasion," *The New York Times*, December 19, 1971, p. Ell.

[31] Quoted in the *NCCD Newsletter*, 50 (May–June, 1971), p. 15.

The Government is gathering information on its citizens in the following reservoirs of facts:

- A Secret Service computer, one of the newest and most sophisticated in Government. In its memory the names and dossiers of activists, "malcontents," persistent seekers of redress, and those who would "embarrass" the President or other Government leaders are filed with those of potential assassins and persons convicted of "threats against the President."
- A data bank compiled by the Justice Department's civil disturbance group. It produces a weekly printout of national tension points on racial, class and political issues and the individuals and groups involved in them. Intelligence on peace rallies, welfare protests and the like provide the "data base" against which the computer measures the mood of the nation and the militancy of its citizens. Judgments are made; subjects are listed as "radical" or "moderate."
- A huge file of microfilmed intelligence reports, clippings and other materials on civilian activity maintained by the Army's Counterintelligence Analysis Division in Alexandria, Va. Its purpose is to help prepare deployment estimates for troop commands on alert to respond to civil disturbances in 25 American cities. Army intelligence was ordered earlier this year to destroy a larger data bank and to stop assigning agents to "penetrate" peace groups and civil rights organizations. But complaints persist that both are being continued. Civilian officials of the Army say they "assume" they are not.
- Computer files intended to catch criminal suspects — the oldest and most advanced type with the longest success record — maintained by the Federal Bureau of Investigation's National Crime Information Center and recently installed by the Customs Bureau. The crime center's computer provides 40,000 instant, automatic teletype printouts each day on wanted persons and stolen property to 49 states and Canada and it also "talks" to 24 other computers operated by state and local police departments for themselves and a total of 2,500 police jurisdictions. The center says its information is all "from the public record," based on local and Federal warrants and complaints, but the sum product is available only to the police.
- A growing number of data banks on other kinds of human behavior, including, for example, a cumulative computer file on 300,000 children of migrant farm workers kept by the Department of Health, Education and Welfare. The object is to speed

the distribution of their scholastic records, including such teacher judgments as "negative attitude," to school districts with larger itinerant student enrollments. There is no statutory control over distribution of the data by its local recipients — to prospective employers, for example.[32]

The war is at home; domestic security is at stake. The government is responding to the challenge, as a government must, by maintaining its control by whatever means necessary.

What began as a governmental war on "crime in the streets" turned into the suppression of any action that threatens the status quo. The presidential elections, and congressional elections as well, of 1964 and 1968 capitalized on the theme of a rising crime rate in America. Each candidate blamed the crime problem on the other candidates. Nixon, in the election of 1968, committed himself to a full-scale attack on the problem. Blaming the rising crime rate on the incumbent administration, Nixon had to deal with lawlessness as soon as he entered the White House. The greatest threat to law and order seemed to be the protests against the war in Vietnam, the draft system, and racial injustice. Nixon and his newly appointed Attorney General, John Mitchell, with the ready assistance of Hoover and the FBI, turned public attention to these politically dissident actions as being the really serious crimes facing the nation.

Shortly after Nixon took office, Attorney General Mitchell announced that he intended to prosecute "hard-line militants," such as those who crossed state lines "to incite riots" on college campuses. Mitchell told the nation, citing evidence collected by the FBI, that "a great deal of evidence has been collected on this aspect of campus disorders," and that "I would say this is a very serious component." [33] A few days later, Assistant Attorney General Jerris Leonard announced to the public that he was prepared to prosecute such militants under the newly enacted anti-riot law. "These statements," Richard Harris writes in his study of the early years of Nixon's Department of Justice, "on top of a promise by Deputy Attorney

[32] Ben A. Franklin, "Federal Computers Amass Files on Suspect Citizens," *The New York Times*, June 28, 1970, p. 42. On the Army's surveillance of the population, see *The New York Times*, January 18, 1971, p. 1; and *The New York Times*, September 7, 1971, p. 39.

[33] Quoted in Richard Harris, *Justice: The Crisis of Law, Order, and Freedom in America* (New York: E. P. Dutton, 1970), p. 186.

General Kleindienst to go after 'radical, revolutionary, anarchistic kids,' suggested that the Department now fully shared Hoover's conviction that most of the trouble in the country was caused by a few radicals and that if they were locked up everything would be fine again." [34]

The government was now prepared to launch a concerted drive against political dissent, whether the dissent was expressed in thought, word, or deed. Political dissent, as a legitimate response to an oppressive system, was now defined as being criminal. A legal structure had been created to define such activity as criminal and to provide for its control. A series of repressive attacks began to be carried out by the government. A trial is held of the "Boston Five" for conspiring to interfere with the operations of the Selective Service system by organizing public rallies, writing and circulating dissident statements, and encouraging draft-age men to resist the draft.[35] Similarly, the government prosecutes the "Chicago Eight" for conspiring to cross state lines, during the 1968 Democratic Convention, with the intent of inciting a riot and committing some illegal act. The "Oakland Seven" are charged with conspiracy to commit the misdemeanors of trespass and resisting arrest in a stop-the-draft demonstration. The "Harrisburg Seven" are tried for, among other things, a plot to kidnap presidential advisor Henry Kissinger. Then there is the trial of Daniel Ellsberg for passing Pentagon documents to the press. And Black Panther groups are harassed in various ways, including being raided and murdered by local and federal agents. The list goes on. Political action against the government, or against policies of the government, has become defined as being such a threat to the existing regime that the most dubious of criminal charges must be made and the most insidious of repressive actions taken.

The government has continued to use a host of legal weapons in its attempt to secure domestic order. Although convictions under the conspiracy law have failed to be upheld on appeal to higher courts, the law and its ensuing trials have nevertheless served to harass dissenters and stifle dissent. In addition to the conspiracy prosecu-

[34] *Ibid.*
[35] On this and other political trials, see *Trials of the Resistance* (New York: Vintage Books, 1970).

116

tions, raids of private premises on false pretenses, and the invasion of human rights in various ways, the government has resorted to a host of tactics available in the legal system. For example, a "preventive detention" law has been enacted to detain "dangerous" persons. As a pretrial detention measure, defendants can be confined to jail without the right of bail on the basis of a judge's decision. And to cite just one more government tactic, and further denial of human rights, there is the use of the mass arrest to detain large numbers of political demonstrators. In the May Day demonstration of 1971 in Washington, nearly 13,000 persons were rounded up and confined in jails and special camps. Although most of the charges were later dropped, the government had sufficiently stopped a legitimate protest against itself. These tactics do not usually result in a successful prosecution, and often are later judged unconstitutional, but they permit the government to repress threatening thoughts and actions. Again, the legal system serves the purposes of the state. Legal order and political order are inseparable, and the economic order is inevitably secured by both.

The initiative for crime control is currently in the hands of the administration. Congress is in the position of legitimizing and enacting the administration's program. The courts, including the United States Supreme Court, being a part of the state elite, are at the disposal of the executive. And the new use of the grand jury symbolizes the administration's initiative in crime control. "The nationwide grand jury network is emerging as a 'chosen instrument' of an Administration strategy to curb dissent and to intimidate and demoralize radicals. What makes this strategy so effective is that federal prosecuting officials — who themselves have no power of subpoena — are using the coercive powers of the grand jury for police and intelligence purposes." [36]

The new grand jury operation is being directed and coordinated by the Internal Security Division (ISD) of the Department of Justice. It reviews thousands of FBI reports about radical activities, determining violations of statutes, most of which are unconstitutional. Further information is provided by the Justice Department's

[36] Frank J. Donner and Eugene Cerruti, "The Grand Jury Network: How the Nixon Administration Has Secretly Perverted a Traditional Safeguard of Individual Rights," *The Nation*, 214 (January 3, 1972), p. 5.

Interdivisional Intelligence Unit (IDIU), now a wide-ranging intelligence system that observes and collects data on a broad spectrum of radical and anti-war activities. With this information, grand juries are activated by the government to hold secret sessions on suspected criminal or subversive activities. Thus, the grand jury has been reformed from a "people's panel," sometimes used in the past to curb prosecutions, to a repressive tool of the state used in the prosecution of political behavior.[37] Further intelligence information is secured by these grand juries through the testimony of subpoenaed witnesses. And on the basis of this testimony, without the protection of counsel, witnesses may in turn be sentenced to jail for contempt or charged with a crime. The grand jury, like the conspiracy charge, belongs to the state.

The new enemy today for the state is the "criminal." Replacing the red menace (internal communism) as the threat to domestic security, is crime. Not only the conventional attacks on private property (robbery and burglary), or the crimes against person (murder and assault), but behavior that has not always been regarded as a threat to domestic order is now being handled as crime — civil disobedience, the verbal expression of political dissent, demonstrations, and organized protest of various forms. Even from the liberal point of view, the nation has entered a new era:

> There are some signs — clear but not clear enough to constitute evidence — that the "crusade" or "war" on crime has been and continues to be used by officials of the Nixon Administration, particularly of the Justice Department, to alter what has long and widely been accepted as the fundamental nature of our society. The danger today is not only that the Constitution will continue to be violated by the government, as it has been repeatedly in the past couple of years, but that the present Administration will rewrite the essential protections contained in that document, with the consent of the governed and the agreement of Congress and the Supreme Court, in the name of private and public security.[38]

The liberal perspective on recent history recognizes the escalation of legal repression. A conclusion as to whether we are in "the grip

[37] *Ibid.*
[38] Richard Harris, "The New Justice," *The New Yorker*, March 25, 1972, p. 44.

of a repressive and authoritarian regime," however, is held in abeyance.[39] From a radically critical perspective, in contrast, the new era is more than another instance of government officials imposing their own will on the people. What is occurring, according to my critique of legal order, is the logical extension of an innately oppressive system. The only way for such a system to survive is to increase its use of repression when the people begin to question its legitimacy. The legal system has long been a tool of repression, but in the last few years we have experienced the true nature of the law. The capitalist state is now resorting to its ultimate weapon to protect the existing order. The contradiction inherent in the capitalist system is being perpetuated by the state's decision to use its legal power rather than face the changes necessary for achieving not only a just existence but one that is basically human. That we will experience greater repression as the capitalist state attempts to survive, rather than create a new existence, is to be expected.

THE TECHNOLOGY OF CRIME CONTROL

The modern era of repression has been realized in the rationalization of crime control. The legal order itself, as a rationalized form of regulation, continues to demand the latest techniques of control. It is only logical, then, that science should come to serve the state's interest in crime control. And this use of science makes the modern legal order the most repressive (and rational) that any society has known.

American society today is well on the way to, or has already reached, what may well be called "the police state." What we are experiencing is the "Americanization of 1984," a police state brought to you with the aid of science and modern techniques of control.

> The enactment of this police state — less conspicuous yet far more threatening than one dominated by the military — is a scientific enterprise. Its low-profiled selective repression is based on surveillance, fear, intimidation, and information control, rather than on the massive deployment of police.
> An underlying drive facilitating development of a police state is the historical governmental trend toward centralization. Information-

[39] *Ibid.*

119

gathering is merely one more example of the federal government's tendency to centralize and coordinate state and local activities. The implications of information concentrated in Washington are clear: Senator Charles Mathias, commenting in 1967 on the government's 3.1 billion records about individual citizens, suggested that "if knowledge is power, this encyclopedic knowledge gives government the raw materials of tyranny."

Technological advances have facilitated the drive to increased concentration of information and power. Computers and Vietnam-perfected hardware applied on the home front are shortening the road to 1984.[40]

The move to apply the latest in science and technology to crime control by the state was made in the mid-1960s with the President's Crime Commission (the Commission on Law Enforcement and Administration of Justice). The state's application of science and technology to crime control was probably inevitable, however, given the tendency to rationalize all systems of management and control. Yet it was with the President's Crime Commission, staffed by scientists, that scientific crime control was justified and presented to the public. The Commission's recommendations were soon made concrete and instituted by the newly created crime control agencies. Science and technology give today's crime control systems their most advanced and insidious character.

The President's Crime Commission included in its coverage of the crime problem a special Task Force Report on *Science and Technology*. The special project was funded by the Office of Law Enforcement Assistance, of the Justice Department, which was also responsible for the staff and organization of the task force. The actual work was conducted by the Institute for Defense Analyses (of the Department of Defense). The project was directed by Dr. Alfred Blumstein, a staff member of the Institute for Defense Analyses. The complete study is contained in the Task Force Report, but the recommendations and arguments of the task force are also included in the final report of the Commission, *The Challenge of Crime in a Free Society*. The message of the task force's research and analysis is (1) that crime control must become more scientific, (2) that crime control must utilize the kind of science and tech-

[40] Jeff Gerth, "The Americanization of 1984," *SunDance*, 1 (April–May, 1972), pp. 64–65.

nology that already serves the military, and (3) that the federal government must institute and support such a program. The chapter on "Science and Technology" in the Commission's final report begins:

> The scientific and technological revolution that has so radically changed most of American society during the past few decades has had surprisingly little impact upon the criminal justice system. In an age when many executives in government and industry, faced with decisionmaking problems, ask the scientific and technical community for independent suggestions on possible alternatives and for objective analyses of possible consequences of their actions, the public officials responsible for establishing and administering the criminal law — the legislators, police, prosecutors, lawyers, judges, and corrections officials — have almost no communication with the scientific and technical community.[41]

That there is a science and a technology available for crime control, on a military model, is the good news presented in the opening lines of the task force's own report:

> The natural sciences and technology have long helped the police to solve specific crimes. Scientists and engineers have had very little impact, however, on the overall operations of the criminal justice system and its principal components: police, courts, and corrections. More than 200,000 scientists and engineers have applied themselves to solving military problems and hundreds of thousands more to innovation in other areas of modern life, but only a handful are working to control the crimes that injure or frighten millions of Americans each year. Yet, the two communities have much to offer each other: science and technology is a valuable source of knowledge and techniques for combating crime; the criminal justice system represents a vast area of challenging problems.[42]

The Science and Technology Task Force goes on to list the kind of equipment and tactics that should be used in the war on crime:

[41] President's Commission on Law Enforcement and Administration of Justice, *The Challenge of Crime in a Free Society* (Washington, D.C.: U.S. Government Printing Office, 1967), p. 245.
[42] *Science and Technology*, Task Force Report of the President's Commission on Law Enforcement and Administration of Justice, Prepared by the Institute for Defense Analyses (Washington, D.C.: U.S. Government Printing Office, 1967), p. 1.

121

In the traditional view, science and technology primarily means new equipment. And modern technology can, indeed, provide a vast array of devices beyond those now in general use to improve the operations of criminal justice agencies, particularly in helping the police deter crime and apprehend criminals. Some of the more important possibilities are:

- Electronic computers for processing the enormous quantities of needed data.
- Police radio networks connecting officers and neighboring departments.
- Inexpensive, light two-way portable radios for every patrolman.
- Computers for processing fingerprints.
- Instruments for identifying criminals by their voice, photographs, hair, blood, body chemistry, etc.
- Devices for automatic and continual reporting of all police car locations.
- Helicopters for airborne police patrol.
- Inexpensive, reliable burglar and robbery alarms.
- Nonlethal weapons to subdue dangerous criminals without inflicting permanent harm.
- Perimeter surveillance devices for prisons.
- Automatic transcription devices for courtroom testimony. Many of these devices are now in existence, some as prototypes and some available commercially. Others still require basic development but are at least technically feasible and worthy of further exploration.[43]

The similarities between military operations and domestic crime control are made clear, and the Crime Commission is advised to pursue the militarization of crime control.

Crime control, being largely a social problem, may appear to be outside the realm of the scientists' skills. Indeed, many aspects of the problem do fall outside their scope. The experience of science in the military, however, suggests that a fruitful collaboration can be established between criminal justice officials on one hand and engineers, physicists, economists, and social and behavioral scientists on the other. In military research organizations these different professions, working with military officers in interdisciplinary teams, have attacked defense problems in new ways and have provided in-

43 *Ibid.*

122

sights that were new even to those with long military experience. Similar developments appear possible in criminal justice.[44]

The stage is reached where military operations abroad and crime control at home have become one — in objective and technique.

The remainder of the Science and Technology Task Force Report is devoted, in great detail, to "the applications of science and technology to the problems of crime, and especially to improving the criminal justice system." And at the same time, the task force director, Alfred Blumstein, was appearing before John McClellan's Senate subcommittee, making the same recommendations to the committee that was in the process of creating the Omnibus Crime bill. Blumstein made the suggestion, which served to reinforce McClellan's initial intentions, that the federal government must play the crucial role in mounting the new form of crime control.

It may very well be that the application of science and technology to criminal justice has been retarded so long as a result of the fragmentation of the criminal justice system. We have over 40,000 separate police agencies, and several thousand court systems and correctional systems. Only a handful of these are large enough and rich enough to undertake major reasearch or equipment development projects on their own. There is little incentive for them to do so, since that would probably be an inefficient investment of resources for any one of them. Although the results would benefit all, the innovator alone would have to bear the high cost. Even if the individual agencies independently conducted their own projects, we would probably see many of them pursuing identical questions not knowing of the work and results of the other. Furthermore, there would be little incentive for an individual agency to disseminate the results of its work to other agencies that might be able to use them.

This is a typical situation in which it is appropriate for the Federal Government to take a leading and coordinating role. The Federal Government could provide the risk capital to conduct the research or to develop the new technology at a cost that would be small by Federal standards but would swamp the budget of any individual criminal justice agency.

It could also assure that a coordinated and mutually supporting program is developed, and it could foster the implementation of the results. Without such a major Federal involvement, it appears un-

44 *Ibid.*, p. 2.

likely that there can be significant innovation in the operation of the criminal justice system. And all recent trends in crime rates, arrest rates, and recidivism rates indicate that what we are doing today is inadequate to cope with the crime problem.[45]

This federally sponsored program, Blumstein continued, would:

- Undertake basic research into the causes of crime and into the consequences of actions taken to control it.
- Provide for the development of equipment that could be widely used by criminal justice agencies throughout the country.
- Create a coordinated program whose parts would complement and build upon each other.
- Assure that the results of the program are made available in a form that would be usable by criminal justice agencies throughout the Nation.
- Provide technical assistance and guidance to State and local agencies in planning and implementing their programs and to the Federal Government in administering its subsidy program.[46]

The government's response is now history, but it continues to shape our lives.

WAR ON CRIME: STRATEGY AND ACTION

The technological war on crime has been launched. The military strategy toward domestic disorder now prevails. LEAA began by creating and sponsoring a host of counter-insurgency and military-like projects for the home front. States, upon receiving block grants, have distributed their funds to local agencies for the development of a broad range of anti-crime programs. Some of these "Discretionary Grants" are listed below, as briefly described in the LEAA annual report:[47]

Grantee — City of Riverside, Riverside, California ($150,000).
Title — Project "ACE" (Aerial Crime Enforcement).
Project Summary — Because of terrain and structural features, it is

---

[45] "Controlling Crime Through More Effective Law Enforcement," *Hearings* Before the Subcommittee on Criminal Laws and Procedures of the Committee on the Judiciary, United States Senate, 90th Congress (Washington, D.C.: U.S. Government Printing Office, 1967), pp. 1070–1071.
[46] *Ibid.*
[47] *LEAA*, 3rd Annual Report, pp. 269–377.

necessary to use an aerial enforcement unit of two helicopters and three crews to maintain police capabilities.

Grantee — Metropolitan Dade County, Miami, Florida ($94,910).

Title — Behavior and Attitude Modification in a Jail Setting.

Project Summary — To initiate a program of attitudinal and behavioral change both in inmates and officers of the Dade County Jail through the introduction of scientifically-tested correctional methods, classification systems and a training program for officers in custodial roles.

Grantee — Oakland Community College, Bloomfield Hills, Michigan ($51,145).

Title — Campus Security: Control of Student Revolt, Oakland Community College.

Project Summary — This project will support a four-day conference on campus disorders for 100 persons from state campus police and security department heads. Top-level professionals in relevant fields will provide conference resources in an effort to begin early stages of development of professional expertise for handling campus disorders.

Grantee — City of Long Beach Police Department, Long Beach, California ($132,488).

Title — Selective Enforcement and Crime Prevention Teams.

Project Summary — Suppression of burglaries and street crime will be accomplished by concerted use of teams of personnel on foot, in cars and in helicopters, with electronic and mechanical equipment necessary to keep constant communication between them. They will work in areas found to have high burglary and robbery incidence. LEAA support will be for equipment and an evaluation component, while the grantee will provide the personnel component.

Grantee — West Virginia Department of Public Safety ($120,000).

Title — State Police Crime Lab Expansion.

Project Summary — This three-fold projected plan calls for expansion and improvement of the chemical and fingerprint sections of the state criminalistics laboratory, using three additional chemists and obtaining additional equipment. The third lab improvement will be in drug identification and routine criminalistics. By adding these provisions, more time may be devoted by local police to preservation and identification of evidence.

Grantee — Spartanburg Police Department, Spartanburg, South Carolina ($73,310).

Title — Comprehensive Police Cadet In-Service Training and Community Relations Program.

Project Summary — This program will generally establish better understanding by the citizens of the programs, priorities and problems of the police role in the community. Three major components of the program consist of establishing a three-man police civil-disorders prevention unit, a training division and community relations unit and a 30-hour police/community relations in-service training program for all members of Spartanburg Police Department and a police cadre training program. The program will be evaluated by an independent organization.

Grantee — Union County Board of Chosen Freeholders, Elizabeth, New Jersey ($25,000).

Title — Union County Tactical Force.

Project Summary — The Tactical force will be comprised of two 50-men units from all municipalities in Union County, on a force-strength ratio, with a minimum of two men from each department. Extensive training will be given at Ft. Dix, N.J. in civil disorder-related subjects, to be followed by one training day per month for each unit at local National Guard Armory. Each unit will be made up of unit leader, assistant unit leader, two 20-man squads, a three-man gas squad, a three-man sniper squad. An attorney will be attached to assist in legal matters. Senior level officers will be sent to Ft. Gordon, Georgia, for special training.

Grantee — Department of Law and Public Safety, Trenton, New Jersey ($30,000).

Title — Expanded Court Disposition Reporting System.

Project Summary — More than 1,200 units will supply input data, and they will receive accurate offender histories on instant request from this expanded criminal statistical information system, which will include data on detention and adjudication of over 23,000 individuals. Contributors will receive training by six field representatives in proper recording procedures to be developed by a consulting firm.

Grantee — Blackfeet Tribal Business Council ($48,830).

Title — Court Improvement and Reform, Browning, Montana.

Project Summary — The purpose is to initiate a demonstration project for improvement of the reservation court system. The proposal is designed to provide a legally trained and experienced person to act as tribal court judge and administrator; develop and sustain effective court management programs including procedures, scheduling, forms and staff utilization devices and offices of public defender and prosecutor; and develop a comprehensive tribal court system which will effectively and fairly administer the reservation criminal justice system.

Grantee — Tennessee Department of Safety ($25,700).

Title — Civil Disorders Technical Assistance Unit.

Project Summary — This project is to assist the Commissioner of the Department of Safety in planning, training and coordinating efforts by all law enforcement agencies within the state in the field of civil disorder prevention, detection and control. The functions and responsibilities of this unit include: (1) to provide civil disorders technical assistance between local and state agencies; (2) to gather pertinent data concerning quantities and quality of equipment and training at local and state levels so that resources can be utilized in mutual aid situations; and (3) to review grant applications for special equipment or training requirements submitted to Tennessee Law Enforcement Planning Agency in field of civil disorders prevention, detection, control and potential analysis.

Grantee — Berkeley Police Department, Berkeley, California ($25,000).

Title — Berkeley-Alameda County Disorder and Riot Control Action Plan.

Project Summary — This project will implement the first phase of "a problem definition" stage of a larger plan for the control of civil disorders in Berkeley and Alameda County. Phase II is analysis and Phase III is solutions and recommended plans for implementation of the total program.

A total of 643 such "Discretionary Grant" projects were supported by LEAA in 1970, with over $340 million allocated for the projects. Through these projects, we are told, state and local units of government are able to "improve their criminal justice systems."

In only a few years LEAA, through such funding, has been able to change the nature of criminal justice in America. One author, in reviewing the projects since 1968, has indicated some of the ways in which criminal justice has been affected.

Civil Disorder Assistance

- The sweeping arrest of 894 students (out of a total enrollment of 2500) at all-black Mississippi Valley State College, thereby breaking a peaceful campus-wide strike. The *Washington Post* noted that LEAA's action "marked the beginning of one of the

127

Nixon Administration's potentially most volatile policies — federal 'technical assistance' in local suppression of 'campus disorders.' " The crime in this "disorder" was "obstructing a public road on a campus." Police action was made possible by a LEAA grant of $288,405 to the Mississippi State Commission for "developing plans and procedures for coping with civil disorders (riot control and natural disaster) and organized crime."

- The deaths of four people in the disorders in Baton Rouge, Louisiana were underwritten in part by LEAA grants, one of which was for $48,708 on June 25, 1970, and called for the creation of a "special trouble shooting squad." Another was for $31,942 on November 30, 1970 for "police technical assistance for prevention and control of civil disorders." A special squad made up of city police, sheriffs, and parish county police, equipped with submachine guns and M-16's with bayonets, sealed off the streets where a Black Muslim rally was being held. Soon afterward the shooting began.
- LEAA has to date supplied $750,000 to the cities of San Diego and Miami to develop joint defenses against potential demonstrations at the conventions. . . .

Weapon Stockpiling

- LEAA is arming the police to the teeth. For $16,464 LEAA bought the tank used by Louisiana police to storm a New Orleans Black Panther headquarters September 10, 1970. The same tank, classified by LEAA bureaucrats as a "command and control vehicle," had been used earlier against demonstrating black students.

Clandestine Surveillance

- A LEAA grant in Delaware financed mobile surveillance units hidden in civilian rental trucks. The grant provided for operators dressed in the uniforms of dry-cleaner delivery men, salesmen, public utilities workers, and others, "making it possible to be in a neighborhood without being obvious." The trucks are to be equipped with infrared cameras and video equipment for taking pictures night or day of "suspicious persons."
- In Tampa, Florida a LEAA-sponsored surveillance system costing $150,000 will use computers to control a network of videotape cameras and alarms placed in "convenient" grocery stores and overlooking shopping center parking lots. Operators will monitor the cameras constantly, using their zoom lenses for close-ups of any "suspicious activity."

- In San Jose, California; Hoboken, New Jersey; and Mount Vernon, New York; TV cameras are placed throughout the cities' business areas, flashing their images back to the local police headquarters where they are monitored for "suspicious" goings on. The Mt. Vernon equipment, which cost LEAA $47,000, is capable of discerning a man-sized object in extreme darkness for more than a half-mile away.

Data Gathering
- LEAA has sponsored the construction of statewide data banks on "actual or *potential* troublemakers." In Oklahoma, for example, a $29,453 grant enabled the National Guard to compile dossiers on six thousand individuals, only one-third of them Oklahomans. The ACLU and Oklahoma Civil Liberties Union have filed suit in federal court maintaining the dossiers are used to "harass and intimidate." One of the lawyers, Stephen Jones, has evidence that some Oklahomans have been blacklisted as a result of the dossiers. "A number of Negroes and whites who have taken part in peace rallies or racial demonstrations," he told the *New York Times,* began "having trouble finding jobs or getting into college."
- A $46,000 appropriation has been made to the New Haven, Connecticut Police Department for an "exploration of law enforcement utilization of the 1970 Census Bureau Data." The police can use the census data, which will be stored in IBM computers, during "civil disorders" to obtain vital background information (age, schooling, occupation) on the residents of the area.[48]

In addition to financing state and local programs, LEAA is sponsoring a massive project aimed at developing a national intelligence network. Started as a $45 million LEAA pilot project called SEARCH (Systems for Electronic Analysis and Retrieval of Criminal Histories), the project has grown into a computerized "criminal justice information center," operated by the FBI. The information not only includes official records, such as an individual's arrest record, regardless of the eventual disposition of the case, but information compiled from other sources as well. The computerized intelligence system will contain information derived from infor-

[48] Gerth, "The Americanization of 1984," p. 59.

129

mants, wiretaps, employers, and the like.[49] The intelligence gathering network functions through separate computer centers set up by each state. All records, criminal and otherwise, will be stored and then transmitted to the FBI for filing in the National Crime Information Center (NCIC).

> All 50 states will be able to "talk" to each other through the FBI master computer. In addition, every major municipal police department in the country will be hooked into the network, either with its own computer or a less expensive teletype operation. There are already 135 local and state police agencies that are using or will soon be using the memory links to the FBI. Before long, 75 per cent of the nation's police agencies will be plugged in, and by 1975 the figure should rise to 95 per cent.[50]

Each locality decides how much and what kind of information to feed into its computer; and all the information, regardless of its validity or legality, is pumped into the national computer in Washington.

By the time the intelligence system is in full operation (in 1975) law enforcement agents will have instant access to information on any person they regard as "suspicious." Once again, science and technology have come to the aid of the state in providing a system that will enable government agents to control domestic order. In the name of combating crime, the state is now able to obtain information on as many people as it wants to and make it instantly available for use against them. This new anti-crime technology, in the form of a computerized data bank, has serious implications, even from a constitutional standpoint.

> The new technology has made it literally impossible for a man to start again in our society. It has removed the quality of mercy from our institutions by making it impossible to forget, to forgive, to understand, to tolerate. . . . The undisputed and unlimited possession of the resources to build and operate data banks on individuals, and to make decisions about people with the aid of computers and electronic data systems, is fast securing to executive branch

---

[49] See Goulden, "Tooling Up for Repression," pp. 528–529; and Gerth, "The Americanization of 1984," pp. 60–61.

[50] Michael Sorkin, "The FBI's Big Brother Computer," *The Washington Monthly*, 4 (September, 1972), p. 24.

officials a political power which the authors of the Constitution never meant any one group of men to have over all others.[51]

Further weaponry for the war on crime is rapidly being developed. New developments in scientific warfare abroad are being applied to crime control at home. Though a technology for domestic security has lagged behind that for military intervention abroad, the situation is being corrected.

Up until recently the standard arsenal for the patrolman was the sidearm and nightstick. Occasionally a labor strike was met with riot guns and gas bombs. Today's rapid expansion in the variety of the police arsenal illustrates the rapid expansion of domestic counterinsurgency planning. Today's police can employ a number of different gas dispensing devices, from shotguns to helicopters; carry individual two-way radios; fire machine guns on the practice range and high-powered rifles from moving aircraft; wear helmets and body armor; carry MACE in their belts; engage in mock confrontations; as well as use computers to sort out large quantities of information in seconds. Recently, for instance, the Pentagon announced plans to provide $20 million worth of riot control equipment to the National Guard — including face shields, batons, protective vests, shotguns, floodlights, public address systems, radios and tear gas.[52]

The kinds of weapons used against the people of Indochina are now being used at home. Weapons are being developed and manufactured by corporations for local law enforcement. Police departments today are supplied with an arsenal that includes helicopters, infrared detection devices, gas armored vehicles, tanks, hand grenades, explosives, smoke screen equipment, barbed wire, high powered guns, sound machines, and so on. Aided by the federal government, mainly by grants from LEAA, the local police department is equipped with a stockpile of the latest weapons.

The federal government today, through science and technology, has thus armed the police around the country with the weapons necessary to maintain domestic order. The role of the federal government in modern crime control has been summarized by Blum-

[51] Senator Sam J. Ervin, Jr., as quoted in Goulden, "Tooling Up for Repression," p. 528.

[52] Vince Pinto, "Weapons for the Homefront," in National Action/Research on the Military-Industrial Complex, *Police on the Homefront* (Philadelphia: American Friends Service Committee, 1971), p. 74.

stein: "Think of where military technology would be if each battalion commander were responsible for his own research and development. A national agency was needed to represent the combined interests of police departments across the nation. The creation of the Law Enforcement Assistance Administration, and especially its research and development arm, the National Institute of Law Enforcement and Criminal Justice, was an important step in that direction." [53] Whenever the time is right, the government can now launch a full-scale war against its own people. Scientifically and technologically the state has been made ready.

REFORM, REPRESSION, AND RESISTANCE

The contradiction within advanced capitalist society is that a system which violates human sensibilities in turn calls for resistance and rebellion by the population. And the more such resistance occurs, whether in outright political acts or in behavior that otherwise violates the rules of such a society, the more the state must bring its repressive forces to bear on the people. The state's failure to respond would allow changes that would undoubtedly spell the end of the kind of political economy upon which that society rests. Thus today in America we are witnessing the repression of a society that refuses to use its resources to solve its own problems. To protect the system from its own victims, a war on crime is being waged.

The crime control programs of the last ten years have been constructed within the framework of "reform." This is to be expected, since reform is no more than the existing society's way of adjusting the system so that it will survive according to its own terms. Many of the crime control programs have been an integral part of the programs confronting poverty, racial inequality, and campus disorders. Under the guise of working toward "new frontiers," "the great society," and the like, measures have been instituted to preserve the existing social and economic arrangements. At the same time, measures have been developed to control resistance to the reforms and to prevent changes that go beyond them. The state thus activates the option that must accompany reform, namely

---

[53] Alfred Blumstein, "Science and Technology for Law Enforcement: Prospects and Problems," *The Police Chief*, 36 (December, 1969), p. 61.

repression. Reform and repression are not alternative options for the state but complementary ones.

However, as reform reveals itself incapable of subduing pressure and protest, so does the emphasis shift towards repression, coercion, police power, law and order, the struggle against subversion, etc. Faced as they are with intractable problems, those who control the levers of power find it increasingly necessary further to erode those features of "bourgeois democracy" through which popular pressure is exercised. The power of representative institutions must be further reduced and the executive more effectively insulated against them. The independence of trade unions must be whittled away, and trade union rights, notably the right to strike, must be further surrounded by new and more stringent inhibitions. The state must arm itself with more extensive and more efficient means of repression, seek to define more stringently the area of "legitimate" dissent and opposition, and strike fear in those who seek to go beyond it.[54]

The process of repression is cumulative. Further repression can only engender more protest, and further protest necessitates more repression by the state. The transition is to a new kind of control, one that transforms crime control into an expression of a larger system of state authoritarianism.

This transition need not assume a dramatic character, or require a violent change in institutions. Neither its profession nor its end result need be identical with the Fascism of the inter-war years. It is indeed most unlikely to assume the latter's particular forms, because of the discredit which has not ceased to be attached to them, and of the loathing which Fascism has not ceased to evoke. In fact, the usage of Fascism as a reference point tends dangerously to obscure the less extreme alternatives to it, which do not require the wholesale dismantling of all democratic institutions, the total subversion of all liberties, nor certainly the abandonment of a democratic rhetoric. It is easily possible to conceive of forms of conservative authoritarianism which would not be "Fascist," in the old sense, which would be claimed to be "democratic" precisely because they were not "Fascist," and whose establishment would be defended as in the best interests of "democracy" itself. Nor is all this a distant projection into an improbable future: it describes a process which is already in train, and which is also, in the condition of advanced

54 Miliband, *The State in Capitalist Society*, pp. 271–272.

capitalism, more likely to be accentuated than reversed. The gradual transition of capitalism into socialism may be a myth: but the gradual transition of "bourgeois democracy" into more or less pronounced forms of authoritarianism is not.[55]

That we are entering a new kind of America, or rather a modernization of the old one, seems evident from our study of crime control. The state, in its support of advanced capitalism, an economic system that cannot respond to human needs and still exist, must remake itself. The modern state, with its ruling class, maintains its control over internal challenges by developing and institutionalizing the instruments of science and technology. This "new-style" fascism is a complex of modernized control mechanisms. It is a pervasive form of control: indeed, a managed society. As Bertram Gross has described this new order, "A managed society rules by a faceless and widely dispersed complex of warfare-welfare-industrial-communications-police bureaucracies caught up in developing a new-style empire based on a technocratic ideology, a culture of alienation, multiple scapegoats, and competing control networks." [56] Not only will the economy be managed, but the total society will be managed by the modern state.

The police component of the new state will be, as we know from present experience, a network of law enforcement systems decentralized on a geographical basis yet guided by federal agencies. "It will include the Attorney General's office, the FBI, the CIA, the military intelligence agencies, federal-aid crime agencies, and new computer-based dossier facilities tied in with the Internal Revenue Service, the Census Bureau, and credit-rating offices." [57] This control complex will, of course, be integrated into an expanding wel-

---

[55] *Ibid.*, p. 272.

[56] Bertram Gross, "Friendly Fascism, A Model for America," *Social Policy*, 1 (November–December, 1970), p. 46. Gross goes on to suggest that this "new-style" fascism will differ strikingly from traditional fascism: "Under techno-urban fascism, certain elements previously regarded as inescapable earmarks of fascism would no longer be essential. Pluralistic in nature, techno-urban fascism would need no charismatic dictator, no one-party rule, no mass fascist party, no glorification of the state, no dissolution of legislatures, no discontinuation of elections, no distrust of reason. It would probably be a cancerous growth *within* and *around* the White House, the Pentagon, and the broader political establishment" (p. 46).

[57] *Ibid.*, p. 47.

fare system which itself malignly controls the population. We will be bound, finally, by a communications network.

> In toto, the warfare-welfare-industrial-communication-police complex would be the supramodern fascist form of what has hitherto been described as "oligopolistic state capitalism." Its products would be: (1) increasingly differentiated armaments (including more outer-space and under-sea instruments of destruction) that in the name of defense and security would contribute to world insecurity; (2) increasingly specialized medical, education, housing, and welfare programs that would have a declining relation to health, learning, community, or social justice; (3) industrial products to serve warfare-welfare purposes and provide consumer incentives for acceptance of the system; (4) communication services that would serve as instruments for the manipulation, surveillance, and suppression — or prettifying — of information on domestic and foreign terrorism; (5) police activities designed to cope with the new "crime" of opposing the system, probably enlisting organized crime in the effort.[58]

Is there an alternative to this future? Certainly the liberal reform solutions are not the answer; they only lead to further repression and open the way for the neo-fascist state. Only a vision that goes beyond reform of the capitalist system can provide us with a humane existence and a world free of the authoritarian state. Crime control in modern America is a crucial indication of the world that can emerge under present images and theories of society and human nature. Only with a critical philosophy of our present condition can we suggest a way out of our possible future. We are capable of an alternative existence, one that frees us and makes us human. We must think and act in a way that will bring about a world quite different from the one toward which we are currently heading. A socialist future is our hope.

[58] *Ibid.*, p. 48.

135

5
Ideology of Legal Order

The ruling class in capitalist society secures the existing order in several ways. The coercive force of the state, including law and legal repression, is one means of maintaining the social and economic order. Yet a more subtle reproductive mechanism of capitalist society is the perpetuation of a particular conception of reality. In the manipulation of consciousness the existing order is legitimated and secured. Manipulating the minds of the people is capitalism's most subtle means of control.

> The most important reproductive mechanism which does not involve the use of state violence is consciousness-manipulation. The liberal state has an enormous amount of violence at its disposal, but it is often reluctant to use it. Violence may breed counter-violence, leading to instability. It may be far better to manipulate consciousness to such an extent that most people would never think of engaging in the kinds of action which could be repressed. The most perfectly repressive (though not violently so) capitalist system, in other words, would not be a police state, but the complete opposite, one in which there were no police because there was nothing to police, everyone having accepted the legitimacy of that society and all its daily consequences.[1]

[1] Alan Wolfe, "Political Repression and the Liberal State," *Monthly Review,* 23 (December 1971), p. 20.

Through its various reproductive mechanisms, capitalism is able to maximize the possibility of total control over the citizens of the state. Ranging from control of economic resources to manipulation of the mind, capitalism operates according to its own form of dictatorship.

> The dictatorship of capital is exercised not only on the production and distribution of wealth, but with equal force on the manner of producing, on the model of consumption, and on the manner of consuming, the manner of working, thinking, living. As much as over the workers, the factory, and the state, this dictatorship rules over the society's vision of the future, its ideology, its priorities and goals; over the way in which people experience and learn about themselves, their potentials, their relations with other people and with the rest of the world. This dictatorship is economic, political, cultural, and psychological at the same time: it is total.[2]

Hence, the ideology of capitalism must be considered in any radical critique of the institutions of American society.

We have seen that law in capitalist society serves to maintain and perpetuate existing social and economic arrangements, that ruling class interests are secured by the legal system of the state. How the legal order is made legitimate is now our concern. In fostering the ideology that the established legal order is the most appropriate way to manage a society and that crime is to be controlled by the state, the ruling class is able to maintain its dominance over the population. The ideology of legal order is the ultimate form of control in capitalist society.

LEGAL IDEOLOGY IN CAPITALIST SOCIETY

Every society is founded on and supported by some ideology that serves to establish and justify the existing order. But the ideology that prevails is inevitably that of the ruling class. Marx noted the ideological hegemony of the ruling class in the observation that the ruling ideas are the ideas of the ruling class.

> The ideas of the ruling class are in every epoch the ruling ideas, i.e. the class which is the ruling *material* force of society, is at the

2 André Gorz, *Strategy for Labor: A Radical Proposal*, trans. Martin A. Nicolaus and Victoria Ortiz (Boston: Beacon Press, 1967), pp. 131–132.

same time its ruling *intellectual* force. The class which has the means of material production at its disposal, has control at the same time over the means of mental production, so that thereby, generally speaking, the ideas of those who lack the means of mental production are subject to it. The ruling ideas are nothing more than the ideal expression of the dominant material relationships, the dominant material relationships grasped as ideas; hence of the relationships which make the one class the ruling one, therefore, the ideas of its dominance.[3]

Our interest here is in the particular ideology that develops in a capitalist society to secure domestic order. And my argument is that the ideology of law serves as a primary form of control in capitalist society. To establish the ideology that we are to be bound by law in our activities is to secure the existing system. The ideology of law in America is an extension of the prevailing capitalist ideology. Criminal policy, in particular, reflects the capitalistic outlook and interests. The framework for dealing with domestic disorder is always that of the ruling class, which means that criminal policy is articulated within the capitalist framework; in subscribing to the general capitalist ideology, the public accepts the criminal policies of the ruling class. As long as a capitalist ruling class exists, the prevailing ideology will be capitalistic. And as long as that ruling class uses the law to maintain its order, the legal ideology will be capitalistic as well. The ideas of the ruling class therefore extend from the general to the particular. We are led to believe that the legal system is for the benefit of us all. The objective reality is quite different, however; the ideology of law serves the ruling class, establishing the hegemony of the dominant economic interests.

It is usual in any discussion of law to ignore the fact that the legal ideal itself is an ideology. Such lack of awareness, of course, lends support to the official reality of capitalism. If we are to transcend the official reality in thought and practice, we must recognize the ideological nature of the legal order. As Kolko suggests in regard to American ideology in general, "The pervasiveness of this ideological power in American society and its measurable influence on mass culture, public values, and political opinions is the most visible

[3] Karl Marx and Frederick Engels, *The German Ideology,* ed. C. J. Arthur (New York: International Publishers, 1970), p. 64.

reality of modern American life to the contemporary social analyst." [4] This means that we can understand the legal order in America only when we recognize the dominant legal ideology and its relation to ruling class interests.

What then is the nature of the legal ideology in America? And how does that ideology come to prevail in the society? First, it prevails by the very fact that alternatives to legal order are not perceivable within the capitalist framework. An American society without law, one not secured by legal order, is rarely suggested. The ideology of law successfully keeps alternatives from arising. Second, it prevails through the conscious efforts of the ruling class. Through the various means of communication the ruling class and its bureaucracies systematically present the public with the ruling class ideology. It is not stretching the facts to suggest, although conventional liberal intelligence may be offended, that what is involved here is a process of indoctrination.[5] By selectively presenting one view of reality, and by rejecting alternatives to it, the ruling class (with the assistance of organizations that serve it) presents an ideology to the public as being *the* reality.

But whether the process is a deliberate effort to shape public consciousness or simply a general conception of the world, an ideological hegemony is established. Hence, we are all likely to share the ideology that law is good for us and, indeed, that a legal order is the only way to run a society. The legal ideology has done little more than perpetuate an oppressive system that depends on the domination of one class by another. Not to have seen beyond the dominant legal ideology represents a lack of critical imagination. To do better is the objective of a critical philosophy of legal order.

THE MORAL BASIS OF THE LEGAL ORDER

Among the pervasive forces that support the ideology of law are the moral values of the society. In specific instances it is the religion

[4] Gabriel Kolko, *The Roots of American Foreign Policy* (Boston: Beacon Press, 1969), p. 26. Also see David Horowitz, "Introduction," in David Horowitz (ed.), *Corporations and the Cold War* (New York: Monthly Review Press, 1969), pp. 14–16.

[5] See Ralph Miliband, *The State in Capitalist Society* (New York: Basic Books, 1969), p. 182.

of the time that gives legitimacy to legal order. And related to the moral force of the legal ideology is nationalism itself. In fact, nationalism has become the secular moral force of the modern age. So it is that the ideology of law is supported by the moral basis of the existing order. What this means in modern times is that there is a moral basis to capitalism, a morality that supports the interests of the ruling class and, at the same time, underlies the legal system that maintains the prevailing social and economic order.

Social and economic arrangements have always been secured by some ideology of order. Underlying most societies is a belief in a *natural* order. Moreover, this natural order is believed to be regulated by a natural law. Natural law assumes some kind of relation between man-made law ("positive law") and a higher law.[6] The relation of the natural law to the man-made law is recognized in most legal systems. The end result, nevertheless, is a moral basis for an ideology of law.

The prevailing view of law in capitalist societies is basically the Greek conception. That is, the citizen has a moral duty to obey the law, even when that law seems to be immoral. According to the Greek conception "human law may conflict with moral law but the citizen must still obey the law of his state though he may and indeed should labour to persuade the state to change its law to conform with morality."[7] This view has tended to dominate most ideologies of law and order since Greek times.

The Christian notion of law gave further legitimacy to the law of the state. The state — as a law-making and law-enforcing body — was essentially a theological creation. For example, in the thought of John Calvin, the state was a necessary entity. Since man brought the Fall upon himself, a man-made order had to be established. Man had failed, according to Calvin, to remain in the integrity of his original nature:

> Let us realize, then, that not without reason has God established the order of earthly justice; but because He considered the corruption that is within us. We are well warned by that as I have already

[6] For a more detailed discussion of natural law, and the ideology of law, see my article, "The Ideology of Law: Notes for a Radical Alternative to Legal Oppression," *Issues in Criminology*, 7 (Winter, 1972), pp. 1–35.

[7] Dennis Lloyd, *The Idea of Law* (Harmondsworth, England: Penguin, 1964), p. 55.

said, to humble ourselves seeing that our vices require such a remedy. All the more we must extoll the goodness of God because He decided to assure that harmony would prevail and that we should not despair: which would come about if there were no law in the world.[8]

Because of man's inordinate disobedience, the temporal state must exist and secure its power if for no other reason than to protect the sovereignty of God's order. This is the conservative basis of religious political thought.

Nevertheless, Calvin created a dilemma in his thought: How can earthly power be adapted to God's Kingdom? Although Calvin's passion for order on earth was strong, his belief in the progressive character of the Kingdom of God was overwhelming. Ultimately the Kingdom of God cannot coexist with the state. For Calvin the movement of history was from political-legal regulation to the self-determining freedom of the conscience. The coercive element of the state cannot finally be adapted to the free-willing potential of the Christian life. The old order must eventually give way to the new.

The practical tension between positive law and natural law, however, was not reconciled. The Anglican churchmen tended to opt for the conservative aspect of Calvinism. The citizen was simply to conform to the existing political order. The Puritans in the American colonies likewise were not particularly bold in establishing the rights of man. The Massachusetts Bay Colony, as a "City upon a Hill," an example of godliness to the world, was based on the belief that government exists to regulate imperfect man and that political commands must be obeyed.[9] Out of such ideas the Puritans developed a conception of the *covenant*. Under this conception government was viewed as originating in a compact among the people. But more than this, the power of the state was viewed as legitimate because it was a government conforming to what God had decreed.

In the American context, law soon became the moral instrument to establish social order. Though the early American criminal codes applied sanctions for religious infractions, the criminal policies gradually shifted to the regulation of behavior that threatened to dis-

---

[8] Quoted in David Little, *Religion, Order, and Law: A Study in Pre-Revolutionary England* (New York: Harper & Row, 1969), p. 41.

[9] George Lee Haskins, *Law and Authority in Early Massachusetts* (New York: Macmillan, 1960).

rupt the social order of the nation.[10] Criminal policy, especially the institutionalization of the offender, became a means of promoting the stability of the society. Criminal punishment served to incapacitate the violator and deter others from violation, while allowing the emerging social and economic conditions to continue without alteration. Criminal law had a new moral basis: to promote the necessary (natural) order of a capitalist society.

The moral basis of legal ideology continues to this day. It is this ideology that underpins the recent efforts to control crime. And the objectives remain the same, perpetuation of the existing social and economic order. The war on crime — the law and order challenge — is another manifestation of the attempt to preserve the capitalist system. The American way of life is at stake, we are told, in this war on crime. This moral challenge is providing the state and the ruling class with the rationale to institute ever new forms of legal control. Crime today, as always, is a moral problem. This is what gives the ideology of law its force and consequence. The ruling class rules through moral authority fostered by an ideology that it in turn perpetuates.

CIVIL LIBERTIES AND SELECTIVE REPRESSION

In some regimes it may be necessary for the state to repress all forms and instances of opposition. Complete repression, however, is not usually necessary for the political systems of capitalist countries. Capitalist nations are able to preserve their existing social order even in the presence of considerable opposition. Political tolerance, therefore, has been part of the legal ideology of capitalist countries. Organized according to the precepts of "liberal democracy," these countries have held out the notion of "civil liberties," that is, the rights of citizens before the law, and the idea that individuals may conscientiously violate the law on some occasions, in the name of "civil disobedience."

Yet, whenever opposition to the existing order reaches a point where that order is threatened, the state has always been able to withhold or withdraw these "rights." Although in recent years some

[10] See David J. Rothman, *The Discovery of the Asylum* (Boston: Little, Brown and Company, 1971), esp. pp. 57–78.

rights have been totally suspended, for the most part the rulers and agents in capitalist societies tend not to withdraw these rights completely but rather to apply legal sanctions on an individual basis. Legal harassment may become the tactic, rather than massive repression. Nevertheless, the suspension of the legal rights of some citizens is used as an example of what may happen to others who would threaten the established system.

The American social order is founded on the liberal precepts of political tolerance and the right of dissent. The legal ideology thus embodies the notions of civil liberties and civil disobedience. These notions as part of the ideology of law make that ideology appear to serve the interests of the citizen. The truth, however, is that even this part of the legal ideology serves the interests of the state and the ruling class. In thinking about individual freedom, we tend to overlook the fact that civil liberties are administered by those who have authority in the society. When liberties are in the hands of a ruling elite, we do not actually have these rights in practice. The legal ideology about civil liberties, although it claims otherwise, in fact supports the interests of the established order.

The actual lack of civil liberties is obvious in liberal democracy, contrary to all the rhetoric and the pleas for protecting civil liberties that are heard when the government is threatened to the point of becoming unstable. Although the people have the right to resist oppressive government, even to overthrow it, the guarantees can be suddenly withdrawn or reinterpreted. Tom Hayden, in a chapter titled "A Note to Liberals," describes this situation:

> We are in a condition in which the First Amendment freedoms do not work effectively. Citizens have the right to speak, assemble, and protest freely until their actions begin to have a subversive effect on unresponsive authorities. It can be expressed as an axiom: at the point at which protest becomes effective, the state becomes repressive. Constitutional rights become primarily rhetorical. They are not extended to those who might use them to make basic structural change, to those who represent the beginning of a new society.[11]

Thus, abstract freedoms may flourish with ease. And we have these freedoms as long as our protests and actions are ineffectual

[11] Tom Hayden, *Trial* (New York: Holt, Rinehart, and Winston, 1970), pp. 44–45.

144

and as long as we behave according to the rules administered by the governing class. However, when the authority of that class is threatened, a host of laws can be invoked. Not only may civil liberties be abridged, but repressive laws may be used to suppress potentially effective action. "Hence the dissenter has the freedom to become a victim in the social process and history, and a battery of sedition, espionage, criminal anarchy, or labor laws exist in readiness for the appropriate moment of social tension and the breakdown in the social and ideological consensus which exists during periods of peace and stability. The celebrants of American freedom rarely confront the concepts of order that underlie the large body of law for suppression that always exists in reserve." [12]

Contrary to the legal ideology, civil liberties are not a safeguard of human rights. Those liberties that are abstractly guaranteed are the province of the ruling class. That is, those from whom we are to be protected dispense our civil liberties. There is a one-way allocation of civil liberties, from the top down, from those with power to those without. Civil liberties are thus parceled out to us at the discretion of the authority that we wish to dissent from, alter, or destroy. All is on their terms, according to their rules and their application of the rules. The expectation that we should get a fair hearing stretches even the most optimistic liberal imagination. Yet the legal ideology would have us believe the official guarantees.

Even the opportunity to use civil liberties is severely limited in a liberal, ruling class democracy. The positions of power, the economic resources, and the means of communication are possessed by the ruling class. With such an arrangement the chances are slight that the opposition can get into a position to effectively protest or threaten an oppressive government. Only by the most extreme and, by definition, the most illegal of means can the opposition be assured of a voice and possibly of effective action. An opposition can expect little more from civil liberties than a device that gives legitimacy to existing authority.

The same problems are found regarding the ideology of civil disobedience. As with all civil rights, civil disobedience is regulated by the ruling class. The idea of civil disobedience presupposes the concept of legality. Only a legal ideology could raise the issue of

[12] Kolko, *The Roots of American Foreign Policy*, p. 8.

civil disobedience; civil disobedience is a part of the ideology that law is necessary — that social order is to be maintained by a legal system.

The legal ideology holds that disobedience to law may be a *moral* right but that disobedience cannot be *legally* justified. We are clearly warned that a system of law is to be honored no matter how unjust it may be, in its entirety or in part. We are asked to obey the law without any questions of justice. The nature of this law and order approach is illustrated in George Kennan's revealing conclusion to the question of civil disobedience:

> In the final analysis, the question of civil disobedience is, I am sure, a matter of temperament. Humanity divides, it has been said, between those who, in their political philosophy, place the emphasis on order and those who place it on justice. I belong in the first of these categories. Human justice is always imperfect. The laws on which it bases itself are always to some extent unjust. These laws have therefore only a relative value; and it is only relative benefits that can be expected from the effort to improve them. But the good order of society is something tangible and solid. There is little that can be done about men's motives; but if men can be restrained in their behavior, something is accomplished.[13]

As one of the leading liberal spokesmen and government servants, Kennan adds: "The benefit of the doubt should lie, therefore, with the forces of order, not with the world-improvers." The ideological position is quite clear: to preserve the existing order at the expense of a just human existence.

It becomes clear that the legal system really has no place for the practice of civil disobedience, other than to provide a liberal ideology and to assure that the offender is punished. Uncritically the legal ideology tells us to look to Socrates who insisted that he should accept the death penalty for an act he thought was morally right. This is the argument that centuries later goes unquestioned. Former Supreme Court Justice Abe Fortas, in his book on civil disobedience, confirms the doctrine: "Civil disobedience is violation of the law. Any violation of law must be punished, whatever its purpose,

[13] George F. Kennan, *Democracy and the Student Left* (New York: Bantam Books, 1968), pp. 149–150.

146

as the theory of civil disobedience recognizes."[14] Law and order are the paramount values: "For after all, each of us is a member of an organized society. Each of us benefits from its existence and its order. And each of us must be ready, like Socrates, to accept the verdict of its institutions if we violate their mandate and our challenge is not vindicated."[15]

The legal ideology regarding civil liberties and civil disobedience thus works to the advantage of the state and the ruling class. In recent years, as the existing order has been continually threatened, the application of the legal ideology has been realized. Abstract rights have been denied, and various legal qualifications of these rights have been instituted. For example, the government has attacked those who oppose the war in Vietnam. The government attacks (occurring in the administration of Kennedy, Johnson, and Nixon) have been both in words and actions, ranging from statements that demonstrations are dangerous in that they prolong war, to the arrest and prosecution of protesters.[16] Moreover, lengthy congressional hearings have been held "to make a full and complete study and investigation of riots, violent disturbances of the peace, vandalism, civil and criminal disorders, insurrection, the commission of crime in connection therewith, the immediate and longstanding causes, the extent and effects of such occurences and crimes, and measures necessary for their immediate and long-range prevention and for the preservation of law and order and domestic tranquility within the United States."[17]

In addition to the hearings on "urban riots," there have been extensive hearings on "campus disorder."[18] And hearings by the House

[14] Abe Fortas, *Concerning Dissent and Civil Disobedience* (New York: Signet Books, 1968), p. 124.

[15] *Ibid.*

[16] See Ted Finman and Stewart Macaulay, "Freedom to Dissent: The Vietnam Protests and the Words of Public Officials," *Wisconsin Law Review,* 1966 (Summer, 1966), pp. 1–92.

[17] "Riots, Civil and Criminal Disorders," *Hearings* Before the Permanent Subcommittee on Investigations of the Committee on Government Operations, Part 1, U.S. Senate, 90th Congress (Washington, D.C.: U.S. Government Printing Office, 1967), p. 1.

[18] See *Ibid.*, Parts 16, 23, and 24. Also "Riots, Civil and Criminal Disorders: College Campus Disorders," *Second Interim Report* of the Committee on Government Operations, U.S. Senate (Washington, D.C.: U.S. Government Printing Office, 1971).

Committee on Un-American Activities have attempted to link protest to subversive influences. One hearing, on the disruption of the 1968 Democratic National Convention, began by suggesting:

> The free functioning and security of our democratic institutions are threatened by the activities of subversive organizations and individuals. With adherents within the United States numbering in the thousands, such organizations seek to effect changes in our constitutional system of government by violence and illegal means. Although our system of government provides adequate opportunity for lawful and peaceful change, they have rejected the democratic process and seek to achieve their objectives by means totally inconsistent with our libertarian institutions.[19]

The liberal notions of civil liberties and civil disobedience had ceased to be an issue. Or more to the point, the legal ideology has shown its true purpose: to preserve the capitalist order.

The legal ideology has advanced to the point where citizens are told by representatives of the government that it is time to put an end to civil disobedience. The National Commission on the Causes and Prevention of Violence, in its final report, tells the public that "there is every reason to believe that the lesson taught by much of the current disobedience to law is disastrous from the standpoint of the maintenance of a democratic society." [20] We are then warned that "society" will be seriously injured if civil disobedience is allowed to continue. The Commission concludes:

> We believe that the time has also come for those participating today in the various protest movements, on and off the college campuses, to subject their disobedience to law to realistic appraisal. The question that needs to be put to young people of generous impulses all over the country is whether tactics relying on deliberate, symbolic, and sometimes violent lawbreaking are in fact contributing to the emergence of a society that will show enhanced regard for human values — for equality, decency, and individual volition.[21]

[19] "Subversive Involvement in Disruption of 1968 Democratic Party National Convention," Part 1, *Hearings* Before the Committee on Un-American Activities, U.S. House of Representatives, 90th Congress (Washington, D.C.: U.S. Government Printing Office, 1968), p. 2239.

[20] National Commission on the Causes and Prevention of Violence, *To Establish Justice, To Insure Domestic Tranquility* (New York: Bantam Books, 1970), p. 86.

[21] *Ibid.*, p. 88.

This ideology is a blatant attempt to preserve the existing order. We are told in the ideology of law to suspend any action that might effectively change oppressive conditions.

The modern ideology of law — as a logical extension of earlier liberal precepts — has reached the point where the United States Attorney General can insist that the government has license to protect itself against attack and that this must prevail over citizens' rights. In a 1971 speech devoted to a justification of the legal power to wiretap "dangerous" radical persons without court approval, then Attorney General Mitchell declared that the Fourth Amendment's prohibition of unreasonable searches must be balanced against "the right of the public to protect itself." [22] Conditions are serious enough to justify warrantless wiretapping when individuals are suspected of planning "a violent attack on the existing structure of Government." It is up to the government, of course, to determine who and what is a threat to itself.

In the eulogy at the funeral of J. Edgar Hoover, President Nixon could state that "the trend of permissiveness in this country, a trend which Edgar Hoover fought against all of his life, a trend which has dangerously eroded our national heritage as a law-abiding people, is now being reversed. The American people today are tired of disorder, disruption and disrespect for law." [23] The President added: "America wants to come back to the law as a way of life." The ideology of law had reached its finest hour.

SHAPING PUBLIC OPINION ABOUT CRIME

A crucial element in the ideology of law is the concern about crime itself. When the existing order is in crisis, the emphasis on crime is escalated. And related to the increased use of the criminal sanction by the government at such times is the need to convince the public that its own interests are being endangered. Though citizens may indeed be the victims of criminal acts, the official ideology construes this victimization to be the result of certain forces rather than others, and suggests that action must be taken in particular ways. The official ideology, the one that is to be accepted by the public,

[22] *The New York Times,* April 24, 1971, p. 1.
[23] *The New York Times,* May 5, 1972, p. 15.

stresses and rationalizes the concerns and reactive policies of the ruling class. The public is thereby prevented from developing critiques and solutions that would threaten the existing order. True public consciousness is avoided.

Crime became a major concern in the 1960s, a concern that continues unabated in the 1970s — officially and publicly. One observer of the phenomenon reports:

> Sometime during the 1960's — it is not easy to pin-point just when — crime emerged as a predominant public issue. By the end of the decade, some polls revealed that the public ranked crime as the most serious problem facing our society — above the Vietnam war, race relations, and inflation. Certainly there have been other times in our history when this issue has aroused great anxiety, and this is hardly the first time that politicians have exploited America's chronic apprehension that the moral order is breaking down. Nevertheless, at least in its magnitude, the current reaction to crime is unprecedented.[24]

The problem for us in a critique of legal order is to understand the relation of the increased concern about crime to the social and economic order. It is my contention that public reaction to crime reflects the interests of the ruling class and the government that supports that class. Most studies of public reaction to crime are so tied to the official ideology that they fail to critically understand the public's reaction — and how this reaction is related to official ideology.

The explanations for the sharp rise in public concern about crime are generally of two kinds.[25] According to the first explanation, the concern about crime is an irrational response of the public to the rapid social changes that have supposedly taken place in the past decade. According to the second, the public's reaction to crime is largely justified by the increase in the crime rate. The establishment of the President's Crime Commission in 1965 was justified by these kinds of explanation. And the Crime Commission even subjected the public reaction to study: "A chief reason that this Commission was organized was that there is widespread public anxiety about crime.

[24] Frank F. Furstenberg, Jr., "Public Reaction to Crime in the Streets," *The American Scholar*, 40 (Autumn, 1971), p. 601.
[25] See *Ibid.*, pp. 601–602.

In one sense, this entire report is an effort to focus that anxiety on the central problem of crime and criminal justice. A necessary part of that effort has been to study as carefully as possible the anxiety itself." [26] The President's Crime Commission and the resulting Omnibus Crime bill were also justified — officially — by the public's concern about crime.

The critical understanding of the public's reaction to crime, however, argues that public opinion cannot be separated from the ideology fostered by government officials and members of the ruling class. Public opinion must be seen as the result of official indoctrination and ideological manipulation — by and for those who rule and govern. It is not to be doubted that public concern about crime is widespread and has increased sharply in recent years. National public opinion polls and surveys indicate not only that crime is perceived by the public as one of the most serious domestic problems but that a majority of people are greatly concerned about their personal safety and private property.[27] Moreover, the fear of crime has affected people's lives and has prompted the public to alter their behavior and activities. Most important from the official ideological standpoint, however, are the attitudes that people share regarding the control of crime. It is here that officials would like the public to agree that action is needed and that the policies made and the actions taken deserve popular support. Though the public may be concerned about crime, even independent of official ideology, it is in the action against crime that the officials desire a public opinion that supports government policies. Public opinion must be shaped, if necessary, to rationalize official policies of crime control. With the appropriate public opinion, official policies can be instituted without the appearance of exploiting the public and serving the narrow interests of the ruling class.

Public attitudes toward crime control generally *have* been favorable to the government's war on crime. Although the public attrib-

[26] President's Commission on Law Enforcement and Administration of Justice, *The Challenge of Crime in a Free Society* (Washington, D.C.: U.S. Government Printing Office, 1967), p. 49.

[27] See President's Commission on Law Enforcement and Administration of Justice, "Public Attitudes Toward Crime and Law Enforcement," *Task Force Report: Crime and Its Impact — An Assessment* (Washington, D.C.: U.S. Government Printing Office, 1967), pp. 85–95.

utes an increase in crime to the lowering of moral standards, most persons would depend on the police and similar agencies for controlling crime. And connected with this reliance on law enforcement is the generally positive attitude the public has toward the police. According to opinion polls, most of the public has a high opinion of the work of the police. A poll in 1967 showed that 77 percent of the public had a "great deal" of respect for the police, 17 percent had "some" respect, and only 4 percent had "hardly any" respect.[28] Similarly, the national survey in 1965 by the National Opinion Research Center showed that 67 percent of the persons interviewed thought that the police were doing a good to excellent job of enforcing the law.[29]

In spite of some criticism, there is a general public reliance on the police for the control of crime. Associated with this acceptance is the public's willingness to permit the police considerable range in their efforts to control crime. A majority (73 percent) of those interviewed in Washington, D.C. agreed that the police have the right to act tough when they deem it necessary.[30] More than half (56 percent) thought that there should be more use of police dogs. In the national survey, 52 percent of the respondents believed that the police should have more power, and 42 percent believed that police should risk arresting an innocent person rather than risk missing an offender.[31]

Another indication that the public believes that repressive measures, rather than changes in social conditions, are the most effective means of controlling crime is found in attitudes about court actions. A Gallup survey poll in 1969 found that 75 percent of adults believe

[28] George Gallup, "U.S. Public Gives Police Big Vote of Confidence," *The Gallup Report* (Princeton, N.J.: American Institute of Public Opinion, August 30, 1967).
[29] Phillip H. Ennis, *Criminalization in the United States: A Report of a National Survey*, President's Commission on Law Enforcement and Administration of Justice, Field Survey II (Washington, D.C.: U.S. Government Printing Office, 1967), pp. 52–72.
[30] Albert D. Biderman, Louise A. Johnson, Jennie McIntyre, and Adrianne W. Weis, *Report on a Pilot Study in the District of Columbia on Victimization and Attitudes Toward Law Enforcement*, President's Commission on Law Enforcement and Administration of Justice, Field Survey I (Washington, D.C.: U.S. Government Printing Office, 1967), pp. 144–149.
[31] Ennis, *Criminalization in the United States*, pp. 58–60.

that the courts do not deal harshly enough with criminals.[32] (The figure had changed considerably since 1965, at which time 48 percent had said that the courts were not dealing harshly enough with criminals.) Only 2 percent in 1969 said that the courts in their area deal "too harshly" with criminals, whereas 13 percent agreed that the treatment by the courts is "about right." Further evidence of the public's desire to crack down on crime was indicated when 58 percent of the respondents agreed that it was a good idea to give a double sentence to anyone who commits a crime with a gun. Similarly, 71 percent of the sample believed that it is a good idea to deny parole to a person convicted of crime a second time.

That the public would deal severely with offenders is again indicated in a national survey which asked a sample of the public the best way of dealing with an adult convicted of a specific crime.[33] The alternative sentences, from a list of seven crimes ranging from embezzlement to murder, were probation, a short prison sentence with parole, or a long prison sentence. The use of probation found little favor with the public. Considering each of the crimes, only about a quarter of the respondents felt that probation was an appropriate sentence. Only for prostitution, judged more harshly by women than men, did as much as 26 percent of the public feel that probation should be used.

There is no need to continue citing these polls and surveys of public attitudes toward crime and crime control. What I am contending is that these findings have to be placed in the context of the official ideology of law, including the ideology regarding crime and crime control. What is striking is the correspondence between public opinion and official ideology and policy. But rather than follow the traditional assumption that official policy reflects public opinion, I am suggesting that officials use public opinion for their own advantage and that, at the same time, government officials and members of the ruling class manipulate public opinion to suit the policies they are establishing. At this point in time it is to be expected that public opinion and official ideology will be the same. A critical public in-

[32] *The New York Times*, February 16, 1969, p. 47.
[33] Louis Harris and Associates, *The Public Looks at Crime and Corrections* (Washington, D.C.: Joint Commission on Correctional Manpower and Training, 1968), pp. 11–12.

telligence would spell a different attitude and approach toward crime and criminal justice.

Public opinion about crime is conventionally thought to be a major force in determining criminal policy, but given the nature of power and economics in America the opposite is closer to the truth. It is criminal policy and official ideology that shape public opinion about crime. This is also to say that public opinion is shaped by government officials and members of the ruling class. Public attitudes about law and order are influenced greatly by the statements and actions of the President, the Attorney General, the Director of the FBI, the Administrator of LEAA, executives of large corporations, Congressmen, local officials, lawyers of the American Bar Association, members of government commissions, and so on. The public, because of the support an authoritarian political system demands, is ready to follow the words and deeds of government officials and successful professional men and businessmen. Whenever "responsible" leaders utter conclusions and formulate policies we are expected to follow. Such is the force of modern government and such is the way in which public opinion is formed.

And if public opinion should give way, that is, if it should no longer conform to government policies, the government would nevertheless continue to carry out its program. This in the end shows public opinion to be a mere facade for state and ruling class interests. Kolko writes in this regard:

> We must confront anew the meaning of the concept of consensus or public opinion and the way it operates in the policy process. On one hand the seemingly shared beliefs, values, and consensus in society appear more critical than any single interest. But the fact that a ruling class makes its policies operate even when the mass of society ceases to endorse them, and that the voluntaristic and occasionally enforced social goals benefit individuals rather than all of society, is a central reality most analysts perpetually exclude from a descriptive explanation of American society.[34]

And official policy continues even when public consensus withers away.

> That the voluntaristic basis of consensus usually justifies the actions of the men of power is less consequential than that, as we see

[34] Kolko, *The Roots of American Foreign Policy*, pp. xii–xiii.

154

today in the case of the American public and Vietnam, the policy continues when mass agreement withers away and even disappears. For consensus is identifiable with class goals and needs, suitably wrapped in a vague ideology of American nationalism and its global responsibility. These class goals and interests prevail even when the consensus disappears, and it is at this very point we see that administrators base policy on the control of power and interests rather than society's sanction or consent.[35]

Public opinion is thus based on the ideological hegemony of the power elite — on the ideology of the small but ruling element of society. The ruling class determines how we think as well as how we are governed. All of this to serve the predominant interests of the minority, but ruling class. Until we create a critical imagination, to be shared by all, public opinion about crime can be little more than a reflection of the official ideology of legal order.

MASS MEDIA IN THE TRANSMISSION OF OFFICIAL IDEOLOGY

How does the official ideology of legal order get translated into public opinion? Most persons at some time directly experience the force of that ideology, but there are more subtle and continuous ways of transmitting it. The most important means in an advanced technological society is by mass communications. Each day the citizenry is presented with messages from the various media of mass communications. Images of law and order, or simply portrayals of the nature of the "real" America, are presented daily in the newspapers, on the radio, in books and magazines, and on the television screen. Whether the format is "entertainment," news broadcasts and articles, or statements by government officials and community leaders, a message is conveyed regarding the official reality. A world is presented for us to believe in.

This is not to argue simply that the ruling class dictates the substance of social reality in the media of mass communications. Indeed, in modern capitalist countries communications are not the official mouthpiece of the state; a diversity of views is presented, even in opposition to the interests of government and the ruling class. Yet in spite of the diversity, a general reality is being con-

[35] *Ibid.*, p. xiii.

veyed; in spite of a certain freedom of expression the existing order is being legitimated.

The importance and value of this freedom and opportunity of expression is not to be underestimated. Yet the notion of pluralist diversity and competitive equilibrium is, here as in every other field, rather superficial and misleading. For the agencies of communication and notably the mass media are, in reality, and the expression of dissident views notwithstanding, a crucial element in the legitimation of capitalist society. Freedom of expression is not thereby rendered meaningless. But that freedom has to be set in the real economic and political context of these societies; and in that context the free expression of ideas and opinions *mainly* means the free expression of ideas and opinions which are helpful to the prevailing system of power and privilege.[36]

Although the media are not explicitly engaged in the transmission of an official ideology, that ideology is nevertheless portrayed to the exclusion of alternative realities. There may be a variety of viewpoints, and controversies may be presented, but the general framework of the prevailing system serves as the boundary of expression. Hence, "the fact remains that the mass media in advanced capitalist societies are mainly intended to perform a highly 'functional' role; they too are both the expression of a system of domination, and a means of reinforcing it." [37]

The media presentations relating to crime, whether as fiction or reality, are based on a general acceptance of the prevailing social and economic order. And on such a basis the portrayals of crime and crime-fighting inevitably adhere to the existing legal system and the necessity of controlling crime. Crime is viewed in the media as a threat to the American way of life, and the right of the state to intervene in controlling crime is presented as the only legitimate reality. This is the ideology presented by officials when they appear in the media, and this is the message in the fictional accounts of crime and the law.

The content of the mass media must therefore be understood in reference to the underlying ideology and the presentation of a particular reality. The criticism usually made of the media concerns

[36] Miliband, *The State in Capitalist Society*, p. 220.
[37] *Ibid.*, p. 221.

156

such things as the cultural level of programming, commercialism, excessive violence, and the like. And the indictment is justified. "But that indictment also tends, very often, to understate or to ignore the specific ideological content of these productions and the degree to which they are used as propaganda vehicles for a particular view of the world." [38] The specific ideological content of mass media portrayals of crime is shown, for example, in popular detective fiction:

> Furthermore, it is worth noting that much of the "message" of the mass media is not diffuse but quite specific. It would of course be ridiculous to think of such authors as Mickey Spillane and Ian Fleming (to take two writers whose sales have been astronomical) as political writers in any true sense. But it would also be silly to overlook the fact that their heroes are paragons of anti-Communist virtues and that their adventures, including their sexual adventures, are more often than not set in the context of a desperate struggle against subversive forces, both alien and home-grown. As has been said about the anti-communism of the Spillane output, "it is woven into the texture of assumptions of the novel. Anyone who thinks otherwise is taken to be either treasonable or hopelessly naive." This kind of crude "ideology for the masses" does not permeate the whole field of "mass culture"; but it permeates a substantial part of it in most media. Nor of course is the rest of "mass culture" much permeated by counter-ideological material. There are not, on the whole, many left-wing and revolutionary equivalents of James Bond. It may be that the *genre* does not lend itself to it; and the political climate of advanced capitalist societies certainly does not.[39]

How crime is to be fought — and the fact that it is necessary to fight crime — is clearly portrayed in a variety of media presentations. The portrayals are strikingly similar, however, whether presented in the form of Dick Tracy and Superman cartoons, the Lone Ranger and the Green Hornet on the radio, or the latest detective series on TV. Crime is to be "stamped out"; crime-fighters pursue crime impersonally and with anonymity; methods and techniques beyond the law are used, including secret decoder rings, electronic devices, entrapment, and murder — anything that gets results; and the world is divided into "good guys" and "bad guys." Being raised on the games of Cops and Robbers, or Cowboys and Indians, we all

[38] *Ibid.*, p. 226.
[39] *Ibid.*, pp. 226–227.

are prepared to be on the side of law and order. It is the "white hat" rather than the "black hat" that we must wear. The "forces of evil" are to be wiped out, and good is to win over the bad. No wonder that we grow up seeking solutions to problems through law and order, looking to the FBI and LEAA.

The media have been effective in disseminating a particular view of crime and control. Beginning in the 1920s, with cartoons and radio, definite themes regarding the world of crime began to be presented to the American public. A new American hero, continuing to this day, presented the public with specific themes:

A new breed of American heroes — SUPER crime-fighters — was inked on drawing boards and a tradition was born. As these new heroes were created and continued in the media — the comic strips, the comic ("funny") books, radio, television and the wide screen of the neighborhood threatre — several themes emerged about the nature of the crime problem, the crime-fighters and the criminals.

These themes have been generally consistent over time and in the various media and may have produced a "Dick Tracy mentality" in the minds of our citizenry.

The "Dick Tracy mentality" — born in frustration — includes the following concepts:

1. The crime-fighter is no mere mortal, but rather a SUPER crime-fighter.
2. The criminal is distinctive, unique, readily identifiable, and different.
3. The best way to stamp out crime is through the use of gimmicks and hardware.
4. Good always triumphs over evil; crime does not pay.
5. Members of ethnic minorities may fight crime, but only in a supporting role.
6. Violence is central to the crime problem.
7. Uniforms, costumes and masks provide the crime-fighter with anonymity and identity, and conceal any emotional involvement in crime-fighting.
8. Operating outside the law is appropriate in dealing with major crimes and criminals.
9. There are two kinds of people in society — good guys and bad.[40]

[40] Robert M. Carter, "Where Have All the Crime-Fighters Gone?" *Gunsmoke Gazette*, 1 (January–February, 1972), p. 9.

When media content has been subjected to systematic investigation, the findings have consistently shown a uniform presentation of crime and its control. As the Violence Commission found, in one of the research investigations for which it contracted, drama presentations on television constitute a world of violence — over 80 percent of all programs analyzed in the study contained some form of violence.[41] However, violence occurred most often in the programs with a crime-western-action adventure story. And not surprisingly, the collision of the forces of law and lawlessness made up one-fourth of the total of television drama. High proportions of violent acts were committed by and against both criminals and agents of the law. Eighty-two percent of the criminals and 80 percent of the lawmen were engaged in some violence. In other words, when crime was featured, the programs nearly always involved violence. And the violence by the agents of the law was usually portrayed as being justified.

The message for the TV viewer is that crime is commonplace and that it must be fought even with violence itself. That most crime in the real world does not involve violence is ignored, and a reality is portrayed that is quite the opposite. But since crime is presented as being violent and of great danger to the social order, the viewer is expected to believe in the worthiness of the lawmen's cause. Crime, like the enemy, is to be fought in any way.

News coverage on television presents its own version of reality, not so much different from that of TV drama programs. When the Violence Commission turned its attention to news coverage, the question of government influence on the media was specifically raised. The ideal for the media has always been the libertarian belief in the right of free expression unfettered by government intervention. "Objective journalism" is the goal, with a "balancing" of viewpoints. The media industry projects the ideology that diversity is being achieved, primarily because of its own professionalism and its attempt to maintain "independence and integrity" from government control.

Professional pride and morale, high standards of performance, and maintenance of the public interest — all are dependent on con-

[41] National Commission on the Causes and Prevention of Violence, *Violence and the Media* (Washington, D.C.: U.S. Government Printing Office, 1969), pp. 311–339.

tinuing diversity in the channels of expression. Where the pressure for improvement comes through the channels of government, there is an inevitable threat to independence and integrity and thus to professionalism, high standards, and the public interest. Herein lies the dilemma which must be faced in any effort to raise the level of the mass media and thus to improve the quality of life in America.[42]

What this argument totally neglects to tell the pubic is that as long as the media are in the hands of corporate power, removed from those who receive their communications (the public), government regulation and interference have little meaning. As long as communications are controlled by corporate power and journalists are supported by business interests, recommendations that suggest a "balanced coverage" still result in media presentations that fall well within the official reality. The way the media are controlled is in large part the message; the substance of the media establishes one reality rather than another.

As a major American industry, the mass media are not separate from the interests of the state and the ruling class. The mass media industry, in fact, is a solid part of the business and government establishment. Media have, as the Violence Commission euphemistically put it, "an economic base."

> Media, like other social institutions, cannot exist without an economic base, and accordingly are big business in the United States. Daily newspapers are a $7-billion-a-year industry, of which about $5 billion is from advertisers' investments and $2 billion is the direct revenue from the public. Television is supported by $3 billion a year which is paid by advertisers for time and production. Radio yearly draws $1 billion. Magazines are a $2.5 billion industry, with $1.3 billion accounted for by advertising. Book publishing grosses $2.4 billion and motion picture theaters $1.8 billion each year.[43]

Thus there are concrete influences which make the media industry protectors of the status quo.[44] As partners with government and the rest of the corporate business world, the mass media inevitably must

[42] *Ibid.*, p. 184.
[43] *Ibid.*, p. 169.
[44] These influences are discussed in Miliband, *The State in Capitalist Society*, pp. 227–235.

present an ideology that supports and preserves the established system. Being capitalist enterprises, the mass media are bound by the same contingencies as other corporations. The failure of the capitalist system would also mean the end of the mass media industry. Those who own and control the mass media are therefore in ideological agreement with the rest of the ruling class. And this ideology is ultimately presented to the public in network programming.

Just as important as the ownership and control of the mass media in assuring ideological hegemony is the way in which the media are supported — by advertisers. Advertisers, themselves members of the capitalist ruling class, exercise a strong influence over the content of the mass media. And the influence need not be direct:

> The direct political influence of large advertisers upon the commercial media need not be exaggerated. It is only occasionally that such advertisers are able, or probably even try, to dictate the contents and policies of the media of which they are the customers. But their custom is nevertheless of crucial importance to the financial viability, which means the existence, of newspapers and, in some but not all instances, of magazines, commercial radio and television. That fact may do no more than *enhance* a general disposition on the part of these media to show exceptional care in dealing with such powerful and valuable interests. But that is useful too, since it provides a further assurance to business interests in general that they will be treated with sympathetic understanding, and that the "business community" will, at the least, be accorded a degree of indulgence which is seldom if ever displayed towards the labour interest and trade unions: *their* displeasure is a matter of no consequence at all.[45]

Advertising revenue from the large corporations of the capitalist system suggests a favorable portrayal of the world that supports this system.

Finally, there is the pressure that the government, in its own ways, exerts on the media. The government and its agencies "now make it their business, ever more elaborately and systematically, to supply newspapers, radio and television with explanations of official policy which naturally have an apologetic and tendentious character. . . .

[45] *Ibid.*, p. 231.

The state, in other words, now goes in more and more for 'news management,' particularly in times of stress and crisis, which means, for most leading capitalist countries, almost permanently; and the greater the crisis, the more purposeful the management, the evasions, the half-truths and the plain lies." [46]

What all of this means is that the mass media contain an ideology that supports the capitalist system. The media, as an integral part of the capitalist system, effectively present us with an ideology of law that serves to enforce the existing order. Daily a social reality of law and order is constructed for us, according to the interests of the ruling class.

TRANSCENDING THE OFFICIAL IDEOLOGY

Modern American society, then, is not free from ideology. Contrary to much conventional wisdom, an ideology not only exists but is extremely important in promoting existing social and economic arrangements. The American capitalist system is, in fact, dependent upon this ideology. It is another, albeit the most subtle, means of controlling the social order — in this case, through controlling the minds of people. An ideology, reinforced daily in mass communications, serves the ruling class in dominating the minds and lives of the subordinate classes.

An important part of this ideology is the belief that law is the most appropriate (and the only) means for establishing an order that is good for all of us. Crime control, that is, the preservation of domestic order, is supposedly for the "public interest." The ideology of law is made more palatable to us by the inclusion of a rhetoric on civil liberties. That we are often granted due process before the law is supposedly enough to warrant our allegiance to the capitalist legal system. Even when we are given the right of civil disobedience, we are nevertheless expected to accept the punishment for transgressing the law. And when civil disobedience becomes too great a threat to the established order, it too must cease. All of this for the purpose of preserving "the society."

Only a new consciousness will free the subordinate classes from

46 *Ibid.*, p. 232.

162

the hold of the ruling class. As long as our minds and our lives are dominated by the official ideology, we are not free to create a new existence. A critical philosophy is the beginning of a new life. An alternative existence is possible when we allow ourselves to transcend the official ideology and its imposed reality.

6
Toward a Socialist Society

What is to be done? As I have argued and shown with supporting evidence, American society is coercively bound by a legal order that benefits only a portion of the society — the capitalist ruling class. The existing legal system can do little more than assure the perpetuation of the capitalist order. That we have looked to the capitalist legal system for the creation of a better world, as well as the attainment of basic human rights, reflects the lack of a critical intelligence. We must now begin to think about an alternative existence. Our goal is a world that is free from the oppressions produced by capitalism. We must go beyond the existing society — with its supporting legal system — in the search for a better society. It is to a society based on socialist principles that we turn. Notions about crime and law that follow from this alternative conception of society are considerably different from capitalist thinking about legal order. And in the process of such critical thought, we create lives in which our ideas and our actions become one. Theory and practice are united in creating a new existence.

THE CONTRADICTIONS OF CAPITALISM

Marxian theory, in contrast to classical economic thought, views capitalism as a dynamic process, capable of profound transformations.[1] Marx himself thought that as capitalism advances to a modern industrial technology a revolution is inevitable. Technology would become revolutionary, he suggested, changing continuously and rapidly to accommodate to its own advances. But moreover, advanced capitalism could engender a revolution by those who continued to be oppressed by the capitalist mode of production. Under the current conditions, the oppressed workers have the potential of making a revolution that will overthrow the existing capitalist relations. Given these objective conditions, and a revolutionary consciousness on the part of those forced to make a living by giving their time to capitalist production, a revolution will take place.

That capitalism is a dynamic process, subject both to change and resistance, is our starting point in a discussion of an alternative to the existing order. As I have argued throughout, law in capitalist societies is a means of controlling threats to that system from those who are oppressed by it. Dynamic forces within capitalist society assure that change will take place, changes that will benefit mainly the owners, managers, and servants of capitalism. Any changes or resistance from those whom capitalism must continue to subordinate have to be dealt with by means of the coercive and violent force of the state, ultimately through the machinery of the criminal law.

An essential aspect of the dynamic of capitalism is the production of forces that are at the same time destructive of the advances of capitalism. There is, in other words, a dialectic in the development of capitalism. For every advance in capitalism there is also generated a force that opposes this advance. This is what is meant by the *contradictions* of capitalism. "A contradiction of capitalism results when the very process of capitalist development produces simultaneously the conditions needed to transform it fundamentally; that is, when the successes of capitalist development create situations which are fundamentally antagonistic to capitalism itself. Contradictions tend to intensify with time and cannot be resolved within the exist-

---

[1] See Paul M. Sweezy, *Modern Capitalism and Other Essays* (New York: Monthly Review Press, 1972), pp. 127–146.

ing social framework." [2] It is in the contradictions of capitalism that we find the basis for the creation of a new society.

Although capitalism, as Marx first observed, has the potential of liberating human life, in order to expand and survive it also generates forces that lead to its own self-destruction.[3] As capitalism advances, a majority of the people must be exploited in various ways, particularly in being forced to engage in alienating wage and salary work so that the propertied class can profit from their labor. Furthermore, as capitalism advances, dehumanizing needs must be developed in the individual to assure the sale of the goods that other workers are producing in the course of their alienated labor. Commodity consumption, in turn, can bring about its own demise, as individuals realize the true nature of their being:

> In the developed world, where modern capitalism has delivered a wealth of material goods, it has sought to define well-being in terms of individual commodity consumption. But with continued economic growth, the desirability of more individual material consumption fades in comparison to other dimensions of well-being, such as the availability of creative and socially useful work, meaningful community, and liberating education for individual development. Yet, because capitalism must constantly expand, the realization of these needs is incompatible with capitalist relations of production. Instead, capitalist economic growth deepens the alienation of work and community, and poisons the environment, and commercializes all social relationships. People increasingly recognize that well-being consists of more than the individual acquisition and consumption of commodities, and that capitalism cannot meet their felt needs.[4]

On the basis of these fundamental contradictions, as well as many others, the inevitable conclusion is that capitalist society is based on destruction — destruction of the lives of most people as well as its own destruction. The further development of the United States within the capitalist framework can only mean further destruction. In order for the capitalist system to continuously expand, various forms of oppression must be maintained. Capitalism can survive

[2] Richard C. Edwards, Michael Reich, and Thomas E. Weisskopf, *The Capitalist System: A Radical Analysis of American Society* (Englewood Cliffs, N.J.: Prentice-Hall, 1972), p. 462.
[3] Karl Marx, *The Grundrisse,* trans. David McLellan (New York: Harper & Row, 1971), pp. 94–95.
[4] Edwards, Reich, and Weisskopf, *The Capitalist System,* p. 463.

167

only by promoting further inequality, alienation, racism, irrationality of human wants, imperialism, and so on. And according to the argument I have been presenting, crime will continue as long as capitalism exists.

Criminal law with all of its repressive apparatus will have to be used against those who are oppressed by the capitalist system and against those who attempt to remove that oppression. The legal order — as a system of maintaining authority and control in capitalist society — stands ready to suppress any challenges to the capitalist system that cannot be handled by other means of manipulation and control. Capitalism has produced crime as we know it today in America; and it is capitalism that will assure the continuation of the crime problem. To remove the sources of oppression that result in crime, and to dismantle the apparatus that coerces and defines the oppressed as criminal, would be to destroy the capitalist system.

The contradictions of capitalism provide us with the basis for a new future. As the contradictions increase, as capitalism fails to solve the human problems it creates, and as people become aware of these contradictions, we will move to a radically different society. And in the course of this change, the capitalist ruling class (as the privileged and exploiting class) will not give up easily — it has too much to lose. It will continue to mystify our current reality. Not being able to resolve the contradictions of advanced capitalism, the ruling class will resort to any means necessary in the attempt to preserve the system. The repression of legal order will be pushed to its ultimate extremes. Crime will increase as a political phenomenon — as the struggle of the oppressed and as the reaction of the oppressor.

Any critique of law and crime, therefore, has to cope with the transformations and contradictions of advanced capitalism. And in the course of understanding the existing order, we will demystify that which promotes oppression, including the capitalist legal order itself. Finally, we must envision and promote the new society that will emerge in this struggle.

REFORM AS ADAPTIVE MECHANISM

The capitalist system responds to its own contradictions by formulating liberal reforms. These reforms never go beyond the interests of the capitalist system itself; they merely update the existing institutions in order to assure the survival of the system. Reform is the adaptive mechanism of advanced capitalism.

In its modern version reform emerged most dramatically at the beginning of this century in the United States. During the Progressive Era, American capitalism moved from laissez-faire individualism to corporate liberalism.[5] In order to assure the continuing expansion of large corporations, the government intervened in the economy; the state became an apparatus for the promotion of a corporate capitalist system. From then on, reforms consisted of state intervention in the social and economic structure of the country. In spite of conventional wisdom, liberalism in the twentieth century has been an ideology and a means of securing the capitalist order.

Corporate liberalism, with its reforms, has been dominant in the United States since the Progressive Era. The New Deal of Franklin D. Roosevelt was only a further refinement of the corporate ideal in the liberal state. Large business secured its hold over the social and economic order of the nation by the many reforms instituted during the years of the New Deal. Further support was given to corporate capitalism with the economic expansion stimulated by World War II, and subsequently by the Cold War that continued into the 1950s. The Great Society programs (including the "war on poverty") of the Johnson administration continued to protect and promote corporate capitalism through national planning and control. Every recent administration, whether Republican or Democratic, has sought to advance the capitalist system.

Thus, for over half a century the American capitalist system has been able to survive by instituting liberal reforms, as adjustments to the contradictions of capitalism, and has been supported during crucial periods by the markets created either by world wars or by United States military intervention abroad, as in Southeast Asia. In the meantime domestic conditions continue to deteriorate — inequality prevails, crime increases, racism continues, and unemployment remains a problem. From a critical perspective — which also means contrary to the official ideology — nothing else could be expected.

[5] See especially Gabriel Kolko, *The Triumph of Conservatism: A Reinterpretation of American History, 1900–1916* (Chicago: Quadrangle Books, 1967); and James Weinstein, *The Corporate Ideal in the Liberal State: 1900–1918* (Boston: Beacon Press, 1968).

The assumption that it is possible within capitalism to reallocate resources domestically according to social rather than market criteria and on a scale adequate to meet the cumulative social crisis has no foundation in reality. For it is belied by the whole historical experience of capitalist societies and runs counter to the logic of the system itself. Historically, the capitalist state, whether under the formal rule of social democratic radicals or tory conservatives, has never marshaled the funds necessary to even begin a genuine social reconstruction. War and preparation for war have proved the only vast expenditure programs (proportionate to calculated need) that capitalist states have been willing or able to undertake.[6]

Capitalism itself is the problem. Liberal reforms, therefore, can do little more than support the capitalist system, which is also to say that the capitalist problem (and its associated forms of exploitation) cannot be solved within the liberal reformist framework. The liberal state is an integral part of the problem; it is a device for holding down the oppressed classes while at the same time promoting the interests of the capitalist ruling class.

A critical philosophy allows us to uncover another mystification of the liberal state, the myth that law serves the interests of all the people. By believing the "rule of law" ideology, and falling for the related myth that we are "ruled by law not men," we are to assume that the state and its legal system exist for the protection of us all. What is being protected, instead, is the capitalist system — and the class that profits from it. With a critical understanding of the American legal order, however, we know that any legal reforms are inevitably for the further support of the capitalist order. Certainly there have been no reforms in criminal justice that would threaten capitalism. Liberal reforms, by interest and definition, always fall far short of a socialist solution to the problems created by capitalism.

CRIMINAL JUSTICE REFORMS

Continual reform of the criminal justice system has been necessary in this century as new contradictions have arisen in advanced

---

[6] David Horowitz, *Empire and Revolution: A Radical Interpretation of Contemporary History* (New York: Random House, 1969), p. 250.

capitalism. These liberal reforms can be viewed as adaptations of the legal system to the changing needs of capitalism. Thus, businessmen, including the corporate owners and managers, have been instrumental in promoting these legal reforms.

Yet, the day-to-day work of reform has been undertaken by middle-class urban reformers, professionals, and special interest groups. These reformers have not simply been the lackeys of big business. Most have been sincerely interested in relieving human misery and creating a just existence.[7] Nevertheless, most reforms have accepted (and continue to accept) the structure of the capitalist system, seeking to moderate some of its inequities and inconsistencies. What reformers fail to do is question the basic assumptions of the existing system. Because of this failure, reformers and their reforms continue to provide programs that maintain and increase the efficiency of the existing order. This is nowhere more apparent than in the reforms relating to the criminal justice system.

The recommendations of the President's Commission on Law Enforcement and Administration of Justice provide the most recent reformist thinking on crime in American society. The President's Commission was established to find a rationale and procedures for maintaining domestic order when the existing structure of American society was being threatened from within. The Commission served the purpose of the capitalist state and its ruling class, and, as can be expected, its recommendations promoted this purpose.

The President's Crime Commission, in addition to its ruling class commissioners, consisted of a staff of 63 members, 175 consultants, and hundreds of advisers, including social scientists. In spite of the broad range of backgrounds and opinions, the personnel agreed upon 200 specific recommendations — "concrete steps the Commission believes can lead to a safer and more just society." "Basic changes" were called for, not in the capitalist system itself, of course, but in the operations of the police, schools, prosecutors, employment agencies, social workers, and probation and parole officers. The Commission concluded, in its final report, that a significant reduc-

---

[7] Anthony Platt, "The Triumph of Benevolence: The Origins of the Juvenile Justice System in the United States," in Richard Quinney (ed.), *Criminal Justice in America: A Critical Understanding* (Boston: Little, Brown and Company, 1974).

tion in crime is possible if the following objectives are vigorously pursued:

First, society must seek to prevent crime before it happens by assuring all Americans a stake in the benefits and responsibilities of American life, by strengthening law enforcement, and by reducing criminal opportunities.

Second, society's aim of reducing crime would be better served if the system of criminal justice developed a far broader range of techniques with which to deal with individual offenders.

Third, the system of criminal justice must eliminate existing injustices if it is to achieve its ideals and win the respect and cooperation of all citizens.

Fourth, the system of criminal justice must attract more people and better people — police, prosecutors, judges, defense attorneys, probation and parole officers, and corrections officials with more knowledge, expertise, initiative, and integrity.

Fifth, there must be much more operational and basic research into the problems of crime and criminal administration, by those both within and without the system of criminal justice.

Sixth, the police, courts, and correctional agencies must be given substantially greater amounts of money if they are to improve their ability to control crime.

Seventh, individual citizens, civic and business organizations, religious institutions and all levels of government must take responsibility for planning and implementing the changes that must be made in the criminal justice system if crime is to be reduced.[8]

The President's Crime Commission then went on to make specific recommendations. Nothing in these recommendations, regarding the police and the courts, suggests anything that would alter the existing capitalist system. The recommended changes, rather, would make the existing system more efficient, while holding out the promise of just treatment for those who threaten the system.

In particular, regarding the police "in a free society," the Commission observed the following before making its specific recommendations:

Widespread improvement in the strength and caliber of police

[8] President's Commission on Law Enforcement and Administration of Justice, *The Challenge of Crime in a Free Society* (Washington, D.C.: U.S. Government Printing Office, 1967), p. vi.

172

manpower, supported by a radical revision of personnel practices, are the basic essentials for achieving more effective and fairer law enforcement. Educational requirements should be raised to college levels and training programs improved. Recruitment and promotion should be modernized to reflect education, personality, and assessment of performance. The traditional, monolithic personnel structure must be broken up into three entry levels of varying responsibility and with different personnel requirements, and lateral entry into advanced positions encouraged.

The need is urgent for the police to improve relations with the poor, minority groups, and juveniles. The establishment of strong community relations programs, review of all procedures in light of their effect on community relations, recruitment of more minority group members, and strengthening of community confidence in supervision and discipline, all aim at making the police more effective in high-crime areas. Increased effectiveness also requires that law enforcement improve its facilities and techniques of management — particularly that it utilize manpower more efficiently, modernize communications and records, and formulate more explicit policy guidelines governing areas of police discretion. The pooling of services and functions by police forces in each metropolitan area can improve efficiency and effectiveness.[9]

Thirty-five recommendations were then made:[10]

Community Relations

Establish community relations units in departments serving substantial minority population.

Establish citizen advisory committees in minority-group neighborhoods.

Recruit more minority-group officers.

Emphasize community relations in training and operations.

Provide adequate procedures for processing citizen grievances against all public officials.

Personnel

Divide functions and personnel entry and promotion lines among three kinds of officers.

Assess manpower needs and provide more personnel if required.

[9] *Ibid.*, pp. 294–295. Also see the specific task force report, President's Commission on Law Enforcement and Administration of Justice, *The Police* (Washington, D.C.: U.S. Government Printing Office, 1967).
[10] *Ibid.*, p. 295.

Recruit more actively, especially on college campuses and in inner cities.

Increase police salaries, especially maximums, to competitive levels.

Consider police salaries apart from those of other municipal departments.

Set as goal requirement of baccalaureate degree for general enforcement officers.

Require immediately baccalaureate degrees for supervisory positions.

Improve screening of candidates to determine character and fitness.

Modify inflexible physical, age, and residence recruitment requirements.

Stress ability in promotion.

Encourage lateral entry to specialist and supervisory positions.

Require minimum of 400 hours of training.

Improve training methods and broaden coverage of nontechnical background subjects.

Require 1-week yearly minimum of intensive inservice training and encourage continued education.

Require 12–18 months' probation and evaluation of recruits.

Establish police standards commissions.

Organization and Operations

Develop and enunciate policy guidelines for exercise of law enforcement discretion.

Clarify by statute authority of police to stop persons for questioning.

Include police formally in community planning.

Provide State assistance for management surveys.

Employ legal advisers.

Strengthen central staff control.

Create administrative boards of key ranking personnel in larger departments.

Establish strong internal investigation units in all departments to maintain police integrity.

Experiment with team policing combining patrol and investigative duties.

Adopt policy limiting use of firearms by officers.

Pooling of Resources and Services

Provide areawide communications and records coordination.

Pool and coordinate crime laboratories.

Assist smaller departments in major investigations.

Explore pooling or consolidation of law enforcement in all counties or metropolitan areas.

174

Again, there is nothing in these reforms that attacks the existing social and economic arrangements in American society.

The same reformist suggestions regarding the police are made by social scientists when they speak in their own behalf. Rather than questioning the existence of the law enforcement institution in the capitalist state, most social scientists offer measures that would strengthen the police and increase their ability to perform. Suggestions are made in respect to improving recruitment and training, increasing the size of police departments, better deployment of police forces, and changing the public image of the police. The police functions will be enhanced, we are told, by improving community-police relations.[11] What is actually being advocated is further manipulation of the public consciousness so that the police can more effectively fulfill their function of preserving domestic order.

What we are not offered in these recommendations is a change that would get to the basis of criminal justice in a capitalist society. Such current suggestions among social scientists as the development of a "professional" orientation among policemen (with respect for the rule of law), the creation of "civility in police relations with citizens," or making the criminal justice system more "accountable," do not alter the basic purpose of the criminal justice system.[12] Proposals that would go beyond reform of criminal justice would threaten the dominant social and economic system; proposals within the reformist framework have no intention of doing that.

The court system is subject to the same kinds of reform offered for law enforcement. The President's Crime Commission, paralleling its recommendations for the police, made the following proposals:

A number of important reforms are necessary to enable courts to operate with the dignity and effectiveness many now lack. Substan-

[11] See the essays, especially the one by James Q. Wilson, in Robert F. Steadman (ed.), *The Police and the Community* (Baltimore: Johns Hopkins University Press, 1972).

[12] Jerome H. Skolnick, *Justice Without Trial: Law Enforcement in Democratic Society* (New York: John Wiley & Sons, 1966), pp. 230–245; Egon Bittner, *The Functions of the Police in Modern Society*, National Institute of Mental Health Monograph (Washington, D.C.: U.S. Government Printing Office, 1970), pp. 114–122; Albert J. Reiss, Jr., *The Police and the Public* (New Haven: Yale University Press, 1971), pp. 173–221; Marvin E. Wolfgang, "Making the Criminal Justice System Accountable," *Crime and Delinquency*, 18 (January, 1972), pp. 15–22.

175

tial changes in the processing of criminal cases and increases in the number and caliber of judges, lawyers and administrators are essential to fairer and more effective justice. To rationalize procedures in the crucial and often neglected pretrial stage, bail practices must be reformed; guilty plea negotiation regularized; and discovery expanded. Early diversion of appropriate cases to noncriminal treatment should be encouraged. Sentencing reforms — such as revision of criminal codes, improved fact-gathering, sentencing councils and institutes for judges — are needed to promote consistent and informed decisions.

The right of defendants to counsel must be extended and defense counsel's role broadened. Improvements must be made in the methods used to select, compensate, and educate counsel. Better procedures are needed to remove judges from political influence and supervise their performance. Several Commission recommendations are aimed at strengthening prosecutors' offices, and encouraging better formation of policy guidelines and procedures for the exercise of discretion. State governments should take a more vigorous role in coordinating local prosecution through stronger State attorneys general and the creation of State councils of prosecutors.

Court structures should be reformed to unify felony and misdemeanor courts, overhaul or abolish the justice of the peace system, and provide firm, central administrative responsibility within the courts. The procedures used by the courts to monitor and schedule their work should be modernized and professional talent brought to the administration of courts.[13]

Thirty-eight specific recommendations were then made and discussed in the report. The recommendations are listed as follows:[14]

The Lower Courts

Unify felony and misdemeanor courts.

Increase judicial manpower and modernize physical facilities.

Provide prosecutors, defense counsel, and probation officers in courts now lacking them.

Abolish or overhaul State justice of the peace and U.S. commissioner systems.

[13] President's Commission on Law Enforcement and Administration of Justice, *The Challenge of Crime in a Free Society*, p. 296. Also see the special task force report, President's Commission on Law Enforcement and Administration of Justice, *The Courts* (Washington, D.C.: U.S. Government Printing Office, 1967).

[14] *Ibid.*, pp. 296–297.

176

Initial Stages of a Criminal Case

Establish bail projects.

Enact comprehensive State bail reform legislation.

Establish station house release and summons procedures.

Improve decisions on which defendants should and which should not be charged.

Insure fair and visible negotiated guilty pleas.

Develop and share dispositional information early in case.

Court Proceedings

Establish standards for publicity in criminal cases.

Expand pretrial discovery by defense and prosecution.

Provide single, State postconviction procedure.

Extend prosecution's right to appeal from pretrial rulings suppressing evidence or confessions.

Enact general witness immunity statutes and coordinate immunity grants under them.

Eliminate special standards of proof in perjury cases.

Sentencing Policies and Procedures

Revise sentencing provisions of penal codes.

Consider whether to retain capital punishment.

Establish probation services in all courts for presentence investigation of every offender.

Permit defense counsel broader access to presentence reports.

Expand sentencing institutes and conferences.

Abolish jury sentencing in noncapital cases.

Institute procedures for promoting just and uniform sentencing.

Officers of Justice

Improve selection of judges through better screening.

Provide judicial tenure of at least 10 years.

Expand programs for training judges.

Establish commissions on judicial conduct with power to discipline or require retirement.

Institute salary and selection reforms for prosecutors.

Coordinate local prosecutors through State attorneys general and prosecutor's councils.

Establish programs for training prosecutors.

Extend early provision of counsel for indigents.

Institute State-financed, coordinated assigned counsel or defender systems.

Expand training programs for defense counsel.

177

Court Scheduling, Management and Organization
Create single, unified State court systems.
Centralize administrative responsibility.
Institute timetable for completion of criminal cases.
Utilize experts in business management and business machine systems.
Improve facilities and compensation for witnesses and jurors.

There is little here that will offend the capitalist ruling class. And civil libertarians can be thankful that the judicial system has its liberal elements, while at the same time it protects the existing order.

The current crisis in the American criminal justice system can be relieved only temporarily by means of legal reform. As in the past, measures are being instituted to adapt the legal system to the problems generated by the more general social and economic structure. Rather than working toward a society where a monolithic judicial system would be unnecessary, liberal reformers work to make the law serve the interests of the capitalist order. Thus, the legal reforms today deal with such matters as "modernization of the courts," "decriminalization," and "alternatives to the criminal process."

The crisis in the criminal justice systems of the large cities in America is especially acute. As a response, the Mayor of New York City has recently called for "sweeping changes" in the administration of criminal justice. Following the dramatic instances of riots in city jails, police corruption, and an overwhelming backlog of court cases, many reform proposals are being made. The Mayor, at one point, proposed six specific reforms:

- Day and night court sessions until the backlog of criminal cases — estimated at 90,000 to 345,000 — is cleared up.
- An all-out effort by the state narcotics program to treat addicts now in the city jails — an estimated total of 60 percent of the inmates of city institutions.
- A drastic overhaul of bail policies, including reduced bails and the offering of cash-bail alternatives to every defendant, and the establishment of time limits on detention before trial.
- The placing of direct responsibility for the daily operation and efficiency of the judicial system in the hands of the members of the Administrative Board of the State Judicial Conference.

178

- The abolition of the New York City Criminal Court, and the merging of its functions into a single, unified state court system.
- The strict limitation of jurisdiction of the Criminal Courts to serious crimes, and a search for "other ways" to deal with moral conduct and lesser offenses, including gambling, prostitution and other "victimless" offenses.[15]

These recommendations were followed by counter proposals by other state and city groups. New York's chief judge made his own suggestions, dealing primarily with the regulation and extension of court schedules to handle the tremendous backlog of cases.[16] Six months later the Criminal Justice Coordinating Council, an agency established by Mayor Lindsay to decide how federal crime-fighting money should be spent in New York, issued its own critical report on the need for reforming the criminal justice system.[17] This was followed by a task force report by management specialists who called for a series of administrative reforms in the State's court system.[18]

The liberal concepts of social engineering and social efficiency are being applied to criminal justice problems just as they have been to the management of industrial problems. An engineered and managed criminal justice system means a more effective method of dealing with threats to the capitalist order. The report and recomdations made most recently by the Committee for Economic Development, an advisory committee to the federal government, call for a complete overhaul of the criminal court system and the establishment of an independent federal authority to bring order out of "administrative chaos" at the federal, state, and local levels.[19]

The manipulation and control of American criminal justice since the turn of the century has thus been accomplished through the application of modern techniques of management. Moreover, liberal notions of reform have guided this movement. In the transition from laissez-faire capitalism, state intervention (based on welfare benev-

[15] *The New York Times*, October 11, 1970, p. 1.
[16] *The New York Times*, October 18, 1970, p. 1.
[17] *The New York Times*, March 14, 1971, p. 1.
[18] *The New York Times*, July 30, 1972, p. 1.
[19] Committee for Economic Development, *Reducing Crime and Assuring Justice* (New York: Committee for Economic Development, 1972).

olence) has replaced cruder forms of control. Conflicts within the ruling class, between conservative and liberal factions, were temporarily resolved in the victory of the more "enlightened" corporate rulers over the conservative businessmen.

In recent years, however, the right wing faction of the capitalist ruling class has become more prominent in the formation of public policy — and in determining the course of the nation. This movement is being brought about by the contradictions inherent in corporate capitalism. As the reforms of the liberal capitalist state fail to solve the problems produced by this form of political economy, conflicts emerge within the ruling class over the management and control of the nation, its economy, politics, and people. With the victory of the Republican Party in 1968, and the subsequent years of the Nixon-Agnew administration, a real challenge has been presented to the corporate liberal faction of the ruling class. Indeed, the capitalist state is now in the process of becoming transformed as an agency of control and repression. This seems inevitable given the inability of liberal capitalism to solve the crisis of its own making. This transformation in the capitalist state is most evident in the control of crime. In fact, crime control has become one of the major schemes of the conservative ruling class faction in response to the crisis in capitalism. The crime control programs of the last few years can be viewed as the conservative reaction to the failures of corporate liberalism.

The crime control programs of today, then, have been made possible by the liberal reforms of earlier years. Failing to solve the problems created by modern capitalism, these reforms produced an inevitable reaction within the ruling class. Furthermore, the liberal ideology regarding law and crime has provided the framework for any kind of control and manipulation of the population. The crime programs today use this ideology, but qualify some of its libertarian promises for the sake of more certain control. The liberal reforms of this century have therefore furnished both the context and the need for the newer forms of repression. Where we are headed will be determined to a great extent, as always in capitalist society, by the responses of elements within the ruling class. Only a movement by those outside of this class has any possibility of making a different future.

180

THE OPPRESSION OF CORRECTIONAL REFORM

The transition from the reforms of corporate liberalism to the more recent application of capitalist ideology is also apparent in the handling of convicted offenders. As in the case of law enforcement and judicial administration, penal and correctional policies developed in earlier years are readily adapted to the needs of any regime. Therefore, my argument is not that liberal reforms regarding crime control have been overturned, or that crime control policies have been drastically altered, but that the right wing of the ruling class is using the established programs for its own advantage and in its own way. Yet the purpose is the same: to preserve the capitalist order.

The correctional reform movement of corporate liberalism, which had been developing for half a century, reached its finest hour in the recommendations of the President's Crime Commission. In its report, the Commission summarized its position in the following manner:

> The wholesale strengthening of community treatment of offenders and much greater commitment of resources to their rehabilitation are the main lines where action is needed to make correctional treatment more effective in reducing recidivism. Correctional programs of the future should be built around small centers, located in the communities they serve. These would be better suited than present facilities for flexible treatment, combining the short-term commitment sufficient for most offenders with a variety of partial release or community corrections programs in which job training, educational, and counseling services would be provided or coordinated by the center's staff. Careful screening and classification of offenders is essential so that handling can be individualized to suit the needs in each case. So, too, is greater emphasis on evaluation of the effect of various programs on different offenders.
>
> Much can be done to advance corrections toward such goals with existing facilities, but large increases in skilled diagnostic, rehabilitation, and research personnel are needed immediately. A new regime should be inaugurated in institutions to involve all staff, and encourage inmates to collaborate as much as possible, in rehabilitation. Prison industries must give more meaningful work experience. Counseling, education, and vocational training programs for inmates

must be strengthened. Greater use should be made of release for work and education, of halfway houses, and of similar programs to ease the offender's reintegration in society.[20]

This was followed by the presentation of twenty-two specific recommendations:[21]

Community-Based Corrections

Make parole and probation supervision available for all offenders.
Provide for mandatory supervision of released offenders not paroled.
Increase number of probation and parole officers.
Use volunteers and subprofessional aides.
Develop new methods to reintegrate offenders by mobilizing community institutions.
Make funds available to purchase services otherwise unobtainable for offenders.
Vary caseload size and treatment according to offender needs.
Develop more intensive community treatment programs as alternative to institutionalization.

Correctional Institutions

Establish with State and Federal funds small-unit institutions in cities for community-oriented treatment.
Operate institutions with joint responsibility of staff and inmates for rehabilitation.
Upgrade education and vocational training for inmates.
Establish State programs to recruit and train instructors.
Improve prison industries through joint State programs and Federal assistance.
Expand graduated release and furlough programs.
Integrate local jails and misdemeanant institutions with State corrections.
Provide separate detention facilities for juveniles.
House and handle persons awaiting trial separately from convicts.
Provide separate treatment to special offender groups, through pooling or sharing among jurisdictions.

[20] President's Commission on Law Enforcement and Administration of Justice, *The Challenge of Crime in a Free Society*, p. 297. Also see the special task force report, President's Commission on Law Enforcement and Administration of Justice, *Corrections* (Washington, D.C.: U.S. Government Printing Office, 1967).
[21] *Ibid.*, pp. 297–298.

182

Correctional Decisionmaking

Strengthen diagnostic and screening resources.

Appoint parole boards solely on basis of merit, providing training and requiring full-time service.

Develop standards and procedures to insure fairness to offenders in decisions affecting them.

Research and Training

Improve university research and training in corrections.

Correctional reform, following the liberal ideology, has become the control of crime and criminals by means of scientific knowledge and professional management. The business of the state is to maintain domestic peace; and the role of corrections is to "rehabilitate" anyone who threatens the existing order. Prisons are to be made into therapeutic centers, where offenders will be scientifically managed and manipulated, and finally reintegrated into society. This is all to be done, of course, as humanely as possible, according to precepts of liberalism.

In spite of the correctional reforms of recent years, the purpose of corrections (including imprisonment) is to protect capitalist society. The reforms, in fact, are instituted to better accomplish this goal. The true nature of these reforms is illustrated whenever the functions of corrections are threatened by those subject to its operations. For example, in Attica prison, over forty persons were killed by the state when the prisoners demanded, in a political fashion, a few more reforms. At the time of the uprising, in September of 1971, the New York State Corrections Department was instituting a liberal reform program. The Corrections Commissioner, Russell G. Oswald, could write that "the main impact of the new direction for the department is the recognition of the individual as a human being and the need for basic fairness throughout our day-to-day relationships with each other." [22] Under cover of such notions, Governor Rockefeller could order in the state troopers to fire upon and murder the prisoners and their guards.

The liberal reaction to the prison uprising and the murders by the state was a further proposal for "the very minimum reforms." A package of legislative bills was prepared by the New York Civil

[22] *The New York Times*, September 16, 1971, p. 43.

Liberties Union, with the backing of several state legislators. The bills would do the following:

- Abolish censorship of incoming and outgoing prisoner mail, but allow prison officials to open mail in the presence of prisoners to intercept contraband.
- Liberalize visiting rights to permit inmates to see in private any person, except when prison officials have a "substantial basis" for believing that a particular visitor would jeopardize the security of the prison or the rehabilitation of the prisoner.
- Establish basic due-process rights of inmates in prison disciplinary proceedings, including the right to a hearing to confront and cross-examine witnesses and to have the assistance of counsel.
- Require that every inmate upon admission to prison be given written rules of the prison in Spanish or English, setting forth their rights and responsibilities.
- Require parole boards to reach a decision within seven days and provide a written statement of reasons if parole is denied.
- Establish the right to adequate medical and dental treatment for all inmates, including the right to use outside doctors at no cost to the state.
- Require that all inmates receive items of personal hygiene and receive access to bath or shower facilities every day.
- Establish basic due-process rights of inmates in all parole revocation proceedings, including the right to a hearing, the right to confront and cross-examine witnesses and to be represented by counsel.
- Provide that religious diets of inmates be respected and that if an inmate's religion prevents him from eating certain foods, an alternative choice be provided.
- Establish a minimum right to access to prison libraries, including a law library.
- Require that all clothing and bed linens used by inmates be laundered at least once a week.[23]

Many of the simple reforms had been requested earlier by the rebelling prisoners at Attica: Even reforms can be threatening to the state when suggested within a political context.

[23] *The New York Times*, February 3, 1972, p. 37. A commission (the "McKay Commission") later investigated the Attica uprising and murders. See *Attica, The Official Report of the New York State Special Commission on Attica* (New York: Bantam Books, 1972).

184

As we have come to realize in the last few years, the correctional reforms of a conservative administration are indistinguishable from the proposals of liberal reformers. This suggests, once again, that whether the reforms come from the corporate liberal wing or the conservative wing of the capitalist ruling class, the intentions — and to a great extent the methods — are the same. To rehabilitate the offender, even humanely (if that is actually possible), is to make people adjust to the existing system. Liberal reformers and conservatives are thus in basic agreement on corrections. And both use the state as a device to intervene in the daily lives of the people — in the preservation of an order that promotes the interests of a capitalist economy.

The conservative wing of the capitalist ruling class has, however, instituted its own variety of correctional reform during the years of the Nixon administration. We have seen that the establishment of the Law Enforcement Assistance Administration (LEAA) has placed a heavy emphasis on crime control in the preservation of domestic order. The creation of LEAA, nevertheless, was an outgrowth of the commissions and recommendations of a liberal administration. Whether the administration of that agency would have been different under a liberal government is indeed problematic. Probably there would have been little difference. What the conservative program has added to the contemporary scene, however, is a strong fascistic tone to the law and order programs. But perhaps this new tendency toward fascism was merely hastened by conservative elements within the ruling class.

The conservative approach to correctional reform is clearly defined in the programs of the late 1960s and early 1970s. President Nixon began his administration with a "Magna Carta of prison reform," indicating the importance his administration attached to "preparing the offender for assimilation into society." In 1971 Attorney General Mitchell announced, at a meeting of the National Conference on Corrections (assembled at his request), new federal initiatives to assist state and local corrections programs to bring "genuine reform" to prisons and corrections.[24] He disclosed that LEAA is heavily involved in planning and funding various programs

[24] John N. Mitchell, "New Doors, Not Old Walls," an address presented at the National Conference on Corrections, released by the U.S. Department of Justice, December 6, 1971.

185

related to correctional reform. He cited funded projects including community treatment centers, narcotics and drug treatment, job placement, juvenile probation, work release, halfway houses, volunteer aid programs, psychiatric care, and a host of other offender rehabilitation efforts. Most important, the Attorney General made clear that what was occurring was the development and implementation of a national program — federal, state, and local — on the correction of offenders. He announced that the FBI and LEAA were establishing a National Corrections Academy.

> This would serve as a national center for correctional learning, research, executive seminars, and development of correctional policy recommendations. It would cover the whole range of correctional disciplines, from the new employee to the management level. Besides giving professional training of the highest quality, it would provide a continuing meeting ground for the exchange of advanced ideas on corrections. I believe it will be the most effective single means of upgrading the profession and assuring that correction is more than a euphemism for detention. I hope that the members of this Conference will give us the benefit of their ideas of implementing this Academy in the most effective way.[25]

The Attorney General added that such planning and implementation are necessary because improved law enforcement is going to bring "a new wave of offenders" into the nation's prisons. Thus, correctional reform, whether proposed by liberals or conservatives, attempts to accomplish the same objective: the preservation of some version of a capitalist economy, and the continual oppression of most of the population.

We ask at this point: Is there an alternative to where we are headed in the United States? And related to this: How is an alternative existence to be achieved? My suggestion is that only with a socialist vision can we work toward a form of life that overthrows capitalist oppression and releases us to build a truly human society. We must, therefore, think and act beyond the contradictions and reforms of a capitalist society.

THE SOCIALIST ALTERNATIVE

The alternative to a capitalist society — and its associated legal system — is a socialist society. As we struggle to create such a world,

25 *Ibid.*, p. 12.

186

we can only present a vision of the socialist society. We cannc̩
nor should we — specify a utopia, because a socialist society will
constructed only in the course of the creation. Moreover:

> Any *real* alternatives to capitalism will be historically linked to the
> forces and movements generated by the contradictions of capitalist
> society itself. New institutions which liberate rather than oppress
> can only be created by real people confronting concrete problems
> in their lives and developing new means to overcome oppression.
> The political movements arising from capitalism's contradictions
> therefore constitute the only means for society to move from its
> present condition to a new and more decent form, and only out of
> these movements will humane as well as practical new institutions
> be generated.[26]

A socialist society will allow for the fulfillment of certain human
values. As the authors of *The Capitalist System* write, after their
extensive critique of capitalism:

ownership in : social decisions material benefits

> A truly socialist society would be characterized by equality: equality
> in sharing the material benefits of the society; equality rather than
> hierarchy in making social decisions; and equality in society's en-
> couragement to develop one's full potentials. Work must cease to be
> a means of "making one's living" and become non-alienated, a *part*
> of one's living. Arbitrary distinctions by race and sex (or language
> or eye color) would cease to be criteria for particular forms of op-
> pression or for tracking people into limited opportunities. The irra-
> tionality of production for profits would be transformed into the
> rationality of production to satisfy people's needs, and the unequal
> relations of imperialism would be replaced by a cooperative ethic
> recognizing people's responsibility to each other.[27]

These values will be realized in the process of daily life in a socialist
society.

Socialism means many different things and can take a variety of
forms. This is also to say that various systems have been improperly
called socialist. Historically the objective of one kind of socialism
has been to nationalize all major activities in the country and to
centralize the state bureaucracy. This is state-socialism as practiced
in the Soviet Union and some East European countries. In state-
socialism there is government intervention into the economy, some-

---

[26] Edwards, Reich, and Weisskopf. *The Capitalist System*, p. 520.
[27] *Ibid.*

187

times to promote capitalism, as in Sweden. Furthermore, a welfare state may be established as a reform measure to make the contradictions of capitalism, bureaucracy, and class oppression manageable and also tolerable to those subjected to such a regime. There is little in these societies that promotes the true socialist values of cooperation, equality, participatory democracy, and freedom.

In contrast to state-socialism is democratic socialism. As a process, democratic socialism can be described in this way:

> Most fundamentally, socialism means democratic, decentralized and *participatory* control for the individual: it means having a say in the decisions that affect one's life. Such a participatory form of socialism certainly requires equal access for all to material and cultural resources, which in turn requires the abolition of private ownership of capital and the redistribution of wealth. But it also calls for socialist men and women to eliminate alienating, destructive forms of production, consumption, education and social relations. Participatory socialism requires the elimination of bureaucracies and all hierarchical forms and their replacement, not by new state or party bureaucracies, but by a self-governing and self-managing people with directly chosen representatives subject to recall and replacement. Participatory socialism entails a sense of egalitarian cooperation, of solidarity of people with one another; but at the same time it respects individual and group differences and guarantees individual rights. It affords to all individuals the freedom to exercise human rights and civil liberties that are not mere abstractions but have concrete day-to-day meaning.[28]

As we are coming to realize in our study of the unknown Marx, Karl Marx considered democracy to be the basis of socialism. In contrast to other theorists of his time, including other socialists, Marx insisted upon the democratic character of socialism.[29] In his later work as well as in the earlier work, Marx insisted that socialism can only develop in the course of a democratic mass movement. With the emerging contradictions of capitalism and the development of a political consciousness among those subjected to capitalism, a socialist society will be created collectively and democratically.

[28] *Ibid.*
[29] See Michael Harrington, *Socialism* (New York: Saturday Review Press, 1972), pp. 36–54.

In addition to the democratic ideal evident in Marxian theory, there is the socialist image of human possibilities. As we are finding in our reading of *Grundrisse*, the most basic statement of Marx's perspective, Marx held that only under the appropriate conditions can human possibilities be realized.[30] In the course of the socialist revolution, a person is transformed into a new being, into the authentic species-being. This new human nature is one that is totally liberated from the society of acquisitive individualism, as found in capitalist society. In the movement from a capitalist society to a socialist society, then, the human being no longer suffers the alienation otherwise inherent in the relations of capitalism. The socialist vision is one of human liberation.

According to the new understanding of Marxism, therefore, the human being is realized in the struggle for a true democracy, a socialist society. Marx then arrives at the conclusion that this process will lead to the dissolution of the state. The state eventually may be abolished or altered in a socialist society, since the state (at least as constituted under capitalism) is based on class divisions, is characterized by centralized authority, and is dominated by bureaucracy. Without the eventual abolition of the state, these conditions and forces may continue to expand, into state-socialism or state capitalism, negating the realization of a true democratic socialism. The state serves to separate the political person from civil society, dividing members of society among themselves.[31] In a socialist society there is no longer the need for the kind of state we know under capitalism.

Our consideration of the alternatives leads us to the role of law in socialist society. As I have argued throughout, the capitalist state is a tool of the ruling class, maintaining the dominance of that class over the classes oppressed by the capitalist system. The capitalist state, in turn, makes and enforces law for the purpose of securing and perpetuating the interests of the capitalist ruling class. The legal order of the capitalist state is a device to maintain the domestic

[30] Marx, *Grundrisse*, pp. 59–76, 148–152. Also see, James M. Glass, "Marx, Kafka and Jung: The Appearance of Species-being," *Politics & Society*, 2 (Winter, 1972), pp. 255–271.

[31] David McLellan, *Marx Before Marxism* (New York: Harper & Row, 1970), pp. 119–129. Also see Ernest Mandel, *The Marxist Theory of the State* (New York: Pathfinder Press, 1969).

189

social and economic order. It follows from this, then, that the capitalist state and its legal system can continue to exist only as long as there is need to secure the dominance of the ruling class. With the achievement of a socialist society, devoid of classes, bureaucracy, and centralized authority (that is, characterized by equality, participatory democracy, and decentralized control), the state may no longer be necessary. And following this, there may be no state law. Law as we know it today will be relegated to the history of a former age.

It is not my purpose here to outline a socialist society, including details about law. Rather, the exact nature of the society and its own forms of regulation will be worked out in the struggle of building a socialist society. I only want to indicate the direction of a socialist alternative to capitalist society and its legal system. In doing this I begin with the idea that law, instead of being an embodiment of community custom, is symptomatic of the emergence of the state. Stanley Diamond has observed: "Law is the instrument of civilization, of political society sanctioned by organized force, presumably above society at large, and buttressing a new set of social interests. Law and custom both involve the regulation of behavior but their characters are entirely distinct; no evolutionary balance has been struck between developing law and custom, traditional — or emergent." [32] Law is, and continues to serve as, the means of enforcing the interests of the state and the ruling class.

Therefore, a legal order became necessary only when the state broke down communal solidarity and divided the group into conflicting factions. In the early states, crimes were invented to serve the needs of the state; that is, legal sanctions were needed to protect the new interests of the emerging state. Rather than healing any breaches of custom, law protected the sovereign. The state necessarily broke up customary patterns, in the interest of economic and political dominance, and instituted a legal system to enforce its sovereignty.

With this understanding of the legal order, we begin to see that law is the antonym rather than the synonym of order. Law has its

[32] Stanley Diamond, "The Rule of Law Versus the Order of Custom," in Robert Paul Wolff (ed.), *The Rule of Law* (New York: Simon and Schuster, 1971), p. 120.

origins in the pathology of social relations brought about by the state itself. Diamond writes: "Law arises in the breach of a prior customary order and increases in force with the conflicts that divide political societies internally and among themselves. Law *and* order is the historical illusion; law versus order is the historical reality." [33] Modern capitalist society, with its state and legal order, is the one least likely to serve as a guide for building a human society.

In building a socialist society, therefore, we may turn to the idea of custom, rather than law, for the patterning of our daily lives. Life, instead of being controlled by the rigid mechanisms of the state, is to be lived collectively with others, in harmony with nature and fellow human beings. There is no need for a legal order, as known under capitalism, in the social relations of a socialist society.[34]

A contemporary experience that gives support to the possibility of community custom is the case of revolutionary Cuba. The alternative to national law in this case, and a transitional move to the abolition of law, is the emergence of the popular tribunal.[35] Neighborhoods in Cuba now have their own courts, staffed by personnel elected democratically from within the community. Little emphasis is placed on sanctions of any kind. Instead, violators continue to be educated in the community. Custom plays an educative role in the community, rather than a punitive one. What is important is maintaining peace and understanding in the community rather than enforcement of a legal system.

There are, of course, other arrangements that may serve a socialist society. For example, perhaps there will be several different levels of community, according to specific functions.[36] Communities will likely arrange themselves according to territorial considerations. There may be functions that can be best served on a general state level, serving all the people. Whatever forms emerge in a socialist society, they will be achieved democratically and will be for the

[33] *Ibid.*, p. 140.

[34] Michael E. Tigar, "Socialist Law and Legal Institutions," in Robert Lefcourt (ed.), *Law Against the People: Essays to Demystify Law, Order and the Courts* (New York: Random House, 1971), pp. 327–347.

[35] Jesse Berman, "The Cuban Popular Tribunals," *Columbia Law Review*, 69 (December, 1969), pp. 1317–1354.

[36] See Gar Alperovitz, "Notes Toward a Pluralist Commonwealth," *Review of Radical Political Economics*, 4 (Summer, 1972), pp. 28–48.

collective liberation of the people, rather than for the benefit of the ruling class, removing the alienation and oppression of former arrangements. Such an existence is impossible in a capitalist society.

As students of law and crime, and as socialists, our task is to consider the alternative to the capitalist legal order. Further study of the American legal system must be devoted to the contradictions of the existing legal order. At this advanced stage of capitalist development, law is little more than a rigid and repressive means of manipulation and control. We must make others aware of the current meaning of law and crime control in capitalist society. The objective is to move beyond the existing legal order. And this means ultimately that we are engaged in a socialist revolution.

EMERGING REVOLUTIONARY CONSCIOUSNESS AND THE COUNTERREVOLUTION

The contradictions of capitalism do not inevitably lead to the collapse of the existing order. Indeed, the state can continue to consolidate existing arrangements through the various means of repression, including crime control. The movement toward a socialist society can occur only with a political consciousness on the part of the oppressed and the correct political action. The liberating social institutions will only grow out of the struggles against the oppression of capitalism and the construction of a new world.

In other words, a socialist society cannot be willed into being, but requires the conscious activity of those who seek a new existence. We ask at this point: How will this movement take place? From our analysis thus far we know that the existing capitalist society — with its state, ruling class, and legal system — effectively suppresses resistance that threatens its survival. We realize also that the consciousness of the public has traditionally been manipulated by an official ideology that serves the existing order. Therefore, any change must come about with a new consciousness among the oppressed.

A beginning is the realization of the alienation we suffer under capitalism. The contradiction of capitalism itself — the disparity between possibility and actuality — makes large portions of the population ready to consider alternatives to the capitalist system. When we become conscious of the extent to which we are dehumanized under the capitalist mode of production and consumption, when we realize the source and nature of our alienation, we become active in a movement to build a new society. Sooner or later, then, the oppressed begin to struggle against their oppression. As Paulo Freire has written in *Pedagogy of the Oppressed*:

Who are better prepared than the oppressed to understand the terrible significance of an oppressive society? Who suffer the effects of oppression more than the oppressed? Who can better understand the necessity of liberation? They will not gain this liberation by chance but through the praxis of their quest for it, through their recognition of the necessity to fight for it.[37]

How, then, are the oppressed to move beyond the ideology and social reality of the oppressor? There is need of a critical consciousness, led by those who are oppressed.

To surmount the situation of oppression, men must first critically recognize its causes, so that through transforming action they can create a new situation, one which makes possible the pursuit of a fuller humanity. But the struggle to be more fully human has already begun in the authentic struggle to transform the situation. Although the situation of oppression is a dehumanized and dehumanizing totality affecting both the oppressors and those whom they oppress, it is the latter who must, from their stifled humanity, wage for both the struggle for a fuller humanity; the oppressor, who is himself dehumanized because he dehumanizes others, is unable to lead this struggle.[38]

It would be a contradiction in terms, Freire notes, if the oppressors not only defended but actually implemented new institutions. It is the responsibility of those who are oppressed to remove that which is oppressive, that which makes us less than human.

Already large numbers of people are becoming conscious of the many ways they are being oppressed by the capitalist system. In fact, the legitimacy of the existing system is increasingly being questioned; the moral rule of the capitalist state is declining. Both the rebellion of the people and the repressive measures of the government can be interpreted as reflecting the decline in legitimate authority. No longer do we accept the ideology that once automati-

37 Paulo Freire, *Pedagogy of the Oppressed* (New York: Herder and Herder, 1972), p. 29.
38 *Ibid.*, pp. 31–32.

cally granted legitimacy to the state. The older belief in unexamined allegiance to the state no longer prevails. We now base allegiance on will and conscience rather than on blind acceptance of existing power. The social and political world has become "unfrozen" for us.[39]

As the oppressed continue to question and demystify capitalist institutions, the hegemony of the ruling class and capitalist relations is being eroded. This means that law itself is being undermined. As Aronowitz observes, "The revolt of ordinary people against all forms of legitimate authority controlling the institutions of daily life and their simultaneous efforts to establish their own authority over these institutions takes law from its position of preeminence in society and reveals it as an arm of class rule." [40] Consequently, the American legal order is breaking down.

Yet, while the legitimacy of existing institutions is being questioned, and as the legal order is breaking down, there is occurring simultaneously the further development of an authoritarian state. The authoritarian solution to the attacks on existing institutions is apparent in the creation of the recent crime control techniques and programs. The manipulation and control of a large portion of the population become necessary when the capitalist order is in danger. Some of the principles and methods for fighting crime developed earlier under liberal administrations are now being organized and applied in new efforts to preserve domestic order. An attempt to establish an authoritarian, neo-fascist state may be the final phase of advanced capitalism.

It is the *counterrevolution* in America that a Marxian analysis must now confront. Capitalism may well collapse, but as Marcuse has recently observed, the outcome will not necessarily be a socialist revolution.

> A Marxian analysis cannot seek comfort "in the long run." In this "long run," the system will indeed collapse, but Marxian theory cannot prophesy which form of society (if any) will replace it.

[39] John H. Schaar, "Legitimacy in the Modern State," in Philip Green and Sanford Levinson (eds.), *Power and Community: Dissenting Essays in Political Science* (New York: Random House, 1970), pp. 276–327.

[40] Stanley Aronowitz, "Law, the Breakdown of Order, and Revolution," in Lefcourt (ed.), *Law Against the People*, p. 154.

Within the framework of the objective conditions, the alternatives (fascism or socialism) depend on the intelligence and the will, the consciousness and the sensibility, of human beings. It depends on their still-existing *freedom*. The notion of a protracted period of barbarism as against the socialist alternative — barbarism based on the technical and scientific achievements of civilization — is central to Marxian theory. At present, the initiative and the power are with the counterrevolution, which may well culminate in such a barbarian civilization.[41]

This counterrevolution within advanced capitalist society is the context in which we must now work in making a socialist revolution. There are already the tendencies, such as the erosion of legitimacy and a consciousness of oppression, that are necessary for a mass-based revolution — to work against the counterrevolution. In other words, the presence of objective conditions for a socialist revolution is now being joined with the subjective awareness of the need for such a revolution.[42] Millions of people who are subject to the objective oppressions and repressions of advanced capitalism are challenging the capitalist system in various ways. This is a revolution "from below," by those who are oppressed and exploited in many diverse ways by the existing system. This includes the working class, and the "new working class," as well as many other groups. To sum up, Marcuse writes:

> The working class remains the potentially revolutionary class, although it would be a class of different composition and with a different consciousness. In line with the new character of production in advanced monopoly capitalism, it comprises manual and intellectual labor, blue collar and white collar. The impulses for radical change would be rooted, not primarily in material privation but in human degradation (which finds its most brutal expression in the organization of the assembly line), and in the awareness that it can be otherwise, here and now: that technical progress can become human liberation, that the fatal union of growing productivity and growing destruction can be broken. Needs are becoming a material force: the need for self-determination, for a non-repressive organization of

[41] Herbert Marcuse, *Counterrevolution and Revolt* (Boston: Beacon Press, 1972), p. 29.
[42] Ernest Mandel, *The Formation of the Economic Thought of Marx* (New York: Monthly Review Press, 1971), pp. 21–26.

work; the need for a life that has not only to be "earned" but is made an end in itself.[43]

This new radical movement is spreading — and not only within American society. Even more important, there is a worldwide revolt against global capitalism, mainly among the "underdeveloped" and Third World nations.[44] Revolutionary wars are being waged against capitalist domination. Social and economic reconstruction is taking place on a socialist basis in Vietnam, China, Korea, Cuba, and Algeria.

> These victories, taken together with the increasingly obvious inability of the underdeveloped countries to solve their problems within the framework of the world capitalist system, have sown the seeds of revolution throughout the continents of Asia, Africa, and Latin America. Some of these seeds will sprout and ripen rapidly, others slowly, still others perhaps not until after a long period of germination. What seems in any case clear is that they are now implanted beyond any prospect of extirpation. It is no longer mere rhetoric to speak of the world revolution: the term describes what is already a reality and what is certain to become increasingly the dominant characteristic of the historical epoch in which we live.[45]

In spite of the existence of certain objective revolutionary conditions, and in spite of an emerging revolutionary consciousness, we cannot assume that the socialist revolution will occur or be completed soon, or any time in the near future. We are capable of only some advances in our time, due in large measure to the nature of the conditions.

> Man makes his own history, that is true. But as Karl Marx pointed out, he does not make it out of the whole cloth, only from that which is available to him at any given time. Men cannot accomplish what is impossible. Try as they did, the utopians in previous centuries could not establish new social orders based on brotherhood. The time was not yet ripe for that. They could dream of such a society, and dreams

[43] Herbert Marcuse, "Blue-Collar Revolution," *The New York Times*, August 7, 1972, p. 27.
[44] Sweezy, *Modern Capitalism and Other Essays*, especially pp. 147–165.
[45] Paul A. Baran and Paul M. Sweezy, *Monopoly Capital: An Essay on the American Economic and Social Order* (New York: Monthly Review Press, 1966), p. 365.

are of tremendous importance and play a great role in mankind's progress, but they could not yet realize it. The time can be "seized," but only for that which the objective material forces of society has made possible.[46]

We must be aware, at every turn, that we are engaged in a struggle against the oppressions (and contradictions) of the capitalist system. In the course of concrete struggles against existing capitalist relations and state power we will define our future strategies.

In this "long march" we will build humanizing, socialist institutions. With a critical intelligence we will combat the counterrevolution that is taking place in capitalist society. We must make certain that the alternative to the collapse of capitalism is a socialist world — not a totalitarian one. This makes all the more crucial our understanding of the counterrevolution that now relies on the tools and ideology of legal order. A critique of legal order and crime control helps us to demystify those fundamental aspects of counterrevolution. Our objective is to work toward the only alternative that will promote human liberation — a socialist society.

STRUGGLE FOR A SOCIALIST SOCIETY

I conclude this critique of the American legal order with a sense of the work to be done. We have much to do in the further development of a Marxian theory that is appropriate to our times. A critical intelligence requires the expansion of our ideas to meet the challenges of the advanced capitalist society. Much more attention has to be devoted to an understanding of legal repression as a counterrevolutionary force. Only in such critical work can we survive the collapse of capitalism and build a socialist world.

In critically understanding (and demystifying) our current historical reality, we are in a position to act in a way that will remove our oppression and create a new existence. Though we are subject to the objective conditions of our age, as human beings we are also collectively involved in transforming our social reality. Our praxis is one of critical thought and action — reflecting upon the world and

---

[46] Gil Green, *The New Radicalism: Anarchist or Marxist?* (New York: International Publishers, 1971), p. 53.

acting to transform it. We can free ourselves from the oppression of the age only as we combine our thoughts and our actions, turning each back upon the other. Our theory and our practice are formed in the struggle to make a socialist society. This is a critical life.

Index

199

National Institute of Law Enforcement and Criminal Justice, grants of, 34–35, 40–42
National Institute of Mental Health (NIMH), 49
Center for Studies of Crime and Delinquency, grants of, 35–40
Nationalism, 141
National Opinion Research Center, 152
NCCD. See National Council on Crime and Delinquency
Negative thinking, 13–14
New Deal, 169
New Haven College, 33
New York Civil Liberties Union, 183–84
New York State, Corrections Department of, 183
New York Times, The, 103n, 110n, 113–15, 179n, 183n, 184n
New York University, 36
NIMH. See National Institute of Mental Health, Center for Studies of Crime and Delinquency
Nisbet, Robert A., 19
Nixon, Richard M., 103, 115, 149, 185

"Oakland Seven," 116
Ohio State University, 36
Ohlin, Lloyd E., 30n
Omnibus Crime Control and Safe Streets Act, 40, 60, 75–82, 100–01, 151
Oregon Research Institute, 39
Organized Crime Control Act, 103–04
Oswald, Russell G., 183

Packer, Herbert L., 102n
Parsons, James B., 63
Parsons, Talcott, 19, 24
Pedagogy of the Oppressed (Freire), 193–94

Peden, Katherine G., 71–72
Perkins, John A., 83
Petersen, Howard C., 83
Pinto, Vince, 131n
Platt, Anthony M., 44, 73–74, 171n
Plato, 20
Pluralist theory of class structure, 54
Point Park College, 33
Police
local, departments, 99
recommendations of President's Crime Commission for, 172–78
Political dissent, 116
Positivism, failure of, 3
Pound, Roscoe, 22–23
Powell, Lewis F., Jr., 63–64, 68
President's Commission on Law Enforcement and Administration of Justice, 59–68, 120–21, 150–51
membership of, 60–68
recommendations of, 172–78, 181–83
Prison system, 30
Progressive Era, 169

Quinney, Richard, 5n, 7n, 18n, 45n

Reflexivity of social constructionist thought, 6
Rehnquist, William, 90
Reich, Michael, 52n, 167n, 187n
Reiss, Albert J., Jr., 175n
Rehnquist, William, 90
Repression, 132–35
Riot Commission. See National Advisory Commission on Civil Disorders
Rockefeller, Nelson S., 183
Rogers, William P., 64, 67
Roosevelt, Franklin D., 169
Rostow, Eugene, 21–22
Roth, William M., 84
Rothman, David J., 143n

204

= anti war
= women's movement